This careful work is a shining example of an e ... generation of evangelical scholars has redisco ... of our common catholic heritage. Not only liberais but some influential evangelical theologians have rejected key aspects of God's immutability, often misunderstanding even the definition, exegetical basis and historical development. This is a terrific articulation of what Christians mean when they affirm the words of Malachi 3:6: 'For I the LORD do not change ...' And, as Ronni Kurtz points out well, this unchangeable nature and purpose is good news for us: '... Therefore, O Israel, you are not consumed.'

MICHAEL HORTON
J. Gresham Machen Professor of Systematic Theology and Apologetics,
Westminster Seminary California, Escondido, California

Traditionally, from the time of the Church Fathers, the immutability of God was universally held. In the twentieth century, many philosophers and theologians rejected this doctrine. Rather, they argued that God must be conceived as mutable and passible. However, presently there is a theological resurgence defending and promoting God's immutability – both among Catholic and Protestant theologians. Ronnie Kurtz is one of those theologians who admirably represents this retrieval. He creatively and insightfully argues that the biblical, historical and theological traditions rightly profess God's immutability. Far from be a hindrance, divine immutability is the sine qua non for humankind's salvation. Thus, Kurtz makes a profound contribution to the Christian theological and philosophical tradition.

THOMAS G. WEINANDY
OFM, Capuchin, and
Author, *Does God Change?* And *Does God Suffer?*

In *No Shadow of Turning*, Ronni Kurtz explains the doctrine of immutability clearly, defends it exegetically and historically, and demonstrates its importance in systematic theology. If you're looking for a primer not just on immutability but also on the Christian doctrine of God, biblical hermeneutics, the Great Tradition, and the systematic nature of theology, this is it.

MATTHEW EMERSON
Dean of Theology, Arts and Humanities,
Floyd K. Clark Chair of Christian Leadership, Professor of Religion,
Oklahoma Baptist University, Shawnee, Oklahoma

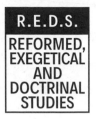

R.E.D.S.
REFORMED,
EXEGETICAL
AND
DOCTRINAL
STUDIES

NO SHADOW OF TURNING

DIVINE IMMUTABILITY AND THE ECONOMY OF REDEMPTION

RONNI KURTZ

SERIES EDITORS J.V. FESKO & MATTHEW BARRETT

MENTOR
Encouraging Christians to Think

Copyright © Ronni Kurtz 2022

Paperback ISBN 978-1-5271-0913-1
Ebook ISBN 978-1-5271-0985-8

10 9 8 7 6 5 4 3 2 1

Published in 2022
in the
Mentor Imprint
by
Christian Focus Publications Ltd,
Geanies House, Fearn, Ross-shire,
IV20 1TW, Great Britain.

www.christianfocus.com

Cover design
by Pete Barnsley

Printed by
Bell & Bain, Glasgow

MIX
Paper from
responsible sources
FSC® C007785

CONTENTS

To Kristen Kurtz,
You are the treasure of my life.

Series Preface

Reformed, Exegetical and Doctrinal Studies (R.E.D.S.) presents new studies informed by rigorous exegetical attention to the biblical text, engagement with the history of doctrine, with a goal of refined dogmatic formulation.

R.E.D.S. covers a spectrum of doctrinal topics, addresses contemporary challenges in theological studies, and is driven by the Word of God, seeking to draw theological conclusions based upon the authority and teaching of Scripture itself.

Each volume also explores pastoral implications so that they contribute to the church's theological and practical understanding of God's Word. One of the virtues that sets R.E.D.S. apart is its ability to apply dogmatics to the Christian life. In doing so, these volumes are characterized by the rare combination of theological weightiness and warm, pastoral application, much in the tradition of John Calvin's *Institutes of the Christian Religion*.

These volumes do not merely repeat material accessible in other books but retrieve and remind the church of forgotten truths to enrich contemporary discussion.

MATTHEW BARRETT
J. V. FESKO

Acknowledgments

In the duration of my working on this project, the world seemed in a state of constant fluctuation. As a small sample size of the change that occurred while writing this book: my wife and I had our first child, my dear mother passed away from cardiac arrest, I moved into my first faculty post, and the world experienced a global pandemic that shut down my country for the better part of a year. And that's not to mention the political, racial, and societal unrest that has permeated and punctuated these last few years.

It was during these ever-altering days that I conducted my research and writing. As I wrote in days riddled with change, the doctrine of divine immutability became more than a theological construction to be examined and moved into a Christian truth to be cherished. While my life was ever changing, my God was ever the same. I can now utter with Kierkegaard, 'in God's changelessness, there is rest.' It is therefore necessary that the first thanks and acknowledgment for this book are made to the Triune God: 'You are unchangeably good and have proven to be the Father of lights in whom there is no shadow of turning. To you, Lord, be every ounce of honor and glory now and forevermore.'

Behind this book is an embarrassment of riches. Many friends, family members, and academic colleagues stand behind its words. First, since this book is a revision of my doctoral dissertation, I'd like to thank my doctoral committee who have now become my editors. Dr Matthew Barrett and Dr J. V. Fesko have been invaluable throughout this process.

Their input was always erudite, and they consistently pushed me to make the project better. They are not only great doctoral supervisors and editors, but they have become great mentors and friends. Without these two, this book would have been an impossibility.

A number of other academic colleagues also made this work possible. I thank Dr Russell Meek who has read every word of the manuscript and edited every syllable. I also thank Dr Matthew Millsap and the entire library staff at Midwestern Baptist Theological Seminary. Any academic knows that librarians are the real heroes and Dr Millsap personally went out of his way on numerous occasions to track down hard-to-find journal articles for me. Thanks also to Jordan Steffaniak for working through a pre-published edition of this manuscript and for offering erudite and thoughtful feedback.

For the majority of the time I was working on this book, I was a pastor at Emmaus Church in Kansas City, Missouri. Therefore, I thank the saints of Emmaus Church as they were gracious with their pastor's time and were more than supportive of my desire to pursue both pastoral ministry and academic theology. Moreover, they kept my soul. Thank you to the members and fellow pastors of this wonderful body of believers.

I also thank my family. Outside of my editors, the only person to read every word of this project was my father – Ron Kurtz, Sr. My dad worked through the material diligently and offered insightful feedback. More important however than the particulars of the feedback he gave is what his reading of each chapter represented – his support. He's been in my corner for as long as I can remember, and I am eternally grateful for him. My thanks also to two other family members, Joshua and Meagan Brown. Most of the hours I spent writing this book, Joshua was within arm's reach. We clocked countless hours at coffee shops in St. Louis, Kansas City, and San Antonio through the years of this project. He and his dear wife are more than family; they are our best friends.

Finally, the most profound thanks belong to my immediate family. My wife, Kristen Kurtz, and our daughter, Finley Jane Kurtz, have my heart. When this book goes to print, my daughter will be turning two. Though she is young in age and small in size, in her I've found a deep well of joy. In her laughs and hugs, I've found the sweetest of writing breaks. Being her dad is a true gift and I pray that she grows to treasure the unchanging Triune God and cherish His gospel.

With joy I dedicate this book to my wife, Kristen Kurtz. I've had to accept the hard truth that there is not an acknowledgment section long enough to capture how important Kristen has been to my life and career. She is my closest friend, my nearest neighbor, my greatest adventure, and in her I have found an ocean of kindness and a lifetime of love. Thank you for the countless sacrifices you have made to make this book possible, Kristen. I love you.

There are many whom I have failed to mention here, and for that I extend my apologies. Each name in these acknowledgments, and many who are not named, are all evidence of James 1:17 that our unchanging Triune God is the Father of lights who is the giver of good gifts – to Him be the glory forever.

Abbreviations

ANF   *The Ante-Nicene Fathers.* Edited by Alexander Roberts and James Donaldson. 10 vols. Peabody: Hendrickson, 1999.

BDPD   John Gill, *The Body of Doctrinal and Practical Divinity.* Paris: The Baptist Standard Bearer, 2017.

CoC   *The Creeds of Christendom.* Ed. Philip Schaff. 3 vols. Grand Rapids: Baker Books, 1984.

CRS   Wilhelmus à Brakel, *The Christian's Reasonable Service.* 4 vols. Trans. Bartel Elshout. Ed. Joel R. Beeke, Grand Rapids: Reformation Heritage Books, 1992.

CT   Benedict Pictet, *Christian Theology.* Trans. Frederick Reyoux. London: Seeley and Sons, 1829.

IET   Francis Turretin, *Institutes of Elenctic Theology.* 3 vols. Trans. George Musgrave Giger. Phillipsburg: P&R Publishing, 1992.

IJST   *International Journal of Systematic Theology.*

JAAR   *Journal of the American Academy of Religion.*

JRT   *Journal of Reformed Theology.*

JTI   *Journal of Theological Interpretation.*

MT   *Modern Theology.*

NPNF1   *Nicene and Post-Nicene Fathers: First Series.* 14 vols. Ed. Phillip Schaff. Peabody: Hendrickson, 2012.

NPNF2   *Nicene and Post-Nicene Fathers: Second Series.* 14 vols. Ed. Phillip Schaff and Henry Wace. Peabody: Hendrickson, 2012.

PRRD   Richard A. Muller, *Post-Reformation Reformed Dogmatics.* 4 vols. Grand Rapids: Baker Academic, 2003.

RCC   James T. Dennison, Jr, *Reformed Confessions of the 16th and 17th Centuries in English Translations.* 4 vols. Grand Rapids: Reformation Heritage, 2008.

RD   Herman Bavinck, *Reformed Dogmatics.* 4 vols. Trans. John Vriend. Ed. John Bolt. Grand Rapids: Baker Academic, 2003.

SBD   Edward Leigh, *A Systeme or Body of Divinity: Consisting of Ten Books.* London: A.M. for William Lee, 1654.

SCG   Thomas Aquinas, *Summa Contra Gentiles.* 5 vols. Trans. Anton C. Pegis. Indiana: University of Notre Dame Press, 1975.

SJT   *Scottish Journal of Theology.*

ST   Thomas Aquinas, *Summa Theologica.* 5 vols. Trans. Fathers of the English Dominican Province. Indiana: Christian Classics, 1948.

TFC   *The Fathers of the Church.* 127 vols. Washington: Catholic University of America Press, 1947.

TPT   Petrus van Mastricht, *Theoretical-Practical Theology.* 3 vols. Trans. Todd M. Rester. Ed. Joel R. Beeke, Grand Rapids: Reformation Heritage Books, 2018.

TS   *Theological Studies.*

WJT   *Westminster Journal of Theology.*

PART ONE

Theological Method and Defining Divine Immutability

CHAPTER ONE

Theology and Economy

'In the Beginning, God': God as the Principle and Source of Theology

The opening salvo of the greatest drama in history begins with the clause, 'in the beginning, God' (Gen. 1:1). In these four words we not only find a robust protology but also insight into proper theological method, which becomes a roadmap in the hands of curious pilgrims. These initial words of sacred Scripture ground the rest of the story in the primary mover and actor in the unfolding narrative – God Himself. As it is with the inaugural lines of Scripture, it should be with our theological method and trajectory: the entirety rests on the foundation of God.

The nature of systematic theology is such that where one decides to start is not a neutral decision; it is a theological one. Where we begin reveals the theologian's prolegomenous intuition and often charts, from the start, where the dogmatic journey will lead.[1] Jumping off the starting block of anthropology, for instance, will cause the theologian to take a different dogmatic course than if he or she began with ecclesiology or eschatology. The voyage that begins with an eschatological focus may

---

1. See Bavinck's two sections, 'The Method and Organization of Dogmatic Theology' and 'The History and Literature of Dogmatic Theology' for a summary of systematic starting points and procedures. He stated, 'From the time the pursuit of dogmatics began, it needed a way of organizing the material treated.' Then, beginning with Clement of Alexandria, Origen, and Theodoret of Cyrrhus, Bavinck works through a large portion of theological antiquity demonstrating dogmatic organization. See Herman Bavinck, *Reformed Dogmatics*, 4 vols. (Grand Rapids: Baker, 2003), 1:95-204.

differ in both order and outcome than the expedition that begins with revelation. Expressing this point, Oliver Crisp and Fred Sanders stated, '*Where* one begins theologically is often as important in shaping the end product as *how* one proceeds theologically.'[2]

Learning the implications of possible theological starting points is an important lesson for the student of theology. However, arguably more important is the lesson that not all doctrines are created equal in terms of capacity for bearing the theological weight of dogmatics. It is not only the case that starting with, say, ecclesiology or soteriology will impact where the theological trajectory leads; it is also the case that these doctrines cannot, and should not, bear the foundational burden of theological reasoning. The doctrine of God alone has the exclusive identity qualified to uphold the weight of all other theological loci and fields. As John Webster stated, 'the only Christian doctrine which may legitimately claim to exercise a magisterial and judicial role in the corpus of Christian teaching is the doctrine of the Trinity, since in that doctrine alone all other doctrines have their ultimate basis.'[3]

Elsewhere Webster described the theological task as having two primary components: 'Christian theology is a work of the regenerate intelligence, awakened and illuminated by divine instruction to consider a twofold object.' That twofold object is, 'first, God in himself in the unsurpassable perfection of his inner being and work as Father, Son, and Spirit and in his outer operations, and second by derivation, all other things relative to him.'[4] Webster makes use of Franciscus Junius

---

2. Oliver D. Crisp and Fred Sanders, eds., *The Task of Dogmatics: Explorations in Theological Method* (Grand Rapids: Zondervan, 2017), 15, emphasis original. The authors continue, 'We might say that where you start and how you get to your goal are two fundamental issues in theological method. It is like preparing to set out on a journey. Before embarking upon the trip, one must consider where it will begin and where it will end.'

3. John Webster, '*Rector Et Iudex Super Omnia Genera Doctrinarum*': The Place of the Doctrine of Justification,' in *God without Measure: Working Papers in Christian Theology*, 2 vols. (London: T&T Clark, 2016), 1:161. It is important to note that Webster would have us be less concerned about the material order of dogmatics as long as each emphasis is rooted in, and conscious of, theology proper.

4. John Webster, '*Omnia…Pertractantur in Sacra Doctrina Sub Ratione Dei*: On the Matter of Christian Theology,' in *God without Measure*, 1:3. Steven Duby, *God in Himself: Scripture, Metaphysics, and the Task of Christian Theology* (Downers Grove, IL: IVP, 2019), 25, articulates a nearly identical understanding, saying, 'the object of theology is principally God himself and then, derivatively, other things as they stand in relation to God.'

in articulating the importance of rooting all theology in the doctrine of God, and for good reason. The sixteenth-century Reformed theologian dedicated many pages to theological prolegomena and throughout his work demonstrated the importance of building from a Trinitarian foundation. In his *Treatise on True Theology*, Junius provided the trustees of the University of Leiden and the consulars of the city thirty-nine theses describing a true theology. Thesis twenty-four stated: 'The material of this theology consists of divine matters: of course God, and whatsoever topics have been arranged with respect to him.' Later in his exposition of thesis twenty-four, Junius continued: 'God is the subject matter of theology … it is God himself that is the subject, or things that are ordered with respect to God, as to the universal principle and end of those things.'[5] Junius' insistence of God as the first principle of theology would make its way into a public disputation in which he stated,

> In most-sacred Theology God is treated not only as the principle upon which it is constructed and the source of our knowledge of it but also as the subject and the foremost, primary locus of theology from which all the others flow forth, by which they are held together, and to which they should be directed. Hence Theology derives its very name from this starting-point.[6]

Lewis Ayres described this theological movement which roots all other theological loci in one controlling emphasis in his discussion of the workings of systematics: 'anyone attempting to conceive the field as a whole is faced with the dual task of finding some guiding principle under which to relate the disciplines and giving an account of the various rationales of the individual disciplines.'[7]

As we have seen, and will see, the 'guiding principle' is none other than the Triune God. That God should be the principle and source of Christian theology ought to come as little surprise as His *a se* essence

---

5. Franciscus Junius, *A Treatise on True Theology* (Grand Rapids: Reformation Heritage, 2014), 177-79.

6. Franciscus Junius, *Synopsis Purioris Theologiae / Synopsis of a Purer Theology: Latin Text and English Translation: Volume 1, Disputations 1–23*, ed. H. van den Belt et al., Studies in Medieval and Reformation Traditions 187 (Leiden: Brill, 2014), 151.

7. Lewis Ayres, *Nicaea and Its Legacy: An Approach to Fourth-Century Trinitarian Theology* (Oxford: Oxford University Press, 2004), 393. While Ayres concedes that systematic theology can be defined in this way, he slightly bemoans the over-fragmented state of theological expertise as one of the contributing factors to non-Nicene reasoning.

renders that not only material matter finds its source in Him, but also intellectual matters as well. Subjecting all corresponding theological fields to this one field – the Triune life of God – seems self-evident, as there is an asymmetrical relationship between the doctrine of God and any other theological field. We can, without much difficulty, think of God without having our mind immediately drawn to ecclesiology, for example. However, there is no contemplating the *ecclesia* without pondering its chief cornerstone, founder, and sustainer. We can consider God's fullness of life in Himself without necessarily considering the divine economy of redemption, but it is unfathomable for the theologian to examine the dramatic salvation of man without reflecting on the Savior. This asymmetrical paradigm could be carried to all fields of theology. All theological truth is grounded and rooted in the Triune life of God: ecclesiology is the study of God's people; revelation and bibliology is the study of God's Word; soteriology is the study of God's redemption; anthropology is the study of God's creatures. The fullness of God's Triune life in Himself is the only foundation fit to shoulder the burdensome weight of theological reasoning. This triune God is the 'orienting factor in all the various loci of dogmatic theology'.[8]

Theology Proper and the Economy of Redemption

'The doctrine of God is prior to the economy of God's works, both materially and so also logically, since the being of God in and for himself is the ground of God's works.'[9] This line from Webster's essay on the place of justification in Christian theology acts as a summary of the previous section: the *opera Dei exeuntia* (God's external operation) is grounded in the *opera Dei immanentia* (God's inner life).

While God is the principle object and source of all theology, and His ontology grounds His economy, the particular focus of this project is the connection between the doctrine of God and the portion of the economy called redemption. In much of modern theology, the intense focus on the functional side of the economy *ad extra* (toward the outside) can come at the expense of the ontological and metaphysical, which has led to atrophy of teaching on the divine life and persons of the

---

8. Duby, *God in Himself,* 25.
9. Webster, '*Rector et iudex super omnia,*' 46.

Godhead. A perusal of modern Christian publications reveals it to be an easier task to find volumes on the work of Christ than a treatise on His ontology or person. This is not confined to the field of Christology, but remains true pertaining to Trinitarianism as well. The worry which drives this study, is that contemporary Christians, especially those in local churches, have a doctrinal diet which focuses more on functional and economic aspects of Trinitarianism, like creation, for example, than they have on the wonder and significance of *perichoresis* or the eternal modes of subsistence. There is a danger in Christians knowing more about the creation than the Creator, more about salvation than the Savior, and more about the gifts than the Giver. Of course, God has permitted the cosmos so that we know and experience Him *via* His economy, and for that we are ever grateful. Yet, as Christians worship the Triune God Himself, it ought not be the case that a steady diet of economic theology comes with a neglecting to contemplate the divine life *ad intra*.

A healthy understanding of the divine life *ad intra* (toward the inside) and sustained focus on Trinitarian metaphysics could serve as an antidote for the ever-increasing degeneration of our doctrine of God. Indeed, an eyeful of the simple, immutable, *a se* (of Himself), impassible essence of our Triune God will not diminish the Christian's love and appreciation for God's work in the economy but, on the contrary, will illuminate it. For, when we gaze at the being of God, we see well that the completion of the economy of redemption is not possible for just *any* god(s) but needed the unique and exclusive identity of *this* God. As Ivor Davidson stated: 'God's attributes are neither dispensable nor separable in anything that God does. God manifests His glory as the one who is all that He is essentially in Himself.' He continued: 'It is this God who is the Saviour of His creatures.'[10] Doing the dogmatic work of making sure the economy of redemption stays connected with the ontology of the redeemer bears much theological fruit, not to mention joy and security in the Christian life.

The point is worth restating, for fear of miscommunication, that Christians can know anything of God's immanent life only because He has, in His loving kindness, accommodated and revealed Himself in His

---

10. Ivor Davidson, 'God of Salvation,' in *God of Salvation: Soteriology in Theological Perspective*, eds. Ivor Davidson and Murray A. Rae (London: Routledge, 2011), 9.

economic works *ad extra*. As Gilles Emery put it in the opening line of his work on the Trinity, 'faith in the Trinity rests on God's revelation of himself in the economy of salvation.'[11] However, there is a theological reciprocation that comes with theology and economy. As the *ad extra* reveals aspects of the divine life *ad intra*, the relationship reciprocates as the economy becomes clear in the light of God's triune life. As the inseparable operations of the Trinity unfold in the economy, the work clarifies and illuminates the Triune being of that economy. So then, it is right, on this side of the incarnation and Pentecost, for Christian theologians to root the *opera Dei exeuntia* in its very source. While this axiom is true in a broad sense, the aim of this book is more focused. Indeed, to further delineate the thesis of this project, we examine one divine perfection – immutability – to assess the soteriological import and significance of the changelessness of the divine life.

Mutualism and Metaphysics: Modernity's Aversion to Classical Divinity

Accomplishing this thesis calls for extended reflection on metaphysics and the *ad intra* life of the immanent Trinity. It has been said that metaphysics is a word that can 'send shivers down the spines of some biblically minded theologians'[12] and that 'metaphysics is a word from which more or less everyone runs away, as from someone who has the plague.'[13]

As we will see in Chapter Two, there is a trend in modern, post-Enlightenment theology to trade in the classical understanding of God for a non-ontic 'being' riddled with parts, potential, and passions. Indeed,

---

11. Giles Emery, *The Trinity: An Introduction to Catholic Doctrine on the Triune God*, trans. Matthew Levering, Thomistic Ressourcement 1 (Washington, D.C.: Catholic University of America Press, 2011), 1.

12. J. V. Fesko, *Beyond Calvin: Union with Christ and Justification in Early Modern Reformed Theology (1517–1700)*, Reformed Historical Theology 20 (Göttingen: Vandenhoeck & Ruprecht, 2012), 35.

13. Kevin Hector, *Theology without Metaphysics: God, Language, and the Spirit of Recognition* (Cambridge: Cambridge University Press, 2001), 1. Hector uses this quote to set up modern distaste for metaphysics; the quote originates from Hegel. See G. W. F. Hegel, *Vorlesungen über die Geschichte der Philosophie*, Glockner, Georg Wilhelm Friedrich Hegel: Samtliche Werke 11 (Stuttgart: Bad Canstatt, 1965), 400. For brief commentary on Hegel's essay, see John Betz, 'After Heidegger and Marion: The Task of Christian Metaphysics Today,' *Modern Theology* 34 (2018): 569.

'being' has given way to 'becoming' as ontology and divine perfections become increasingly outdated in a modern theological world.[14]

Given that this project will make use of several metaphysical categories and since doing work in theology proper often means that the theologian is forced to do philosophical work, it is worth taking a moment to define what we mean by the term 'metaphysics.'[15] Defining metaphysics does not come without controversy or disagreement. In fact, in their helpful introduction to metaphysics, Michael Loux and Thomas Crisp own this outright, saying: 'It is not easy to say what metaphysics is. If one looks to works in metaphysics, one finds quite different characterizations of the discipline.'[16] Although taking a look at the divergent nuances that make up these 'characterizations' of the discipline of metaphysics would be beneficial, for the sake of brevity, I will simply utilize Robin Le Poidevin's understanding of the 'subject matter' of metaphysics. Poidevin writes:

> [Metaphysics is] concerned with what it is to be or be real, with what things there are, with the way that they are, and with the connection between the way things are and what things they are. And all this is pursued at a higher

14. It would, of course, be an overstatement of the case to say that there is *no place* for metaphysics in modern theology. On the contrary, there are a number of theologians and philosophers fruitfully working in the field of metaphysics in erudite and theologically aiding ways. For example, see Eric D. Pearl, *Thinking Being: Introduction to Metaphysics in the Classical Tradition* (Leiden: Brill, 2014); Edward Feser, *Scholastic Metaphysics: A Contemporary Introduction* (Lancaster: *editiones scholasticae*, 2014); Robert Pasnau, *Metaphysical Themes 1274–1671* (Oxford: Oxford University Press, 2011); Matthew Levering, *Scripture and Metaphysics: Aquinas and the Renewal of Trinitarian Theology* (Oxford: Blackwell, 2004); Steven J. Duby, *God in Himself: Scripture, Metaphysics, and the Task of Christian Theology* (Downers Grove: IVP Academic, 2019); and Elenore Stump, *The God of the Bible and the God of Philosophers* (Milwaukee: Marquette University Press, 2016). These names are but a sample of the fruitful work being done in modern metaphysics. Therefore, readers ought not place in the term 'modern' too much disdain. If one examines pertinent literature over the course of the last five decades, it can indeed be disappointing to see classical ontological categories diminishing, but that is not to say there is not good work being done today.

15. However, as a student of theology, I recognize my own intellectual bounds and have no false illusions about the limits of my expertise. When picking up the tools of philosophical theology, I am relying on the brilliance of other thinkers. Especially those referenced throughout this book.

16. Michael J. Loux and Thomas M. Crisp, *Metaphysics: A Contemporary Introduction* (New York: Routledge, 2017), 2. For a brief history of defining and categorizing metaphysics, see Loux and Crisp, 2-10. For a longer history of metaphysics, see Robin Le Poidevin, *et al*, *The Routledge Companion to Metaphysics* (New York: Routledge, 2012), 1-219.

level of abstraction than typifies any of the special sciences like physics, geology, or chemistry.[17]

In short, the discipline of metaphysics is concerned with reality. When utilized in theology in general and in theology proper more specifically, metaphysics concerns itself with conversations pertaining to matters like substance, act, potential, causation, accidents, and essence. Of course, this is but a sampling of what could rightly be called 'metaphysics'; yet for the purposes of this project – which is first and foremost a dogmatic project on the relationship between theology proper and soteriology – these metaphysical categories and metaphysical definition will suffice.

Coming back to our purposes of exploring a growing distaste for metaphysics in some expressions of modern theology, readers can see the willingness to make such a shift in the somewhat pithy line of process theologian, Charles Hartshorne. Hartshorne declared, 'after two thousand years of ontology, why not experiment a bit with hayathology?'[18] Reading twentieth- and twenty-first-century theology might tempt the student of dogmatics to affirm, with the 'unanimous testimony,' that the 'end of metaphysics' is here.[19] John Betz, in a summary fashion, depicts the small avalanche of material contra metaphysics, saying:

> today the 'end of metaphysics' would seem to be a *fait accompli* – after nominalism's critique of universals; after Luther's repudiation of metaphysics as a temptation; after Hume's committing it to the flames; after Kant's doctrine of the *Ding an sich* and denial of any theoretical knowledge of reality; after Nietzsche's repudiation of all 'lying' forms of Platonism; after Barth's rejection of the *analogia entis* and every metaphysics of being; after Heidegger's critique of metaphysics as 'onto-theology' and the source of the evils of modern technology; after Derrida's deconstruction of metaphysics as 'logo-centrism'; after Marion's apophatic critique of metaphysics as conceptual 'idolatry'; after the 'post-metaphysical' pragmatism of Rorty and Habermas; and, last but not least, after the 'therapeutic anti-metaphysics' of Hector, for whom a pragmatic theology inspired by Wittgenstein and Jeffery Stout can do the work that metaphysics used to do and ground truth and meaning otherwise.[20]

---

17. Poidevin, xx. Poidevin is clear that this is merely the 'subject matter' of metaphysics and a well-rounded definition of the discipline would need more than what is provided here.

18. Charles Hartshorne, *The Logic of Perfection: Neoclassical Metaphysics* (Lasalle: Open Court, 1962), 9. The term hayathology is built on the Hebrew verb, *hayah*, 'to become.'

19. Betz, 'After Heidegger and Marion,' 569-70.

20. Ibid.

In modernity there has been a strong current pulling theologians away from not only metaphysics but also theology proper and a classical understanding of the doctrine of God.[21] How have we arrived here? How have we come to the point in which theology must be 'emancipated' from metaphysics and a classical doctrine of God?[22] Several gifted theologians and historians have taken to this very question and have answered with excellence.[23] While it would be a near impossible task to detail all theological and ecclesial impulses that minimize the metaphysics of classical theism's theology proper, a few are worth mentioning as they are addressed throughout this study.[24]

First, one impulse that moves theologians away from a classical under-standing of Trinitarian metaphysics is a desire to preserve reciprocal and relational soteriology. While each of the five movements away from meta-physics are important to understand, this remonstrance against classical Trinitarianism is most pressing for this book. The idea here is that an emphasis on transcendence puts at risk the kind of God needed for the enter-prise of salvation. As David Bentley Hart, with sarcastic rhetoric, quipped:

> Immutability, impassibility, timelessness – surely, many argue, these relics of an obsolete metaphysics lingered on in Christian theology just as false belief and sinful inclinations linger on in a soul after baptism; and surely they always were fundamentally incompatible with the idea of a God of election and love, who proves himself God through fidelity to his own

---

21. See the reasons for the decline listed in Table One in the *Tables and Figures* section at the end of this book.

22. Hector, *Theology without Metaphysics*, 245. Hector ends his volume with a chapter entitled 'Emancipating Theology' in which he restates his thesis, which demonstrates his distaste for the metaphysical in the opening line: 'I have been arguing that theology needs to be freed from metaphysical assumptions about God and language.'

23. For instance, Duby, *God in Himself*, 189, mentions three critiques of metaphysics found in modern theology: 'that it renders God merely a larger version of the creature, that it obstructs God's economic condescension and interaction with us, and that it creates a rift between God *in se* and God *pro nobis*.'

24. Throughout this project I interact with several works that diverge from the kind of metaphysic I propose for theological method. A full bibliography would be much too voluminous to list, but a few are worth mentioning here: Jean-Luc Marion, *God without Being*, trans. Thomas A. Carlson (Chicago: University of Chicago Press, 2012); Jean-Luc Marion, 'Metaphysics and Phenomenology: A Summary for Theologians,' in *The Postmodern God: A Theological Reader*, ed. Graham Ward (Oxford: Blackwell, 1997), 279-97; George Pattison, *God and Being: An Enquiry* (Oxford: Oxford University Press, 2011); Mark Wrathall, *Religion After Metaphysics* (Cambridge: Cambridge University Press, 2003); John Panteleimon Manoussakis, *God After Metaphysics* (Bloomington: Indiana University Press, 2007); and Hector, *Theology without Metaphysics*.

promises against the horizon of history, who became flesh for us (was this not a change, after all, in God?) and endured the passion of the cross out of pity for us. Have we not seen the wounded heart of God, wounded by our sin in his eternal life, and wounded by it again, even unto death, in the life of the flesh? This is why so much modern theology keenly desires a God who suffers, not simply with us and in our nature, but in his own nature as well.[25]

On one hand, this is a commendable attitude, and the very theological perspective that undergirds this project. This concern is rooted in the principle that what we say about the person of Christ or the Trinity bears soteriological significance. With emphasis, we should affirm this theological connection that keeps together theology and economy.

To demonstrate theologians denouncing ontological categories for functional concerns, consider the case of Torrance and Hodge: it is for soteriological reasons that theologians as diverse as these two come together to deny the *non posse peccare* (not possible to sin) position regarding Christ's flesh. Commenting on John's use of 'flesh,' Torrance stated: 'One thing should be abundantly clear, that if Jesus Christ did not assume our fallen flesh, our fallen humanity, then our fallen humanity is untouched by his work – *for "the unassumed is the unredeemed"*, as Gregory Nazianzen put it.'[26] The great Princeton theologian, Charles Hodge, put it this way: 'This sinlessness of our Lord, however, does not amount to absolute impeccability. It was not a *non potest peccare*. If He was a true man He must have been capable of sinning.' Hodge continued: 'Temptation implies the possibility of sin. If from the constitution of His person it was impossible for Christ to sin, then His temptation was unreal and without effect, and He cannot sympathize with His people.'[27]

---

25. D. B. Hart, *The Beauty of the Infinite: The Aesthetics of Christian Truth* (Grand Rapids: Eerdmans, 2003), 159. The first section of Hart's volume, 'The Trinity,' provides a helpful narrative regarding the role of metaphysics in modern theology. See also, idem, *The Hidden and the Manifest: Essays in Theology and Metaphysics* (Grand Rapids: Eerdmans, 2017).

26. T. F. Torrance, *The Incarnation: The Person and Life of Christ* (Downers Grove, IL: InterVarsity Press, 2008), 62-63, emphasis original. Wellum, *God the Son Incarnate*, 235, addressed Torrance's use of Gregory of Nazianzen and made the important point that Torrance might be misappropriating this line: 'Gregory, in fact, deployed this principle against the heresy of Apollinarianism, which denied that Christ assumed a human mind and thus denied he had a full and complete human nature. At stake was whether Christ had a full human nature, not whether that nature was fallen.'

27. Charles Hodge, *Systematic Theology*, 3 vols. (Peabody, MA: Hendrickson, 2013), 2:457. For more on Hodge's view on the doctrine of Christ's impeccability, see James J.

Soteriological concerns like these are the same concerns that caused the downplay of metaphysics, or at least a redefining and recalculation of metaphysics, in the theology of Barth, Moltmann, and a host of modern theologians across denominational and geographical landscapes.

While this book seeks to affirm these theologians' presupposition that our doctrine of God, Christology, and Trinitarianism have significant soteriological consequence, my aim is to invert their claim. Swimming upstream from these theologians, and others like them, the aim of this project is to show the vital soteriological significance of a classical understanding of our Triune God. Instead of looking at theology proper through the lens of soteriology, we instead aim to examine soteriology with our feet planted in theology proper.

Second, there seems to be a gradual decline of contemplative metaphysics or theology proper replaced by an overemphasis of the practical and pragmatic. There is a gravitational pull toward the 'practical,' which in many cases is not entirely wrong, for indeed theological contemplation ought to lead to the Christian life. The problem arises, however, when forms of theological contemplation are forsaken as they are seen as non-pragmatic. This trend can be seen in movements of emphasis; for instance, the movement of emphasis from ontology to function, or from *ad intra* to *ad extra*, from immanent to economic, etc. The growing dichotomy between divine person and divine action within either Trinitarianism or Christology is predicated on a faulty understanding of meaningful 'practice' in the Christian life. As Matthew Levering stated:

> Theocentric metaphysics belongs to the pedagogical intention of theological wisdom: Aquinas's treatise on the triune God is intended to *form* the reader into a particular kind of knower, by guiding the reader through intellectual exercises that enable the reader to experience, through contemplation, the God of salvation history.[28]

Or as Lewis Ayres put it:

> Claims about the metaphysical bondage of Christian thought are not simply part of modernity's dislike of metaphysics per se: they are closely related to post-Enlightenment thought's suspicion of the idea that contemplation

---

Cassidy, 'No "Absolute Impeccability:" Charles Hodge and Christology at Old and New Princeton,' *The Confessional Presbyterian* 9 (2013): 143-56.

28. Matthew Levering, *Scripture and Metaphysics: Aquinas and the Renewal of Trinitarian Theology* (Oxford: Blackwell, 2004), 36, emphasis original.

of the divine might be the goal and root of theology, wanting instead to focus Christian attention on the 'practical' and on the narrative of Christ's ministry as transformative of human possibility.[29]

The desire for the practical is not wrong in itself. Indeed, given that nearly every theological proposition written in the New Testament was intended for some sort of ecclesial body, theologians would do well to make sure that the *telos* of their theological task is the glory of God and the good of their neighbor, in a meaningful and practical sense.

However, the impulse which downplays contemplative theology and metaphysics commits the double mistake of (1) prioritizing the economic such that it might swallow the immanent, and (2) failing to see that contemplation on the divine life is 'practical' as it aids our beholding the glory of the Lord such that we might be transformed from one glory to another (2 Cor. 3:18).

Third, as we have noted, there is an increasing reprioritization of theological categories, removing the doctrine of God from its proper place of primacy. Like Barth's project to move Christology into the center of Christian theology, there are a number of attempts to orient all of theology from a starting block other than the Triune essence and perfections. This gives rise, as Darren Sumner put it, to models of 'Christocentrism, anthropocentrism, soteriocentrism, and ecclesiocentrism.'[30]

Putting these theological categories at the methodological foundation, acting as a 'center' of theology, runs the risk of reversing the methodological order of theology and economy in the dogmatic task. Instead, in the move to make derivative fields theologically transcendental, we aid the effort to diminish the true principle and source of theology – God in Himself.[31]

Fourth is the demise of pre-critical hermeneutics. As Fesko noted, metaphysics has the unwavering ability to cause the spines of some biblical theologians to shiver.[32] This is why, in his work on the Thomistic understanding of the relationship between metaphysics and Scripture,

---

29. Ayres, *Nicaea and Its Legacy*, 389.

30. Darren Sumner, 'Christocentrism and the Immanent Trinity: Identifying Theology's Pattern and Norm,' in *The Task of Dogmatics*, 155.

31. On the concept of 'transcendental anthropology,' see Darren Sarisky, 'Theological Theology,' in *Theological Theology: Essays in Honour of John Webster*, ed. R. David Nelson, Darren Sarisky, and Justin Stratis, T&T Clark Theology (London: T&T Clark, 2018), 3.

32. Fesko, *Beyond Calvin*, 35.

Levering 'puts it bluntly' and asks, 'now that God has revealed himself in Scripture, why would Christian theologians still rely on the insights of Greek metaphysics?'[33]

In an age of the Enlightenment and scholastic criticism, the worry is that readers would impose a system of thought alien to the textual data on the Scripture and treat the interpretive process differently from any other piece of literature. In this hermeneutical context, focus on God's immanent life is rendered as mere scholasticism as opposed to true exegesis. The dangerous dismissal of metaphysically informed hermeneutics lies not just in procedure but in theory as well. For, in modern biblical studies exegetical practitioners often take to the task of asking *how* we should handle the Bible before addressing *what* the Bible is. The fundamental presupposition of this project is that ontology impacts function. This is true not only for the immanent and economic life of the Trinity but also for the inspired Word of the Triune God. Putting the functional cart before the ontological horse matters since Scripture is 'inherently located within the doctrine of God.'[34] Since all speech proceeds from a speaker, the speech of Scripture must not be divorced from the speaker. It is for this reason that Webster quipped, 'bibliology is prior to hermeneutics.'[35]

Reorienting the divine speech around the divine author in order to deal with matters of ontology before function makes room for an intact doctrine of God which bears methodological import in the interpretive enterprise. This gives the doctrine of divine inspiration some teeth as the divine origins of Scripture actually entail interpretive significance. This will, of course, give rise (to the often addressed) cry of Hellenization.

---

33. Levering, *Scripture and Metaphysics*, 8. Levering, using Thomas as a paradigm, demonstrates that any opposition between metaphysics and exegesis need not be. Rather, 'metaphysics illumines the meaning of scriptural revelation.'

34. Matthew Barrett, *God's Word Alone: The Authority of Scripture* (Grand Rapids: Zondervan, 2016), 271. For more on this relationship, see Matthew Barrett, *Canon, Covenant and Christology: Rethinking Jesus and the Scriptures of Israel* (Downers Grove, IL: IVP, 2019). See also Scott R. Swain, *Trinity, Revelation, and Reading: A Theological Introduction to the Bible and its Interpretation*, T&T Clark Theology (New York: T&T Clark, 2011), 72-94.

35. John Webster, *The Domain of the Word: Scripture and Theological Reason*, T&T Clark Theology (New York: T&T Clark, 2012), viii. Webster extrapolates the significance of divine inspiration and its tie between these two fields in John Webster, 'ὑπὸ πνεύματος ἁγίου φερόμενοι ἐλάλησαν ἀπὸ θεοῦ ἄνθρωποι: On the Inspiration of Holy Scripture' in *Conception, Reception, and the Spirit: Essays in Honor of Andrew T. Lincoln*, ed. J. G. McConville and L. K. Pietersen (Eugene, OR: Cascade, 2015).

This decry of a metaphysically informed approach to the Scriptures appears in Walter Brueggemann's *Theology of the Old Testament:*

> But because the Old Testament does not (and never intends to) provide a coherent and comprehensive offer of God, this subject matter is more difficult, complex, and problematic than we might expect. For the most part, the Old Testament text gives us only hints, traces, fragments, and vignettes, with no suggestion of how all these elements might fit together, if indeed they do. What does emerge, in any case, is an awareness that the elusive but dominating Subject of the Old Testament cannot be comprehended in any preconceived categories. The God of the Old Testament does not easily conform to the expectations of Christian dogmatic theology, nor to the categories of any Hellenistic perennial philosophy.[36]

Though theologians are not short of responses to this bemoaning of dogmatics' intrusion in biblical studies, Craig Carter's recent work has been exemplary in rebuttal. As Carter points out, *everyone* comes to the text with a working metaphysic – Brueggemann and his contemporaries included. Far from being a-metaphysical when approaching the Scripture, Carter demonstrated that while many modern theologians decry 'Hellenization,' they may be guilty still of 'Hegelianization.'[37] Interpreters cannot help but to have a presuppositional metaphysic as they come to the text; the question is whether or not it is one consistent with the Christianity they seek to study.[38]

---

36. Walter Brueggemann, *Theology of the Old Testament: Testimony, Dispute, Advocacy* (Philadelphia: Fortress, 2012), 117.

37. Craig Carter, *Contemplating God with the Great Tradition: Recovering Trinitarian Classical Theism* (Grand Rapids: Baker, 2021), 5. This is, of course, not to conclude that all minimizations of a classically informed theology proper are in debt to Hegel; for this would be an over-generalization. However, it is nevertheless a helpful statement to demonstrate the near impossibility of coming to the theological task as a-metaphysical. See also idem, *Interpreting Scripture with the Great Tradition: Recovering the Genius of Premodern Exegesis* (Grand Rapids: Baker, 2018), which demonstrates the 'genius of premodern exegesis.' On the complaint of Hellenization, Ayres, *Nicaea and Its Legacy*, 388-89, says: 'there is a strategy of presenting classical Christian theology as unsustainable because of its debt to "Greek metaphysics," or because of its "Platonizing" of Christianity.' Ayres continues: 'This debt is taken either to result in a speculative theology unrelated to Christian social practice, or it is taken to result in the overcoming of some fundamental "biblical" themes, frequently present as "dynamic" in distinction from "static" ontological categories.' Ayres then gives a substantial footnote giving examples particular to biblical studies.

38. While numerous responses to the Hellenization thesis exist, I was served by Paul Gravrilyuk, *The Suffering of the Impassible God: The Dialectics of Patristic Thought* (Oxford: Oxford University Press, 2004), 1-47.

Fifth, and finally, is the rise of theistic personalism and mutualism. The terms 'theistic personalism' and 'theistic mutualism,' while deriving from two separate theologians and emphasizing two different points, describe a similar phenomenon. That phenomenon is to trade in the Anselmian view of God, captured in his oft-repeated line wherein God is 'something than which nothing greater can be thought,'[39] for a God of lesser transcendence.[40]

The term 'theistic personalism' comes from Brian Davies as he juxtaposed two different means of conceptualizing theism – classical and personalism.[41] With theistic personalism we see a God of mystery, but the mystery is not beyond comprehension. Indeed, in the theistic personalist's understanding of God, God is a disembodied person with whom we can relate by varying degrees. God has wisdom, but we have wisdom and can therefore relate. God has love, but we have love and can therefore contemplate the true person of God. While God might have an infinite measure of these attributes, the theologians can relate as they too possess these communicable traits. This is, of course, contrary to the classical notion of God, which insists on a doctrine of divine incomprehensibility such that theological wisdom and articulation is analogical and the Creator differs from the creature not by varying degrees but in kind altogether. As Gregory of Nazianzus put it in his second theological oration, 'To know God is hard, to describe him impossible.'[42] Van Mastricht anchored the imperceptibility of God, who dwells in 'inaccessible light' (1 Tim. 6:16), in three realities: His simplicity, His infinity, and His unity.[43]

---

39. Anselm, *The Major Works*, ed. Brian Davies and G. R. Evans (Oxford: Oxford University Press, 2008), 87.

40. I recognize the imperfection of these two labels as they are designated not from *within* a theological tradition, but instead by that 'traditions' dissenters. However, they both serve our discussion well here as summary statements only with careful definition. In short, *mutualism* is the prediction of a kind of relationship between the creator and creature such that there is genuine and *mutual* change in both parties due the relationship; *personalism* should be taken to mean a model of God such that God is an infinitely greater being, but not an altogether different being, which will have implications of theological language and method.

41. Brian Davies, *An Introduction to the Philosophy of Religion*, 3rd ed. (Oxford: Oxford University Press, 2004), 12-15.

42. Gregory of Nazianzus, *On God and Christ: The Five Theological Orations and Two Letters to Cledonius*, trans. Frederick Williams and Lionel Wickham, Popular Patristics 23 (New York: St. Vladimir's Seminary Press, 2002), 39. Another translation rendered it: 'It is difficult to conceive God but to define him in words is an impossibility' (Gregory of Nazianzus, *The Second Theological Oration* [*NPNF* 7:289]).

43. Petrus van Mastricht, *Theoretical-Practical Theology*, 2 vols. (Grand Rapids: Reformation Heritage, 2019), 2:75-76.

The term 'theistic mutualism' was popularized by James Dolezal's work, *All That is in God*.[44] Dolezal claimed that those who espouse this view hold that God is involved in a 'genuine give-and-take relationship with his creatures.'[45] This, again, deals with the nature of theological language, for theistic mutualists, *contra* classicists, insist on the creature's ability to univocally articulate God and His essence. While personalists emphasize the relatability of God by degree and mutualists emphasize the relational moldability of God, both are modern movements away from a being of pure actuality and simplicity.[46]

Of course these five criticisms – (1) a desire to preserve a reciprocal and relational soteriology, (2) the prioritization of theological pragmatism over contemplative theology proper, (3) the reprioritization of theological loci that removes the doctrine of God as the principal and source of theology, (4) the demise of pre-critical and pre-modern hermeneutics and its metaphysically informed exegesis, and (5) the rise of theistic personalism and theistic mutualism – do not comprise an exhaustive list of impulses that minimize Trinitarian metaphysics and theology proper, they nevertheless describe the theological climate and some of the current pulling at Christian theologians today.

'Light Thrice Repeated': Trinitarian Lessons from the Great Tradition

Even the briefest survey of theological antiquity will give way to the conclusion that it has not always been this way. Ontic and metaphysical realities are foundational to conciliar Christianity. We see, even in the earliest creeds of the church, utilization of ontic semantics. The deployment

---

44. James Dolezal, *All That Is in God: Evangelical Theology and the Challenge of Classical Christian Theism* (Grand Rapids: Reformation Heritage, 2017). Another option besides theistic personalism and theistic mutualism, as Dolezal points out, is D. B. Hart's 'mono-polytheism.' See D. B. Hart, *The Experience of God: Being, Consciousness, Bliss* (New Haven, CT: Yale University Press, 2013).

45. Dolezal, *All That Is in God*, 2. Dolezal, like Davies, contrasted this understanding of theism with the classical conception, which he defined as 'the underlying and inviolable conviction [that] God does not derive any aspect of His being from outside Himself and is not in any way caused to be' (*All That Is in God*, 1).

46. The concept of *actus purus* (pure act) will appear throughout this volume. The doctrine takes its most prominent role in Chapter Six, on divine immutability and the economy of redemption. It is worth pointing out the location of the most prolonged discussion of the doctrine given its significance to the thesis of this project and presence throughout.

and corrections of *ousia* (essence) and *hypostasis* (person) gave creedal guidelines for the church's theological reasoning regarding Trinitarianism and Christological studies.[47] Opening his time-tested treatise on the Trinity, Hilary of Poitiers stated that 'there is nothing more characteristic of God than to be.'[48] Contra the post-Enlightenment dream to exchange the being of God for the becoming of God, the fathers proclaimed that being is proper to divinity.[49] As Ephrem the Syrian quipped in his *Sermon Against Rash Inquirers*, this God is not only being, but 'absolute being. His being is as glorious as his name.'[50] Augustine picks up this language: 'Through him do we see that whatever exists in any way is good. For, it is from him who does not merely exist "in some way," but is absolutely.'[51] The absoluteness of this being's essence is a far cry from the processed existence of some expressions in modern theology proper.

From the forerunners in the great tradition we learn the lesson that the Triune being of God is not something to flee nor demote in our theological reasoning. In fact, it is the very Trinitarian being of God that gives light to all theological realities. In his fifth theological oration, oration thirty-one, Gregory of Nazianzus declared that God is 'Light thrice repeated.'[52] This thrice-repeated light illuminates all other theological realities in the rays of His own light. As Gregory stated, 'now we have both seen and proclaim concisely and simply the doctrine of God the Trinity, comprehending out of Light (the Father), Light (the Son), in Light (The Holy Ghost).'[53] The Cappadocian father so

---

47. For an important discussion regarding the development of these two terms, see R. P. Hanson, *The Search for the Christian Doctrine of God: The Arian Controversy, 318–381* (Grand Rapids: Baker, 2005), 181-207. Cf. also, Ayres, *Nicaea and Its Legacy*, 92-98.

48. Hilary of Poitiers, *De Trinitate*, transl. Stephen McKenna (Washington, D.C.: Catholic University of America Press, 1954), 6.

49. Ibid., 7.

50. Ephrem the Syrian, *Sermons Against Rash Inquirers*, as quoted in *We Believe in One God*, ed. Gerald Bray, Ancient Christian Doctrine 1 (Downers Grove, IL: IVP Academic, 2009), 39.

51. Augustine, *Confessions* (TFC:21, 450-51).

52. Gregory of Nazianzus, *O31.III* (NPNF 7:318).

53. Ibid. Christopher A. Beeley provides a perhaps clearer translation, 'Out of the light (Father) we comprehend the light (the Son) in light (the Spirit).' See Beeley, *Gregory of Nazianzus on the Trinity and the Knowledge of God: In Your Light We Shall See Light* (Oxford: Oxford University Press, 2008), 197. Beyond translations, Beeley's volume is insightful in demonstrating Gregory's devotion to Trinitarianism in theological and ecclesial perspective.

emphasized Trinitarianism as the bedrock of all doctrinal formulation that he penned that the doctrine of the Trinity is 'the only true devotion and saving doctrine'[54] and that the Trinity is the doctrine which is the 'crown [over] all' other doctrines.[55] Far from neglecting the divine being, Gregory – in line with much early Christian theology – understood the Triune doctrine of God to be the principle and source of theological wisdom and reasoning.

Though there are a number of varying streams which flow into what is known as 'the great tradition,' the rather consistent pattern of orthodox thinking knowns not of a 'being' that is lacking as seen in some,[56] and therefore the only thing He lacks is passive potency and contingency.[57] He has fullness of life in His complete and simple essence and stands as the head of all things, the unmoved mover, in and to whom all things were created. Not only do the saints of the past model for us exceptional articulations of God's being, but they show us as well the systematic connections between God's ontology and His work in the economy of redemption. Athanasius, the great Nicene defender from Alexandria, demonstrated time and again a theological method that holds together God's theology and economy. We can compare his *Four Discourses Against the Arians*, which is riddled with soteric concern, and his *On the Incarnation*, which is riddled with ontic theology, and see that the great Alexandrian theologian noted the importance of connecting theology and economy in showing that God's being is needed to perpetrate God's work in salvation.[58]

---

54. Gregory of Nazianzus, O43.XXX (NPNF 7:405).

55. Gregory of Nazianzus, O2.XXXVI (NPNF 7:212).

56. For a helpful discussion on the metaphysical properties of matter and form, see Robert Pasnau, *Metaphysical Themes 1274–1671* (Oxford: Oxford University Press, 2011), 17-71; 549-78.

57. Aquinas, *ST,* Ia2.2

58. Athanasius, *Four Discourses Against the Arians* (*NPNF* 4:303-448). See especially the first of the four discourses in which Athanasius, before moving into polemic and apologetic exegesis, gives a constructive understanding of the divinity of Jesus and its soteric importance. Idem, *On the Incarnation*, trans. John Behr, Popular Patristics 44B (New York: St. Vladimir's Seminary Press). See especially Athanasius' ninth point in connecting the divine nature of Jesus to the wonder of the incarnation for the salvation of His people. For more on the soteriology found in the pages of *On the Incarnation*, see Thomas G. Weinandy, *Athanasius: A Theological Introduction* (Burlington: Ashgate, 2007), 27-45. We will treat Athanasius at length in Chapter Three.

Therefore, in alignment with the voices of the past, we move not with the current of modernity *away* from a robust theology proper but, on the contrary, recognize that God is the full and final 'object' of Christian theology and move *toward* a lifetime of gazing at our triune God.[59]

Thesis and Method: A Dogmatic Account of the Soteric Significance of Divine Immutability

Pulling all the above data together, this project has a twofold burden – a general thesis and a specific thesis. The general thesis is a larger concern than this individual work can address but it deserves stating. The specific thesis is what we focus on in the pages of this book. The first burden, which acts as the general thesis, is that all soteriology should be rooted in the principle and source of Christian theology – the doctrine of God. As this first chapter has sought to articulate, the thinking Christian community might be able to conceive of God without contemplation of salvation, but we ought not try to articulate a Christian doctrine of redemption without first describing the redeemer. The economy of redemption must not be divorced from the person(s) of the redeemer.

This first burden, the general thesis, has been the primary focus of Chapter One. However, in the coming chapters we move in from the general thesis to the specific thesis. The specific thesis is to articulate and demonstrate the variegated soteriological implications for a classical understanding of divine immutability. Namely, the aim of this project is to demonstrate how a classical articulation of divine immutability both protects and promotes God's work in the economy of redemption. Establishing the soteric import of divine immutability acts as an example of the beauty and worth of anchoring all the economy of redemption in theology proper.[60]

---

59. Along with the many references earlier in this chapter that described God as the object of theology, see also, Francis Turretin, *IET,* I.V.1–I.VIII.15.

60. A foundational hope I have for the current project is that the following pages act as an invitation to join the task of connecting the *ad intra* life of our Triune God to His graceful work *ad extra*. Divine immutability is but one ontological category that bears significant soteriological implications. The hope is to produce a reproducible model that could be applied to future projects on, say, divine simplicity, aseity, atemporality, and more. Chapter Six will work through other possibilities as they relate to the doctrine of divine immutability.

Therefore, this project should be thought of as primarily a work on the divine perfection of immutability and, by derivation, soteriology.[61] This order of emphasis is a nod to the methodology behind the book and the rationale for emphasizing immutability prior to economy in the title. As Webster stated, 'Soteriology is a derivative doctrine, and no derivative doctrine may occupy the material place which is properly reserved for the Christian doctrine of God, from which alone all other doctrines derive.'[62] The following content focuses on this particular doctrine as we excavate the biblical and theological material on our way to demonstrating the soteric import of God's changelessness.

A justifiable question at this point could be, why immutability? Why not use another divine perfection as the specific thesis to demonstrate the importance of rooting the economy in the doctrine of God? While maybe unsatisfactory to some, the answer is twofold. First, as Stephen Charnock stated, the doctrine of divine immutability is 'a glory belonging to all the attributes of God' and 'a thread that runs through the whole web, it is the enamel of all the rest [of the perfections].'[63] Charnock's point is important and we will discuss what he means in greater detail come Chapters Five and Six. For now, suffice it to say that in the doctrine of immutability we get all the other divine perfections. The second reason for focusing on divine immutability is simply due to a lack of literature. Students of theology are hard-pressed to find full-length monographs focusing exclusively on God's changelessness.[64]

---

61. Further discussion pertaining to the definition of divine immutability will come in Chapter Two, yet it is worth noting here that immutability is referred to as a 'divine perfection' only in a loose sense, not a technical sense of predication. Immutability is ultimately an apophatic, or *negative*, predication and therefore Christian theologians have varied in willingness to signify it as a 'perfection.' For our purposes, I will refer to immutability as a perfection throughout this project to demonstrate the difference in God's changelessness from the 'changelessness' that might be inherited by creatures – such as angels or humans in glory. Also, I will use this title to help readers understand that divine immutability is vital in protecting what could properly be predicated as a positive perfection of the divine being. Of course, I am not alone in using the term this way as some thinkers throughout variegated traditions have but I acknowledge the nuance needed in naming God.

62. Webster, '"It was the Will of the Lord to Bruise Him": Soteriology and the Doctrine of God,' in *God of Salvation*, 16.

63. Stephen Charnock, *Discourse on the Existence and Attributes of God*, The Works of Stephen Charnock 1, 5 vols. (Edinburgh: Banner of Truth, 2010), 381.

64. This is not to claim that none exist. See, for example, Michael J. Dodds, *The Unchanging God of Love: Thomas Aquinas and Contemporary Theology on Divine*

The journey to achieve the specific thesis – demonstrating the soteric significance of divine immutability – will take a number of turns. As mentioned, in this opening chapter, I have sought to set the stage by discussing modernity's relationship with Trinitarian metaphysics as we get an eyeful of the immanent life of God in our pursuit of dissecting the doctrine of divine immutability. The second chapter aims to provide a working definition for divine immutability while also describing departures from this definition. The interlocutors of the second chapter will span multiple centuries and theological traditions. Not only will there be diversity in era and tradition, but also diversity in the severity with which these theologians break with a classical understanding of God's changelessness. From the harsh cuts of open and process theism to the lesser lacerations of modern evangelicals, I seek to examine those theologians who wish to add movement and motion to the unmoved mover.

In the wake of these departures from divine immutability, Chapters Three through Five aim to develop a constructive and dogmatic case for immutability as an essential divine attribute. These three chapters act as a threefold witness to immutability: a historical witness, a biblical-theological witness, and a metaphysical witness. In Chapter Three we examine the consistent acceptance of God's changelessness throughout theological antiquity. As we move era by era, the hope is to usher in a monumental amount of support for divine immutability through the voices of the past. The following chapter, Chapter Four, a biblical witness, seeks to employ biblical theology as a means to positively affirm immutability as a textual and biblically explicit doctrine. The final chapter of this threefold witness, a theological-metaphysical witness, makes use of philosophical theology in demonstrating the necessity of divine immutability in a systematic connection with the other divine perfections. Utilizing constructive and systematic theology, in this chapter we establish the simple and essential relationships between all divine perfections and immutability. In this fifth chapter, we again turn our attention to the Scriptures as a unified story bearing witness to the

---

Immutability (Washington, D.C.: The Catholic University of America Press, 2008); and Thomas G. Weinandy, *Does God Change? The Word's Becoming in the Incarnation* (Petersham: St. Bede's, 1985). Yet, book-length treatments from modern evangelical scholars that do not deviate from a classical understanding of divine immutability are hard to come by, which is lamentable.

Triune God whose immutable person provides the unique qualification to provide an immutable work.

The final chapter of the project, 'Divine Immutability and the Economy of Redemption,' turns from a constructive articulation of the doctrine of divine immutability to exploring the soteriological significance of God's changelessness for the economy of redemption. This connection takes place over the contours of multiple headings. First, in looking at the biblical paradigm and context for divine immutability, we see that the biblical authors themselves often tied closely matters of God's changelessness and the salvation of His people. Second, zooming in from the canon as a whole to Jesus in particular, we examine the role of divine changelessness within the life of Christ, paying special attention to the soteriological implications of Christology. Third, we again examine corollary divine perfections in hopes to show that not only does divine immutability have soteric implications, but even more so in its systematic connection to the other divine perfections. Finally, the chapter comes to a close by observing the relationship between divine changelessness and union with Christ.

This enterprise takes the harmonious implementation of the major fields of theology – exegesis, history, philosophy, and systematics. The purposeful use of multiple disciplines both attests to the consistent truth which undergirds the doctrine of divine immutability and a methodological preference that seeks to break down barriers between theological disciplines. I aim to build from the *principium externum* (the external principle) of the inspired Scriptures while bringing philosophical insight to bear and linking arms with brothers and sisters in the great tradition. Making use of the theological tools of multiple fields ensures that, in the end, this is a product of systematic and dogmatic theology, demonstrating, as Bavinck stated, not only what confessors and confession *do* believe, but what they *ought* to believe.[65] Namely, that by the testimony of Scripture, reason, and the great tradition, we worship the Triune God who has 'no variableness, neither shadow of turning' (James 1:17 KJV), who is the 'same yesterday, today, and forever' (Heb. 13:8), as the immutable Redeemer who secures an immutable redemption.

---

65. Bavinck, *Reformed Dogmatics*, 1:88.

CHAPTER TWO

Definitions, Deviations, and Denials of Divine Immutability

Toward a Definition of Divine Immutability

The first chapter set the stage for the rest of the project by arguing that a metaphysically informed doctrine of God should ground the theological enterprise as the only *locus* of theology suited to hold the weight of theological method. Now, we zoom in to our example: the relationship between divine immutability and soteriology. Examining the relationship between divine immutability and the economy of redemption will be an example of the benefit of rooting the economy in theology. The first ingredient needed for a project aimed at demonstrating immutability's soteriological import, however, is a working definition. The conversation surrounding this doctrine is a mutable conversation about an immutable God, so clarity of terms is crucial. Therefore, this chapter provides a working definition of divine immutability and then uses that definition to articulate the growing deviations and denials of divine immutability.

There is no shortage of attempts to define divine immutability. Given the doctrine's prevalence throughout theological antiquity, it should come as no surprise that definitions abound. Turretin articulated God's changelessness, saying, 'Immutability is an incommunicable attribute of God by which is denied of him not only all change, but also all possibility of change, as much with respect to existence as to will.'[1] Another oft-quoted definition comes from the Lutheran scholastic theologian, Johannes Quenstedt, who expressed immutability as 'the perpetual identity of the divine essence and all its perfections, with the absolute negation of all motion, either physical or ethical.'[2] A final definition comes from the Early Modern Reformed theologian, Stephen Charnock, who penned, 'The essence of God, with all the perfections of his nature, are pronounced the same, without any variation from eternity to eternity.'[3] Though Charnock only mentions the immutable nature of God's essence, he goes on to expand the definition of immutability to include God's essence, His knowledge, and His will and purpose.[4]

Though we could examine an abundance of supplementary definitions, these three serve our purpose in this chapter; they include several caveats that a proper definition of immutable should include, along with a number of points that opponents will deny. Moreover, while bringing more voices to bear in our efforts of defining divine immutability would prove helpful, further examination of the historical development of the doctrine will come in Chapter Three. Pulling from these three voices, along with a host of theological antiquity, let us proceed with our working definition of divine immutability: The doctrine of divine immutability is the Christian teaching, held by the vast majority of the historic Christian tradition, that declares that God is free from change and that alteration in God is an impossibility. This means that God is not in danger of nor prone to any alteration, including actualization, potentiality, and accidents, nor any kind of increase or decrease. This unchangeableness should be understood to extend to all that is in God, including His essence, His will, His knowledge, etc. The doctrine of immutability is related to the other divine perfections, and together they present a God who is free from change in parts, passions, time, and space. Instead, God is a God who is pure act and possesses no accidents, a God who is *a se* and the supreme contingency of all life, a God who

---

1. Turretin, *IET*, III.XI.1

2. Johannes Quenstedt, *Theologia Didactico-Polemica*, cited in Heinrich Schmid, *The Doctrinal Theology of the Evangelical Lutheran Church* (Philadelphia: Lutheran Publication Society, 1876), 137.

3. Stephen Charnock, *Discourse on the Existence and Attributes of God*, 1:379.

4. Ibid., 1:382-87.

is the unmoved Mover and Creator of all things who is not altered by that which He created.

In sum, God is free from change and indeed it is impossible for Him to change. While defining immutability as God's freedom from alteration – whether increase or decrease – is satisfactory, the following are a few alliterated categories which give handrails to speak theologically regarding God's changelessness: God is immutable in respect to process, processions, potentiality, parts, passions, perfections, and plans. Before moving on to deviations from a classical understanding, we will here say a brief word about each of these seven.[5]

(1) *Process*: Contra modern process theology, God is not in the act of *becoming*. Rather, God is pure act and is the fullness of *being* in Himself.

(2) *Processions:* That which distinguishes the persons of the Trinity – eternal relations of origin – are eternal and unchanging. The Father is the ever-unbegotten, the Son is the eternally generated, and the Spirit eternally proceeds from the Father and Son. The personal properties of the eternal modes of subsistence are unchanging in the Trinity.

(3) *Potentiality*: Since God is pure act, that is, He possesses no passive potency, there is nothing in God that needs to be awakened to actuality.

(4) *Parts*: Since God's essence is unified and not composed of parts, He is simple. Therefore, He does not experience change in virtue of addition or subtraction of compositional parts.

(5) *Passions*: Since there is nothing in God which needs to be actualized, He will not undergo an addition or change of passions. Instead, God is pure act and as He is without body and parts, He is also without passions.

(6) *Perfections:* Closely related to God's immutability by virtue of His 'parts,' what we mean by saying that God is immutable in His perfections is that all God's attributes are not merely items He possesses and one day might possess more or less of them. Rather, God's attributes are to be understood as perfections and stand therefore immutably perfect.

And (7) *Plans*: God's perfection of immutability renders Him perfectly consistent. Volitional swings are not to be predicated of God; rather He is faithful in accomplishing His immutable will.

---

5. See this alliterated list defining divine immutability in chart form in Table Two of the *Tables and Figures* section at the end of this book.

With this working definition in hand, the remainder of this chapter examines the growing number of deviations and denials of the doctrine, before constructing a positive affirmation of the classic understanding of divine immutability in Chapters Three through Five.[6]

Deviations and Denials of Divine Immutability

A survey of recent theological literature surrounding divine immutability reveals the discussion of God's changelessness to be a mutable conversation about an immutable God. Denials of God's unchanging nature have compounded in the last century and now flow from several springs. Repudiations of immutability are not confined to one denomination, continent, or theological era. Rather, the cast whose pen writes of a mutable God seems to be increasingly diverse. From process theists to evangelicals, and many variations in between, modern remonstrances against immutability proliferate. One dissenter, Isaak August Dorner (1809–1884), put the reality this way: 'The traditional axiomatic immutability of God is nowadays in dispute by a majority of contemporary thinkers from a variety of perspectives,' which led Dorner to conclude that 'there must be a renewed theological investigation of this question in order to prepare a more satisfactory doctrine of God.'[7]

These deviations from a teaching of an unalterable God are not going unnoticed. Indeed, it would prove difficult to remain ignorant of the rising tide of literature against classical immutability, especially

---

6. A point worth restating at the end of this section on defining divine immutability is that there is no shortage of understandings and articulations of divine immutability. Even while writing this project, I proof-read a chapter on immutability for a forthcoming publication. At the time of this book's publication, Jordan Steffaniak's forthcoming volume on classical theism espouses four models of immutability. They are (1) Global Divine Immutability, (2) Local Divine Immutability, (3) Essential Divine Immutability, and (4) Weak Immutability. Steffaniak argues that either of the first two models can maintain consistency with Classical Theism (Jordan Steffaniak, forthcoming volume, Lexham Press). While Jordan's project is erudite and helpful (and I hope aids in recovering a classical articulation of divine immutability), I still chose here to go with the definition given in this chapter. There will, no doubt, continue to be articulations of immutability as theologians work together in trying to best describe our unchanging God. This footnote is simply to mention the diversity and variety of definitions concerning divine immutability.

7. Isaak August Dorner, *Divine Immutability: A Critical Reconsideration*, trans. Claude Welch and Robert T. Williams, Fortress Texts in Modern Theology (Minneapolis: Fortress, 1994), 81.

as the theological conversation pushes into the modern era. In his 1983 essay, Richard A. Muller points to the ingenuity of Kant, Hegel, Fichte, and Schelling and says that under their tutelage, 'the older ontology of immutable being was replaced by an idealist ontology of the gradual self-realization of the absolute idea, in short, an ontology of becoming or of the becoming of being.'[8]

Muller's insightful point picks up on the trend in modern theology to move from the absolute to the unactualized. As we will see, a trade such as this stems from a number of sources, as the impulse to diminish the absoluteness of God's unchanging nature is invoked for different reasons. Brian Davies, working on the interconnectivity of God's attributes of simplicity and immutability, helpfully lists five such reasons theologians might be prone to deviate from a classic understanding of an unchanging essence in God: (1) if God lives and acts, then He changes; (2) if God loves, then God changes; (3) if God is immutable, then God is not free; (4) if God knows, then God is changeable; and (5) the Bible says that God changes.[9]

While the impulses to deny immutability are variegated, enough time has passed – and enough deviations published – to reveal theological patterns. One could use any number of several strategies to traverse the arguments *contra* classical immutability in hopes to provide a taxonomy of deviations and denials away from the doctrine. For instance, you could cover the pertinent material chronologically, examining the denials of immutability as they appear throughout history. You could opt to cover the literature via the lens of denominational affiliation, showing the denials by way of tribal affirmations and denials. Or one could organize the arguments by theological position; this method would treat groups instead of individuals and look at entire segments, such as

---

8. Richard A. Muller, 'Incarnation, Immutability, and the Case for Classical Theism,' *Westminster Theological Journal* 45 (1983), 22. Muller continues to demonstrate the impact of these theological architects, saying, 'The impact of this alternative ontology upon theology was enormous, particularly in Germany. Theologians like Dorner, Thomasius, Biedermann, and Gess all concluded that change, becoming, could be predicated of God.'

9. Davies, *Introduction to the Philosophy of Religion*, 165. Dolezal, *All That Is in God*, 9, puts the significance of this discussion in perspective when he claims, 'Perhaps no question more clearly illuminates the conflict between the older teaching of classical Christian theism and the newer commitments of theistic mutualism.'

process theologians, open theists, or evangelicals. While each of these models is helpful in its own right, this chapter instead seeks to explore the deviations and denials of divine immutability by categorizing them inductively. Like we have said, patterns emerge as theologians work through the pages of theological literature which seek to deny, or at least alter, the doctrine of divine immutability. Using these patterns, we can develop a taxonomy of denials and deviations to catalog why modern theologians are willing to ascribe movement to God. While others may exist, there are five major 'problems' leveraged against a classical articulation of divine immutability that become apparent in working through the literature. Moreover, it would not do justice to the breadth of theological literature to argue that deviations of divine immutability are monolithic. On the contrary, even within this taxonomy of denials, arguments are variegated. As pertaining to deviations and denials of divine immutability the following five categories will be our working taxonomy for the remainder of this chapter: (1) the problem of relations and soteriology; (2) the incarnation; (3) creation and divine action; (4) volition and knowledge; (5) and divine freedom and contingency.[10]

The remaining space of this chapter works through each problem respectively, discussing key ideas, theologians, and groups who have contributed to and ascribed that particular change to God. Of course, an exhaustive treatment of each problem is impossible and is out of line with the *telos* of this project. Instead, each category focuses on a few representative examples. It should also be noted that when theologians deny immutability, they often do so on multiple fronts. So, when we treat representatives for each ascribed remonstrance, we will focus on an aspect of their denial while other aspects may remain.

Furthermore, since the ultimate goal of this project is to articulate the soteriological significance of a classical understanding of divine immutability, we will not seek to respond to each deviation or denial point-by-point. Rather, the subsequent three chapters develop a constructive understanding of divine immutability and interact with the movements as needed to articulate a positive understanding of immutability as it relates to soteriology.

---

10. See this taxonomy of denials and deviations in chart-form in Table Three in the *Tables and Figures* section at the end of this book.

(1) The Problem of Relations and Soteriology

Of the problems ascribed to God above, the relational/soteriological dilemma is both the most important for this project and the most frequently used deviation from a classical approach to divine immutability. The former is true because this remonstrance against divine immutability shares the impulse of our thesis. These theologians worry that a strong conception of changelessness renders God unable to save in the manner the biblical data seems to depict. The concern that drives their reasoning is soteriological in nature; and, in this way, these theologians share the foundational conviction of this work, namely, that our theology of God's being influences and impacts our theology of God's redemption. This connection is why Richard Swinburne referred to the classical notion of God as a 'lifeless thing,' saying if God possessed 'Fixed intentions "from all eternity" he would be a very lifeless thing; not a person who reacts to men with sympathy or anger, pardon or chastening because he chooses too there and then.'[11]

The latter reason for the importance of this complaint is true since the cast that employs this line of argumentation is not confined to one theological era, denomination, or tribe. On the contrary, asserting the seeming negative soteric effects of classical immutability found favor across the theological spectrum. Given the size of the pertinent literature, some delineation is needed; we will confine our survey to three theologians who represent both the strength of this argument and the diversity – Isaak August Dorner, Charles Hartshorne, and Bruce Ware.

Isaak August Dorner

No treatment of divine immutability would be complete without interaction with I. A. Dorner. Between 1856 and 1858, Dorner wrote a collection of three essays, published originally in *Jahrbücher für deutsche Theologie*, which have had a remarkable influence on the conversation of God's changelessness.[12] The ghost of his articulation of

---

11. Richard Swinburne, *The Coherence of Theism* (Oxford: Oxford University Press, 1993), 221. This is why Swinburne declares that God must have 'continual interaction' with men such that God is 'moved by men.'

12. One needs to only look at the explosion of secondary literature interacting with Dorner to witness his significant impact on the conversation. While this list is far from exhaustive, see: Robert Brown, 'Schelling and Dorner on Divine Immutability,'

divine immutability outlived him through the pens of many theological children. The most prominent of these theological children is Barth. Introducing his section on immutability, Barth nods to Dorner: 'I. A. Dorner has made this clear in a way that is illuminating for the whole doctrine of God. ... [T]hose who know the essay will recognize as they read this sub-section how much I owe to Dorner's inspiration.'[13]

The occasion for Dorner's three essays on immutability was a response to the growing popularity of kenotic Christology. In Robert Williams' fine introduction to Dorner's essays, he states: 'Dorner's analysis of kenoticism reveals that it both fails to solve the christological problem, and errs in simply rejecting divine immutability.'[14] Dorner believed that an aspect of divine immutability must remain for there to be hope in God's consistent goodness and benevolence. Moreover, if we rid every shred of divine immutability, Dorner feared that the end result would inevitably be a pantheistic problem. However, Dorner found the Thomistic conception of immutability less than satisfying in its attempt to articulate God's real relations with His creatures. Dorner had a multifold thesis, but the most pertinent to this discussion follows:

> Exhibiting in a positive dogmatic way the necessary and true union of the immutability and vitality of God in a higher principle, which will contain at the same time the supreme norm for correctly determining the relation of

Journal of the American Academy of Religion 53 (1985); Stephen Duby, 'Divine Immutability, Divine Action and the God-World Relation,' International Journal of Systematic Theology 19 (2017); Matthias Gockel, 'On the Way from Schleiermacher to Barth: A Critical Reappraisal of Isaak August Dorner's Essay on Divine Immutability,' Scottish Journal of Theology 53 (2000); Piotr J. Malysz, 'Hegel's Conception of God and Its Application by Isaak Dorner to the Problem of Divine Immutability,' Pro Ecclesia 15 (2006); Robert Sherman, 'Isaak August Dorner on Divine Immutability A Missing Link Between Schleiermacher and Barth,' Journal of Religion 7 (1997); and Robert R. Williams, 'I. A. Dorner: The Ethical Immutability of God,' Journal of the American Academy of Religion 54 (1986).

13. Barth, Church Dogmatics [Peabody: Hendrickson, 1957], II.1, 493. Richard Muller, Incarnation, Immutability, and the Case for Classical Theism, 23 (cf. fn. 3), praising Dorner's essay in God and the Incarnation in Mid-Nineteenth Century German Theology (Oxford: Oxford University Press, 1965), says: 'In all honesty, Dorner's essay in this volume (pp. 105-80) on the problem of divine immutability is a brilliant exposition and must be seen as a primary dogmatic source for all subsequent reflection (cf. Barth, Moltmann, Pannenberg) on change in God.'

14. Robert Williams, 'Introduction,' in Dorner, Divine Immutability, 19.

the trans-historical life of God to his historical life, of God's transcendence to his immanence in the world.[15]

The tension in Dorner's thinking appears in that he aims to keep together both the 'trans-historical' life and the 'historical' life of God. In doing so, Dorner proposes that we can maintain the constancy of essence needed for divine benevolence while upholding a form of mutability that allows for reciprocal relations with God's creatures. Since Dorner argues that these features in God must not be thought of as rooted in God's essence, Dorner fits in our categorical movement of will and knowledge.[16] However, while Dorner would affirm mutability of knowledge and will, this is ultimately foundational to his relational understanding of mutability. Any articulation of immutability that presses for more absoluteness without these concessions, according to Dorner, is a 'defect [in] the doctrine of God' that is 'taken over from scholasticism.'[17]

Ultimately, Dorner's three-part essay sought to root God's immutability in His ethical nature. After denying the immutability of God 'in his relation to space and time' and 'in his knowing and willing of the world and in his decree,' Dorner then asks, 'In what then does the center and the essence of divine vitality consist?' He continues: 'We answer: in the same thing in which the center of his immutability also consists, namely, not in his being and life as such – for these categories, which in themselves are still physical, lead us forever to Deism or pantheism in restless interplay – but in the ethical.'[18]

The move to ascribe ethical immutability to God saves Dorner from a rigid immutable essence found in the Thomistic conception of the doctrine while also saving him from the kenotic and pantheistic notion of a being who has no actuality apart from the creation. Avoiding these two theological pitfalls – both of which he saw as soteriological nightmares – was crucial for Dorner. Summarizing Dorner's position

---

15. Dorner, *Divine Immutability*, 131.

16. The same can be said for the movement of creation/divine action, as Dorner stated: 'The idea of *creation* also is certainly in general not compatible with a doctrine of God's simple, unmoving, rigid essence' (Dorner, *Divine Immutability*, 141, emphasis original).

17. Ibid., 133.

18. Ibid., 165.

as a *via media* between rigid absoluteness and pantheistic dependence, Robert Williams stated:

> Dorner seeks a middle ground between these concepts. However, he does not engage in purely speculative metaphysical inquiry for its own sake; rather he contends that Christian theology has an important stake in this debate. For Christian faith makes soteriology central. The soteriological interest has two requirements for the doctrine of God: 1) some concept of divine mutability is necessary as instrumental to salvation, and 2) some concept of divine immutability is necessary as grounding the finality of salvation in God's goodness. God's ethical goodness is perfect and cannot change. Hence God must be conceived as immutable in some respects and as mutable in other respects.[19]

Dorner ascribed significant movement to God in his articulation of God's mutable vitality and immutable ethics. From his pen we see our first example of using the movement of relations/soteriology to deviate from and deny the classical understanding of immutability, yet it is far from the last.

Charles Hartshorne and Process Theism

Conversations on the doctrine of God took a decisive turn in the late-nineteenth and early twentieth centuries with the rise of process theism. The consequences of process theism were severe, and theologians working after the rise of process literature will inevitably have to deal with the repercussions of this theological movement. As Bruce Ware stated, 'any responsible assessment of the doctrine of God's changelessness must devote special attention to process theology's proposal, both for its own sake, and because of its pervasive impact on current discussions of the doctrine.'[20] The process proposal has caused a number of theologians to re-examine their thinking regarding the doctrine of God, especially as it pertains to divine immutability.[21] Process theist Barry Whitney, writing

---

19. Williams, *I. A. Dorner*, 721. We see in this quote a prime example of Chapter One's burden. Beginning the theological task from soteriology has dramatic negative consequences for the doctrine of God, and for soteriology in return. Rather, we avoid Dorner's tragic misstep by beginning the theological task with God and then relate all things back to God.

20. Bruce Ware, 'An Evangelical Reexamination of the Doctrine of the Immutability of God' (Ph.D. diss., Fuller Theological Seminary, 1984), 249.

21. Writing on modern interactions between process theists and Catholic theologians, Whitney states: 'A number of contemporary Roman Catholic theologians are now in

of the process concern, says: 'Process thinkers insist that the traditional Christian interpretation of the doctrine of divine immutability (as formulated by St. Thomas and others) cannot be reconciled with the Bible's revelation of divine love and care for the world.'[22] While we could debate Whitney that the *telos* for all process theists was biblical fidelity since Hartshorne 'develops his entire doctrine of God without reference to the biblical texts,'[23] nevertheless, divine immutability – along with most divine perfections – went under the critical microscope in process thought. Whitney followed up this claim, concluding,

> An immutable God, being eternally and fully complete in himself, would remain the same whether or not the world was created, whether or not there was an incarnation, whether or not we pray or suffer, and so on. How could such a God love us? How indeed could we love such a God?[24]

While a number of process theologians have come and gone, arguably none stood taller than Charles Hartshorne (1897–2000). Hartshorne, together with Alfred North Whitehead (1861–1947), provided the process movement with its metaphysical framework. The Hartshorne-Whitehead framework made use of two theological and philosophical categories that proved to be vital to the process understanding of God – a dipolar view of God and the theory of surrelativism.[25] Both of these philosophical tools shape Hartshorne's denial of classic immutability. Hartshorne found the concept of an unalterable God abhorrent and did not attempt to hide his distaste for the idea. In a 1967 essay he stated, 'I

dialogue with the Whiteheadian-Hartshornean challenge.' He then works through ten Roman Catholic theologians who have been, in some way, impacted and influenced by the process proposal. The list includes James Felt, Norris Clarke, Joseph Donceel, Piet Schoonenberg, Walter Stokes, William Hill, John Wright, Anthony Kelly, Martin D'Arcy, and Karl Rahner. See Barry L. Whitney, 'Divine Immutability in Process Philosophy and Contemporary Thomism,' *Horizons* 7 (1980): 52-59.

22. Ibid., 50.

23. Jay Wesley Richards, *The Untamed God: A Philosophical Exploration of Divine Perfection, Simplicity, and Immutability* (Downers Grove, IL: InterVarsity Press, 2003), 172. However, as Richards points out, Hartshorne was convinced that his articulation of dipolar deity was more in tune with the biblical data than his classical counterparts.

24. Whitney, 'Divine Immutability,' 50.

25. While both theologians were important to the development of the process framework, they certainly differed. See David Ray Griffin, 'Hartshorne's differences from Whitehead,' in *Two Process Philosophers*, ed. Lewis S. Ford (Tallahassee: American Academy of Religion, 1973), 35.

regard the unqualified denial of divine change (in the form of increase of content) and the unqualified denial of relativity or dependence as catastrophic errors, and of course I am far from alone in this.'[26] These 'catastrophic errors' were so egregious to Hartshorne, that he said in the same essay: 'If I were to accomplish nothing else than to bring about the definitive abandonment of the traditional notion of God's *pure* necessity, not simply for existence and essence but for all properties whatever, I would not have labored in vain.'[27]

The dipolar depiction of deity in process theism gets at God being simultaneously absolute and relative. This, of course, is contrary to any articulation of the divine that would insist on a monopolar emphasis of absoluteness. Hartshorne defines 'absoluteness' as the 'independence of relationships' and states that God is metaphysically unique in the sense that He is the only being who can be described as 'maximally absolute, and in another aspect no less strictly or maximally relative.'[28] While this may ring as a contradiction in the ears of Hartshorne's hearers, he argues this is not the case on the basis of an asymmetrical relationship between the absolute and relative. About this asymmetrical relationship he says, 'The same reality may in one aspect be universally open to influence, and in another aspect universally closed to influence.'[29] In short, God can have absolute properties such that it would be appropriate to ascribe immutability to them while also having properties that are open to influence. Hartshorne's major concern in his exposition of dipolar deity is to bring balance to the emphasis on the transcendence and immanence of God. He is motivated by what he sees as an unfair emphasis of the absolute essence in classical theism found in doctrines like pure actuality, aseity, and immutability.

---

26. Charles Hartshorne, 'The Dipolar Conception of Deity,' *The Review of Metaphysics* 21 (967): 273.

27. Ibid., 273.

28. Charles Hartshorne, *The Divine Relativity: A Social Conception of God* (New Haven: Yale University Press, 1948), 31. Richards, *The Untamed God*, 191, helpfully summarizes Hartshorne's dipolar view, saying: 'The concept of divine dipolarity has an important metaphysical function. It allows Hartshorne to attribute certain dualities or contrasts, such as abstract-concrete, necessary-contingent, absolute-relative, to God without contradiction.'

29. Charles Hartshorne, *Creative Synthesis and Philosophic Method* (London: Open Court, 1970), 233.

As for the second philosophical category, surrelativism, Hartshorne's 1948 publication, *The Divine Relativity*, is significant. In this work, Hartshorne describes what he means by God's relativity and ability to receive influence. Hartshorne writes, 'my proposition is that the higher the being the more dependence of certain kinds will be appropriate for it.'[30] To illustrate this point, Hartshorne calls his readers to play a 'mental experiment' with him. This mental experiment called readers to consider a poem being read before a number of characters. These characters include: (1) a glass of water, (2) an ant, (3) a dog, (4) a human being who does not speak the language of the poem, (5) a human being who knows the language but is not sensitive to poetry, and finally (6) a person who is both sensitive to poetry and who speaks the language. About this cast of characters, Hartshorne says, 'Now I submit that each member of this series is superior, in terms of the data, to its predecessors, and that each is more, not less, dependent upon or relative to the poem as such, including its meanings as well as its mere sounds.'[31] His point, with this seemingly silly mental exercise, is to show that the cup of water is the most impassible and immutable object amongst the bunch, yet an outside observer to the situation would not ascribe worth on this basis to the glass of water. Instead, we would say that the final individual – the one who knows the language of the poem and is sensitive to poetry – is most worthy of praise for superiority in ability to be impacted.

For Hartshorne, this experiment is aimed at demonstrating the 'metaphysical snobbery toward relativity' that classical theists display.[32] For it could only be with an abstract deity, and nothing else, that hardness toward being influenced would be a praiseworthy virtue. Instead, Hartshorne argues that God demonstrates His superiority in being constantly impacted by the happenings of those He has created and, in this way, demonstrates His immutability – He is immutably changing as He is constantly influenced by, and is the supreme recipient of, the actions and emotions of that which He created.

---

30. Hartshorne, *Divine Relativity*, 48.

31. Ibid., 49.

32. Ibid., 50.

Bruce Ware and Evangelical Reexaminations

Our final representative of relational/soteriological movement is evangelical scholar Bruce Ware. In comparison to Dorner and Hartshorne, Ware is closer to articulating a classic understanding of divine immutability, as he would drastically break from Hartshorne's mutable essence as well as from Dorner's mutable knowledge and will.[33] Though closer to classical theism than Dorner and Hartshorne, Ware still deviates from a classical definition of divine immutability on account of his ascribing change to God by virtue of relational movement, repentance, and change in emotions.[34]

An important feature of Ware's approach to the conversation is his understanding of what it means for a doctrine to be 'evangelical.' He explains his methodological approach: 'theologizing, then, bases itself squarely upon God's self-revelation as given us in the Scriptures and proceeds or builds from this foundation alone.'[35] Ware worries that classical theism has put too much emphasis on 'speculative concepts' instead of the biblical data. He states:

> The modern criticism of classical theism here is in part valid, for indeed the tradition stemming from Augustine through the medieval scholastics and protestant orthodox did tend to take as primary a certain philosophic or speculative conception of the divine perfection which then regulated all its subsequent talk of God's relatedness to the world.[36]

However, Ware intends to set himself up as a mediating position as he claims that modernity is guilty of the inverse error – ascribing relativity to God such that it becomes the driving principle in the face of data

---

33. See Ware's critique of Charles Hartshorne and process theism in Bruce Ware, 'An Exposition and Critique of the Process Doctrines of Divine Mutability and Immutability,' *Westminster Journal of Theology* 47 (1985):175-96. See also, Ware, 'Evangelical Reexamination,' 404, in which he 'utterly rejects' the process project.

34. In the end, I ultimately break from Ware's proposed tweaks to the doctrine of divine immutability. However, I do wish to express gratitude to him for his work on the subject. While I disagree in the end with his conclusions, his work treats the Scripture with the utmost reverence, and it is obvious to me that he arrives at his conclusions in trying to do the most justice to the biblical data.

35. Ware, 'Evangelical Reexamination,' 380. See also Ware's essay-length summary of his dissertation, 'An Evangelical Reformulation of the Doctrine of the Immutability of God,' *Journal of the Evangelical Theological Society* 29 (1986), 431-46.

36. Ware, 'Evangelical Reexamination,' 384.

that suggests independence of essence and being.[37] His claim is that neither position does justice to *all* of the biblical material, as each overemphasizes either transcendence or immanence.

The method of the *via media* approach is made possible, for Ware, by affirming that there are proper ways to speak of God's immutability *and* proper ways to speak of His mutability. Ware declared that this indeed is the depiction of 'revealed immutability,' that 'the incredible and humbling testimony of God's self-revelation is that God is *both* self-sufficient (i.e., transcendently self-existent) *and* wholly loving (i.e., immanently self-relating).'[38]

Ware gives two ways regarding how it is proper to speak of God's immutability – ontological and ethical – while giving three ways that are proper to speak of God's mutability – relational, repentance, and emotions. Of the former two, Ware states: 'God is immutable not only with regard to the fact of his eternal existence but also in the very content or make-up of his eternal essence, independent of the world.'[39] Also, as it relates to His ethical immutability, Ware wrote: 'The God of the Bible is also unchangeable in his unconditional promises and moral obligations to which he has freely pledged himself.'[40]

After describing the 'onto-ethical immutability' of God, Ware moved into what he called the 'proper sense' in which we can speak of God's mutability. While he gave three examples of God's mutability, the most important of the three is relational mutability. Ware wrote:

> The Scriptures affirm one predominant sense of God's changeability under which specific manifestations of it are evident, and this may be called God's 'relational mutability.' From the creation of Adam and Eve to the

---

37. Ibid., 387.

38. Ibid., 406.

39. Ibid., 417. He defines ontological immutability, saying: 'The God of the Bible is unchangeable in the supreme excellence of his intrinsic nature. This may be called God's "ontological immutability"—that is, the changelessness of God's eternal and self-sufficient being' (ibid., 434).

40. Ibid. 436. While Ware affirms, like Dorner, an ethical immutability in God, he nevertheless desires to separate his understanding of ethical immutability from Dorner's, saying: 'The problem with Dorner's view, however, is that he bases the ethical consistency or faithfulness of God strictly on God's unchanging ethical nature (e.g., that God is always loving, holy, just) rather than on a more complete sense of the fullness and supreme excellence of God's immutable being' (ibid., 437).

consummation of history, God is involved in pursuing, establishing and developing relationships with those whom he has made .... That God changes in his relationship with others is abundantly clear from Scripture.[41]

Ware gives credit to both Dorner and Barth and cites Barth's conception of a 'holy mutability of God'[42] such that God changes in 'his attitudes, conduct, and relationships with humans' which allows for genuine reciprocal relationships.[43]

Ware goes on to describe two more ways in which we can 'properly' speak of God's mutability – repentance and emotions, albeit with much less detail than his discussion of the relational model. Though Ware offered them as unique modes of talking about divine mutability, he said of repentance that 'these passages refer fundamentally to God's relational mutability as discussed above.'[44] Passibility, or Ware's third proper way to speak of God's mutability, is also related to his relational dynamic of change. Ware said, 'The abundance of Scriptural evidence of God's expression of emotion and a more positive understanding of their nature lead to the conclusion that the true and living God is, among other things, a genuinely emotional being.'[45] Ware correlated this to the relational dynamic by elaborating that while God is immutable in His essence, He has nevertheless chosen to relate with us, and His relational dynamism predicates His variability in terms of emotional experiences and change.

While Ware has the most sophisticated and robust study of divine immutability, he is not the only evangelical theologian to deviate from a classical understanding of divine immutability. In fact, this writing faced a last-minute revision due to the publication of *The Mystery of the Trinity* by Vern Poythress which was released during the construction of this project.

In the introduction, Poythress states six key problems his book seeks to address. The second in the list is, 'How can God be immutable

---

41. Ware, 'Evangelical Reformulation,' 438-39.

42. Barth, *Church Dogmatics*, II.1, 496.

43. Ware, 'Evangelical Reformulation,' 440.

44. Ibid., 443. After discussing the hermeneutical concept of anthropomorphism regarding the passages where God is depicted as repenting, Ware concludes, 'In general it seems best to understand God's repentance as his changed mode of action and attitude in response to a changed human situation.'

45. Ibid., 446.

(not able to change) and act toward the world?[46] In answering this question, Poythress – through his work – advises Christians to avoid two 'suction pools' relating to both God's transcendence and immanence. The first suction pool, which is a danger in overemphasizing immanence, is 'mutuality theology' or, as Poythress playfully calls it, 'quicksand theology.' The other suction pool, which is overemphasizing transcendence, is 'monadic theology' or, as Poythress playfully calls it, 'black hole theology.'[47]

Taking time to note and appreciate that Poythress works with carefulness is important. He even gets close to affirming a classical understanding of immutability in multiple instances throughout the book. For example, Poythress writes, 'God does not change. Indeed, he *cannot* change, because he is God and he cannot be other than the God he is.'[48] Or, elsewhere, Poythress writes, 'It is not right, but misleading, to say that "God changes," even if the speaker's intentions are good. There are better and clearer ways of saying what we need to say in order to make the point that God is active in many ways in the world.'[49]

However, after examining Aquinas, Turretin, and Charnock and looking at doctrines such as immutability, simplicity, and infinitude, Poythress asserts that classical theism does not, at this point, have the tools to avoid both suction pools. Indeed, Poythress goes as far as saying that 'Classical Christian theism needs enhancement, not merely reiteration, in order to go forward.'[50] Poythress' worry is that the classical articulation of divine immutability, while partially correct, relies on unnecessarily complex theological terminology and has a hard time doing justice to the real relations which the Scriptures seem to attribute to God in His covenant-making relationship with man.

---

46. Vern Poythress, *The Mystery of the Trinity: A Trinitarian Approach to the Attributes of God* (Phillipsburg: P&R Publishing, 2020), xxiv. Beyond the second question listed, others in Poythress' list have relevance for our discussions here. For example, Question 1 asks, 'How can God be independent and yet have relations to the world and things in the world?' and Question 6 asks, 'How can God's attributes be identical with God and also be distinguished from one another?' (Poythress, xxiii–xxv).

47. Ibid., 440-41; 475-76; 505.

48. Ibid., 57.

49. Ibid., 585.

50. Ibid., 485.

While not residing within the walls of evangelicalism, it is important to note that another publication came out during the construction of this book which would not only agree with Poythress but states his conclusion with more emphasis. John C. Peckham's 2021 publication, *Divine Attributes,* focuses on the 'nature and attributes of God' in search of 'what we have biblical warrant to affirm with respect to such questions, in order to better understand the living God whom Christians worship and to whom Christians pray.'[51] For Peckham, this includes examining questions such as 'Does God Change? Does God have emotions? Does God know everything, including the future? Is God all-powerful?'[52]

Peckham makes several affirmations that align well with classical theism. For example, he affirms a strong Creator/creature distinction.[53] He also makes a similar methodological move as classical theists when it comes to the economic and immanent life of God; he writes that a proper theological interpretation of Scripture, 'carefully attends to biblical depictions of God, seeking to affirm all that Scripture teaches about God without conceptually reducing God to the way he is portrayed in the economy.'[54]

While Peckham affirms these aspects of classical theism, he eventually deviates from classical theism, and its account of divine immutability, due to what he says is his hope to allow Scripture to norm all theological articulation. He puts forward what he labels 'covenantal theism.'[55] In the end, his methodology leads him to deny the doctrine of pure actuality and to deviate from a classical understanding of divine immutability. In sum, he writes:

> The claim that God is pure act, then, runs directly counter to the way Scripture consistently depicts God. The situation relative to biblical

---

51. John C. Peckham, *Divine Attributes: Knowing the Covenantal God of Scripture* (Grand Rapids: Baker Academic, 2021), 1.

52. Ibid., 1.

53. Ibid., 2.

54. Ibid., 17. Peckham later gives a great analogy of collapsing God's essence to what is revealed in the economy. He writes: 'At the same time we must be careful not to conceptually reduce God to the way he represents himself to humans in the economy of biblical revelation. It would be a mistake to take a letter I wrote to my nine-year-old son and assume on the basis that my vocabulary is fourth-grade level. God is always greater than can be revealed to creatures' (Ibid., 35).

55. Ibid., 37.

warrant, then, is this. Abundant biblical data depicts God as undergoing changing emotions, but there appears to be no biblical warrant for *pure* aseity, *strict* immutability, *strict* impassibility, or the interpretive move of negating biblical depictions of changing divine emotions. In light of this and other data, I believe the view that God undergoes changing emotions is biblically warranted, and if God undergoes changing emotions, then God is neither strictly immutable nor strictly impassible.[56]

Outside of Bruce Ware, another well-known evangelical theologian to reconsider a classical articulation of divine immutability is John Frame. We will deal with Frame's view later when dealing with methodology and language for God. However, he ought to be noted here as his concern is like those we have seen above. Frame is concerned that the classical articulation of divine immutability, while having some true things to say, does not do justice to all the biblical data concerning the life of God. For example, he is worried with the methodological move of chalking all instances of change depicted in Scripture to a mere anthropomorphism. He writes: 'The historical process does change, and as an agent in history, God himself changes. On Monday, he wants something to happen, and on Tuesday, something else. He is grieved one day, pleased the next. In my view, *anthropomorphic* is too weak a description of these narratives.'[57]

Frame can still hold to a measure of immutability while affirming the above quote by predicating two existences to God. He argues that God possesses an atemporal existence and a historical existence. Frame states that 'neither form of existence contradicts the other. God's transcendence never compromises his immanence, nor do his control and authority compromise his covenant presence.'[58]

While we will not treat his work at the same length as the others, it is important to note that another evangelical, Scott Oliphant, finds

---

56. Ibid., 62.

57. John Frame, *Systematic Theology: An Introduction to Christian Belief* (Phillipsburg: P&R Publishing, 2013), 377.

58. Ibid, 377. Frame goes on to admit that his view of God's having two existences 'bears a superficial resemblance' to modern process theology. He notes that process theology also recognizes two 'poles' to God's existence – the primordial and consequent natures of God. However, using Charles Hartshorne, Frame makes significant differences between his view and process theology and ultimately determines that process theology is 'deeply unscriptural' (Ibid., 378).

Frame's argumentation here persuasive. Oliphant also worries that a classical understanding of anthropomorphism is simply too weak to do justice to the variegated biblical data. Moreover, he argues that Christology is the primary way Christian theologians should look to the perfections of God. Therefore, in presenting attributes considering God's condescension and His 'covenantal properties,' Oliphant writes: 'When Scripture says that God changes his mind, or that he is moved, or angered by our behavior, we should see that as literal.' He continues, 'We should also see that the God who really changes his mind is the accommodated God, the *yarad-cum*-Emmanuel God who, while remaining the "I AM," nevertheless stoops to our level to interact, person-to-person, with us.' He continues: 'His change of mind does not affect his essential character, any more than Christ dying on the cross precluded him from being fully God. He remains fully and completely God, a God who is not like man that he should change his mind, and he remains fully and completely the God who, in covenant with us, changes his mind to accomplish his sovereign purposes.'[59]

These three representatives – Dorner, Hartshorne, and Ware – exemplify modern deviations from the classical understanding of divine immutability with a relational/soteriological impulse. Though all three examples predicate change to God based on *more* than just relational dynamism, the soteriological impulse is strong behind all three lines of reasoning.

Now, we turn to the remaining four arguments which seek to ascribe movement to God. We treat three of the arguments with much more brevity than the first because, while the following three are important and prevalent, the first category proves most relevant to our thesis as we seek to articulate the inverse of their conclusions. While Dorner, Hartshorne, Ware, and many like them seek to deviate from or deny the classical understanding of divine immutability for fear that it impedes a robust soteriology, this project moves in the opposite direction and aims to demonstrate the soteriological significance of absolute immutability. Yet, first, let us examine, in brief, four more alterations predicated to God.

---

59. Scott Oliphant, *God With Us: Divine Condescension and the Attributes of God* (Wheaton: Crossway, 2012), 124.

(2) The Problem of the Incarnation

With cosmic consequence, the Second Person of the Trinity took on flesh and dwelt amongst us. Two key texts depicting this event have been used by those wishing to describe movement in God via the incarnation – John 1:14 and Philippians 2:6-11. In the former, John writes four words that caused theological marvel and mystery for millennia, 'the Word became flesh.' In the latter text, Paul describes the incarnation as Jesus' 'emptying' Himself as to be found in the form of a servant.

Both these texts in particular, and the divine mission of the incarnation in general, have led some to conclude that God is alterable since it is hard to make sense of the incarnation if He were not. The two primary lines of argumentation built on the foundation of these texts are kenoticism and Christological mutability.

Kenoticism and Christological Mutability

Kenotic Christology insists that the 'emptying' described in Philippians 2 entails a literal detraction in the Godhead. Oliver Crisp, who helpfully delineates between two forms of Kenoticism – functional and ontological – defines the movement, saying, 'the view, drawn from New Testament passages such as Philippians 2:7, that, in becoming incarnate, the second person of the Trinity somehow emptied himself of certain divine attributes in order to truly become human.'[60] C. Stephen Evans helps readers understand what the kenotic theologians mean when they describe God 'emptying' Himself: the Son 'in some way limited or temporarily divested himself of some of the properties thought to be divine prerogatives, and this act of self-emptying has become known as a "kenosis".'[61]

While a number of theologians have espoused something like kenotic theology throughout the last two centuries, the view finds its origins in German theologian Gottfried Thomasius (1802–1875). His most important work, which launched a small avalanche of subsequent

---

60. Oliver D Crisp, *Divinity and Humanity* (Cambridge: Cambridge University Press, 2007), 118. Stephen Wellum, *God the Son Incarnate: The Doctrine of Christ* (Wheaton, IL: Crossway, 2016), 355-421, also uses the distinction of functional and ontological when describing kenoticism.

61. C. Stephen Evans, 'Introduction,' in *Exploring Kenotic Christology: The Self-Emptying of God*, ed. C. Stephen Evans (Oxford: Oxford University Press, 2006), 4.

volumes, was *Christi Person und Werk*.[62] In it, Thomasius described the event of the incarnation, saying, 'a divesting of the divine mode of being in favor of the humanly creaturely form of existence, and *eo ispo* a renunciation of the divine glory he had from the beginning with the Father.'[63] This 'divesting' of the divine mode renders immutability impossible as the Second Person of the Godhead changes in His shedding of divine properties. Thomasius assures readers that this is not a shedding of divinity as Christ still possesses the essential perfections that are necessary for God to be God. However, even if this was not a violation of divine simplicity, it would still violate divine immutability. Torrance, offering a varying interpretation of the pertinent passage, opines: 'There is nothing here about any so-called metaphysical change in God the Son such as an emptying out of God the Son of any divine attributes or powers.'[64]

Though kenoticism jeopardizes divine immutability, it is not alone in its ascribing change in God via the event of the incarnation.[65] For example, Hans Urs von Balthasar contends that the incarnation 'shatters' a classical understanding of divine immutability. He writes:

> It implied coming through a narrow pass: not so to guard the immutability of God that in the pre-existent Logos who prepares himself to become man nothing real happens and on the other hand not to let this real happening degenerate into divine suffering … one has to say that P. Althaus is right: 'On this realization, the old concept of the immutability of God is clearly shattered. Christology must take seriously that God himself really entered into suffering in the Son and therein is and remains completely God.'[66]

---

62. Gottfried Thomasius, 'Christ's Person and Work,' in *God and Incarnation in Mid-Nineteenth Century German Theology*, ed. Claude Welch (Oxford: Oxford University Press, 1965).

63. Thomasius, 'Christ's Person and Work,' 48. Cf. Wellum, *God the Son Incarnate*, 358.

64. Thomas Torrance, *The Incarnation: The Person and Life of Christ* (Downers Grove: IVP, 2008), 75.

65. See, for example, Thomas G. Weinandy, *Does God Change? The Word's Becoming in the Incarnation* (Still River: St. Bede's Publications, 1985). Weinandy works through patristic, medieval, kenotic, and process literature in a survey of deviations from classical immutability and impassibility in the incarnation.

66. Hans Urs von Balthasar, 'Mysterium Paschale,' in *Mysterium Salutis*, ed. J. Feiner and Magnus Löhrer (Einsiedelm: Benziger, 1969), 151-52, cited in, Dodds, *The Unchanging God of Love*, 199. Dodds, however, correctly concludes: 'When properly understood, the incarnation, far from denying the immutability of God, rather requires it. For if God

Like the relational/soteriological movement, those theologians who predicate movement to God by virtue of His incarnation vary chronologically, geographically, and denominationally. However, what they share is a view that deviates from the great tradition's understanding of divine immutability.

Moltmann, Pannenberg, and the Theology of Hope

Theology is never done in a vacuum and therefore the cultural context in which theologizing takes place is important in considering any theologian's program. This is especially true for those theologians who studied and wrote under the umbrella of 'the theology of hope.' Coming off the heels of global war and confusion in the 1960s the theologians of hope constructed their volumes in an era where the horrors of the Third Reich and Hiroshima were still fresh in the mind of society. The cultural context of these few decades meant that the confusion which persisted because of national turmoil longed for architects of hope that could divert the gaze of society away from their current plight and toward a future glory. It would, of course, be disingenuous to conclude that the theologians of hope reached their conclusion by virtue of their cultural context alone. However, the theology of hope became an ever-important outlet of theology in this particular cultural moment.

Describing the theological confusion which persisted in the climate of the 1960s, Stanley Grenz and Roger Olson write:

> In the middle of the confusion a book appeared from a virtually unknown young German theologian, which seemed to many to provide the needed new approach for theology in the latter half of the century. The book was *The Theology of Hope* written by a thirty-nine-year-old professor of systematic theology at Tübingen, West Germany – Jürgen Moltmann. In this work Moltmann called for a shift to eschatology, to the traditional doctrine of last things but reinterpreted and understood afresh, as the foundation for the theological task.[67]

The methodological move of resetting theology's foundation toward eschatology had significant Christological implications. For, as Grenz

---

changed in becoming human, he would no longer be truly God, and Jesus Christ would not be truly God and human' (Dodds, *The Unchanging God of Love*, 200).

67. Stanley J. Grenz, Roger E. Olson, *20ᵗʰ Century Theology: God and the World in a Transitional Age* (Downers Grove: IVP, 1992), 171.

and Olson note, the pre-eminent theme of the body of Moltmann's literature became, 'hope for the future based on the cross and resurrection of Jesus Christ.'[68] For this reason, even while we could point to a number of divergent paths in which Moltmann and Pannenberg break from a classical conception of divine immutability, we can rightly treat their view under 'the problem of the incarnation.'

The incarnate life of Jesus Christ was, for Moltmann, of supreme importance for articulating a doctrine of God. In fact, Moltmann so emphasized the economic aspects of God's *ad extra* life that he eventually affirmed Rahner's rule verbatim. Moltmann wrote, in affirmation of Rahner, 'The economic Trinity *is* the immanent Trinity, and the immanent Trinity *is* the economic Trinity.'[69] By collapsing the economic and immanent Trinity, Moltmann's understanding of the divine life was captivated by observing the incarnate life of Jesus Christ as the primary mode of revelation and reason. Doing theology proper from the starting point of Christ's incarnation was, for Moltmann, a way to not 'speculate in heavenly riddles' and therefore, 'Anyone who really talks of the Trinity talks of the cross of Jesus.'[70]

This discussion of methodology is important in discussing Moltmann's doctrine of inalterability because it is in his methodological decisions that Moltmann separates himself from both the classical theists and the process theists. Contra classical theism, Moltmann is weary of philosophical speculation regarding the divine life. Yet, at the same time, Moltmann did not hold to a process view over God's relativism. Instead, Moltmann's approach to God's change was one of self-change. He writes: 'God is not changeable as creatures are changeable. However, the conclusion should not be drawn from this that God is unchangeable in every respect, for this negative definition merely says that God is under no constraint from that which is not God.'[71] According to

---

68. Ibid., 172.

69. Jürgen Moltmann, *The Crucified God* (Minneapolis: Fortress Press, 1993), 207. Moltmann is quoting Rahner here; see Karl Rahner, *The Trinity* (New York: Seabury, 1974), 22. For more on Moltmann and Rahner's doctrine of divine immutability, see Susie Paulik Babka, *'God is Faithful, He Cannot Deny Himself': Karl Rahner and Jürgen Moltmann on Whether God is Immutable In Jesus Christ* (PhD Dissertation, University of Notre Dame, 2004).

70. Moltmann, *The Crucified God*, 207.

71. Ibid., 229.

Moltmann, God's freedom actively allows changes to Himself, which is what happens in the case of the incarnation and suffering of Christ. In the theology of hope, the glory of God is seen primarily through God's willingness to share in our suffering which means we will ultimately share in His eschatological resurrection.

Comparing Rahner and Moltmann's view of God's unchangeability, Susie Paulik Babka concludes:

> Especially in the Incarnation and Cross, as revealing God's personal identity as willing in love to 'become' for the sake of the other (Rahner) or to 'suffer' for the sake of the other (Moltmann). Because Moltmann endorses Rahner's *Grundaxiom*, both believe that God's self-communication to what is finite, or not-God is a radical sharing of God's very being ... they [both] move beyond traditional metaphysics of absolute divine immutability and impassibility.[72]

Wolfhart Pannenberg, while differing from Moltmann in some points, affirmed his colleague's eschatologically minded ontology. Pannenberg argued, like Rahner and Moltmann, against dichotomizing the economic and immanent Trinity. Pannenberg stated that, in the Scriptures, 'the divine name is not a formula for essence.'[73] Rather, the divine name is 'a pointer to experience of his working.' Therefore, 'the question of essence thus becomes that of the attributes that characterize God's working.'[74] Just a few pages later, Pannenberg asserts, 'the qualities that are ascribed to him rest on his relations to the world which correspond to the relations of creatures to him.'[75]

Maybe the most important piece of methodological consideration for this project comes in Pannenberg's pages on the Trinity. In the Trinitarian section of his *Systematic Theology*, he bemoans the 'one-sided' development of philosophical theism and writes that as early as Athanasius' work against the Arians we can see the regrettable detachment of the economic from the immanent. Pannenberg is worth quoting at length here as he directly relates this faulty practice to divine immutability.

---

72. Babka, 357.

73. Wolfhart Pannenberg, *Systematic Theology* (Grand Rapids: Eerdmans, 1988), 1:360.

74. Ibid., 1:360.

75. Ibid., 1:364. See also, 'The Appropriation of the Philosophical Concept of God as a Dogmatic Problem of Early Christian Theology' in Wolfhart Pannenberg, *Basic Questions in Theology*, Volume 2 (Minneapolis: Fortress Press, 1971), 119-83.

Understandable, too, is the fact that in the provisional outcome of this history of interpretation in the dogma of Nicea and Constantinople, the thought of the eternal and essential Trinity broke loose from its historical moorings and tended to be seen not only as the basis of all historical events but also as untouched by the course of history on account of the eternity and immutability of God, and therefore also inaccessible to all creaturely knowledge. If the Son and Spirit were known to be of the same substance as the eternal and unchangeable Father, then under the conditions of Hellenistic philosophical theology this Trinity had to be at an unreachable distance from all finite, creaturely reality. The immanent Trinity became independent of the economic Trinity and increasingly ceased to have any function relative to the economy of salvation.[76]

Pannenberg continues and calls for revision of what he perceives to be a dangerous theological error:

Today we see that differentiating the eternal Trinity from all temporal change makes trinitarian theology one-sided and detaches it from its biblical basis. This situation obviously calls for revision. But the related problems are greater than theology has thus far realized. Viewing the immanent Trinity and the economic Trinity as one presupposes the development of a concept of God which can grasp in one not only the transcendence of the divine being and his immanence in the world but also the eternal self-identity of God and the debatability of his truth in the process of history, along with the decision made concerning it by the consummation of history.[77]

Like Moltmann, the justification for treating Pannenberg under 'the problem of the incarnation' lies in his collapsing the immanent and economic Trinity. For, instead of language of divine immutability in the *ad intra*, Pannenberg preferred language of divine faithfulness in the *ad extra*. Since, for Pannenberg, the immanent and economic are identical, our theologizing of theology proper ought to arise out of an explicit examination of the economic activity of God, since this is what is available to us. Pannenberg makes this point explicit, saying, 'whereas the predicate of immutability that derives from Greek philosophy implies timelessness, the truth of God's faithfulness expresses his constancy in the actual process of time and history, especially his holding fast to his

---

76. Pannenberg, *Systematic Theology*, 1:332-33.
77. Pannenberg, *Systematic Theology*, 1:333.

saving will, to his covenant, to his promises, and also to the orders of his creation.'[78]

As a final point showing the connection between the items treated in this section which are: (1) the theology of hope, (2) deviations from a classical articulation of immutability, and (3) the problem of the incarnation, Pannenberg summarizes his understanding of divine changelessness in relation to the incarnation saying:

> In distinction from the idea of immutability, that of God's faithfulness does not exclude historicity or the contingency of world occurrence, nor need the historicity and contingency of the divine action be in contradiction with God's eternity. If eternity and time coincide only in the eschatological consummation of history, then from the standpoint of the history of God that moves toward this consummation there is room for becoming in God himself, namely, in the relation of the immanent and the economic Trinity, and in this frame, *it is possible to say of God that he himself became something that he previously was not when he became man in his Son.*[79]

(3) The Problem of Creation and Divine Action

As we will see, there is an inseparable connection between God's immutability and His eternality. This is the exact relationship that comes into question as God acts throughout history. Surely, some scholars insist, God's gracious involvement in the world – whether it be His creation *ex nihilo*, incarnation, or simply His providential interfering in the lives of His people – calls into question any understanding of a non-successive life of God. Does it not suppose, for example, that there must have been a change in God as He moved from passivity to actuality in the creation of all things? This was the view of Thomas Torrance (1913–2007), who wrote:

> While God was always Father and was Father independently of what he has created, as Creator he acted in a way that he had not done before, in bringing about absolutely new events – this means that the creation of the world out of nothing is something *new even for God*. God was always Father, but he *became* Creator.[80]

---

78. Ibid., 1:437.

79. Ibid., 1:438. Emphasis added.

80. Thomas F. Torrance, *The Christian Doctrine of God: One Being, Three Persons* (London: T&T Clark, 1996), 208.

Torrance applies the same logic to the divine action of the incarnation and Pentecost. These movements, for Torrance, seem to indicate a Triune mover who acts and changes in time as each member of the Godhead moves in time and space. Ultimately, for Torrance, these three acts – creation, incarnation, Pentecost – display the freedom of God. Furthermore, Torrance argues they 'tell us that far from being a static or inertial Deity like some "unmoved mover," the mighty living God who reveals himself to us through his Son and in his Spirit is absolutely free to do what he had never done before, and free to be other than he was eternally.'[81]

R. T. Mullins also articulates an issue with a classical understanding of divine immutability by virtue of creation and divine action.[82] Mullins states that it is 'utterly baffling' to him to conceive of a God who creates and does not undergo real change in a real relationship with the creation. Mullins uses the analogy of a builder to demonstrate his point: 'It seems quite clear that the builder who decides to start building does in fact undergo change. It also seems that a God who is not creating and then creates does undergo a change. He is not standing in a causal relation to anything, and then he is standing in a causal relation to creation.' Mullins continues: 'Activity out of a capacity involves change and time, for it at least creates before and after in the life of an agent.'[83] Ultimately, Mullins concludes: 'The Christian God cannot be timeless, strongly immutable, and simple.'[84]

Colin Gunton sees a similar issue and writes about the 'tangled web' of a classical doctrine of God.[85] He writes: 'there is a tendency to identify

---

81. Torrance, *The Christian Doctrine of God,* 88. For a response to Torrance, and others like him, see Steven J. Duby, 'Divine Action and the Meaning of Eternity' in *God of Our Fathers: Classical Theism for the Contemporary Church* (Idaho: Davenant Institute, 2018), 87-104. In *Divine Immutability, Divine Action and the God-World Relation,* Duby deals with divine action as it relates to the doctrine of immutability and utilizes John of Damascus, Aquinas, and Johann Alsted and the 'virtual distinction' to provide proper grammar in speaking about God's external and temporal acts. Duby's conception of these matters influenced the thinking behind this project, which will show throughout.

82. This is not Mullins' only difficulty with immutability; his work primarily deals with atemporality and only by derivation the doctrine of immutability. See, R.T. Mullins, *The End of the Timeless God* (Oxford: Oxford University Press, 2016).

83. Ibid., 114.

84. Ibid., 126.

85. Colin Gunton, *Act and Being: Towards a Theology of the Divine Attributes* (Grand Rapids: Eerdmans, 2002), 22.

the divine attributes by a list of "omni's" and negatives ... and then paste on to them conceptions of divine action, especially that central to the Bible's account of what is called the economy of creation and redemption.'[86] Later, he explicitly defines 'divine action' as 'personal and intentional acts designed to bring about some purpose or change in the world.'[87] This definition leads him to insist that the presence of divine action means that we should be 'against the necessity of constructing God's immutability in a Platonizing manner.'[88] Gunton brings Barth to bear in his line of argumentation, who says:

> God is constantly one and the same. But ... his consistency is not as it were mathematical .... The fact that he is one and the same does not mean that he is bound to be and say and do only one and the same thing, so that all the distinctions of his being, speaking and acting are only a semblance, only the various refractions of a beam of light which are eternally the same. This was and is the way that every form of Platonism conceives God. It is impossible to overemphasize the fact that here ... God is described as basically without life, word or act.[89]

We can see from the pens of Torrance, Mullins, Gunton, and Barth that substantial concern exists that a classical conception of divine immutability leaves little room to do justice for the divine movement of creation and divine action. Indeed, much of modernity would affirm that to impose a metaphysically absolute, changeless God on the textual data and experiential realities of apparent dynamic interaction is to promote a lifeless, immobile being.

(4) The Problem of Volition and Knowledge

The fourth category of movement ascribed to God is movement of the will or knowledge. Though there are several variations of arguments that insist on the denial of God's immutability based on His apparent volitional alterations or advances in His knowledge, we will briefly look at two – open theism and the exegetical decision to interpret the 'divine repentance' passages literally.

---

86. Ibid., 22.
87. Ibid., 77.
88. Ibid., 57.
89. Barth, *Church Dogmatics,* II.1, 496, cited from Gunton, *Act and Being,* 57.

Open Theism and Intellectual Movement

Open theism is an appropriate place of examination in this sub-section treating the apparent movement of God's will and knowledge; however, one could argue that it would be just as pertinent to cover it in the relational/soteriological sub-section because open theists articulate God's self-limiting of His knowledge to His desire for a real relationship with His creatures. What is at stake in a God who immutably knows all things is the freedom of His people. Therefore, though He could control all things, He has nevertheless chosen to limit His own epistemic life to establish freedom. As Clark Pinnock states: 'It holds that God could control the world if he wished to but that he has chosen not to do so for the sake of loving relationships.' He continues: 'Open theism does not believe that God is ontologically limited but that God voluntarily self-limits so that freely chosen loving relations might be possible.'[90] This self-imposition is relationally aimed. Again, Pinnock is a useful example of this point, as he writes: 'Had God not granted us significant freedom, including the freedom to disappoint him, we would not be creatures capable of entering into loving relationships with him. Love, not freedom, is the central issue. Freedom was given to make loving relations possible.'[91]

If God knew beforehand what creatures would do, they would not be free to do otherwise at the risk of God's being incorrect in His knowing. Therefore, for the sake of creaturely freedom God welcomes self-imposed ignorance. Consequently, not only does God change, but He is also in constant change as He continually learns as His creatures act and live. In this way, the Creator/creature distinction is absolved as the Creator's knowledge mirrors creaturely knowledge in that epistemic advancement is relationally limited as we grow in knowledge with the happenings of time. For example, I only know what my Australian shepherd dog will do next as he does it. My knowledge is therefore relationally tied to the actions and progression of my dog. So too, says the open theist, it is with God and those He loves. An immutable God

---

90. Clark Pinnock, 'Open Theism: An Answer to My Critics,' *Dialogue: A Journal of Theology* 44 (2005): 237. Pinnock explicitly states the relational motivation: 'The main emphasis of open theism is that God created the world for loving relations' (ibid., 238).

91. Clark Pinnock, *The Most Moved Mover: A Theology of God's Openness* (Grand Rapids: Baker, 2001), 45.

is an impossibility in the open model, which predicates significant movement of the mind.

Another popular open theist, Greg Boyd, points to the vast number of texts throughout Scripture which seem to indicate an openness of mind by virtue of God intellectually relenting. Boyd writes: 'Unfortunately for the classical interpretation, the text does not say, or remotely imply, that it *looks* like the Lord intended something then changed his mind.' Boyd continues, 'Rather, the Lord himself tells us in the plainest terms possible that he intended one thing and then changed his mind and did something else.'[92]

One need not be an open theist, however, to ascribe mental change to God. We could point to a few theologians, especially in the last one hundred years, who would predicate mental movement in God. Jay Wesley Richards gives an example of how one might deny the concept of divine immutability, or at least alter it in substantial ways, by virtue of atemporality's relationship with changelessness. Richards writes:

> To this point, then, the argument is that God's knowledge relation can and does change, for the simple reason that, in order for God to know what is the case, he will have to know what is the case at a time. And what is the case at time t will usually differ from what is the case at time $t +1$. So, given God's omniscience, if John Brown is running at time t, and John Brown is not running at $t + 1$, then God will know *John Brown is now running at t,* but he will *know John Brown is not now running at t +1.* So presumably, if God is omniscient, then his knowledge will change to account for changes in what is the case.[93]

While Richards' example is simply an intellectual hypothetical, William Lane Craig gives us an actual example of asserting this conception of atemporality and immutability when he says:

> We have seen that God's real relation to the temporal world gives us good grounds for concluding God to be temporal in view of the extrinsic change he undergoes through his changing relations with the world. But the existence of a temporal world also seems to entail intrinsic change in God in view of his knowledge of what is happening in the temporal world.

92. Greg Boyd, *God of the Possible: A Biblical Introduction to the Open View of God* (Grand Rapids: Baker Books, 2000), 77.

93. Richards, *The Untamed God*, 202.

For since what is happening in the world is in constant flux, so also must God's knowledge of what is happening be in constant flux.[94]

Whereas Craig would denounce the conclusion of open theism, the relationship between God and temporal items means that we are forced to predicate intellectual movement to God. What is more, as we will see, what often accompanies intellectual movements in God as He increases or decreases in knowledge is volitional movement as particular revelations entail a change in action for God.

The Volitional Movement of a Repenting God

A more comprehensive analysis of the passages that describe God as repenting or having volitional movement will come in Chapter Four. However, given that theologians usher in these passages as justification for denying a classical conception of divine immutability, it is worth mentioning them here as well. The argument for this denial of immutability is fairly straightforward – a plain reading of particular passage necessitates the conclusion that God changes at least as it pertains to His volitional action seen in His repentance. Genesis 6, for example, describes a God who examines the wickedness within humans, which leads to His regretting that He ever made them. A similar kind of regretful change is expressed in 1 Samuel 15 as God divulges that He regrets making Saul king.

Moreover, there are passages within the prophetic oracles that indicate a volitional dependency. Meaning, for threats or promises to be genuine, God's volitional decision making must be *reactive* to the obedience or disobedience of His people. For example, God says in Jeremiah 18:10, 'and if it does evil in my sight, not listening to my voice, then I will relent of the good that I had intended to do to it.'

Terrence E. Fretheim points out that there are '40 explicit references to divine repentance.'[95] He defines repentance as 'a metaphor whose roots are to be found in the dynamics of interpersonal

---

94. William Lane Craig, *Time and Eternity: Exploring God's Relationship to Time* (Wheaton, IL: Crossway, 2001), 97.

95. Terrence E. Fretheim, 'The Repentance of God: A Key to Evaluating Old Testament God-Talk,' *Horizons in Biblical Theology* 10 (1988): 47. For this point, I am indebted to Steve Duby and his article, '"For I am God, not a Man", Divine Repentance and the Creator-Creature Distinction' in *Journal of Theological Interpretation* (Vol. 12.2, 2018) 149-69.

human relationships.' He continues: 'Generally, the use of the word "repentance" presupposes that one has said or done something to another and, finding that to be hurtful or inadequate or dissatisfactory in some way, seeks to reverse the effects through contrition, sorrow, regret, or some other form of "turning".'[96] Fretheim correctly notes that biblical instances of God's 'repentance' 'is a metaphor.' However, Fretheim argues that every metaphor contains 'both a "yes" and a "no" (an "is" and "is not") with respect to God.'[97] This understanding leads Fretheim to conclude that the 'no' of the divine-repentance metaphor is that God does not repent like humans, i.e., from sin toward righteousness. Nevertheless, the 'yes' of the metaphor demonstrates there is real volitional turning in God.[98]

(5) The Problem of Divine Freedom and Contingency

The problem of divine freedom and contingency is related to the problem of creation and divine action. The mere existence of creation entails, so some argue, a problem for classical theists. Often, the problem of divine freedom is brought up as an issue pertaining to the doctrine of divine simplicity. However, the conversation necessarily blends into consideration of divine immutability as well. Simply put, the problem references the dilemma proponents of divine immutability and divine simplicity face regarding the choice between divine freedom and divine contingency in relationship to divine action and knowledge.

For example, if we affirm the apophatic predicate of simplicity and renounce composition in God, His actions are necessary given that His *ad extra* acts – such as creation – are necessary expressions of His simple essence, so the argument goes. This follows from attributes such as God being called 'Lord, Creator, Redeemer, and Refuge' since if these

---

96. Fretheim, 51.

97. Ibid., 51.

98. A similar strategy to divine repentance can be found in Ware, 'An Evangelical Reexamination,' 431-37; and Rob Lister, *God is Impassible and Impassioned: Toward a Theology of Divine Emotion* (Wheaton, IL: Crossway, 2013), 194-96. For a response to Fretheim and those like him, see Steven J. Duby, '"For I Am God, Not a Man", Divine Repentance and the Creator-Creature Distinction,' *Journal of Theological Interpretation* 12 (2018): 149-69.

attributes are said to exist in a simple God, they must exist necessarily.[99] Therefore, in this model, God lacks freedom as He *must* create or He *must* redeem, etc.

Those who wish to deviate from or deny classical immutability by virtue of the problem of divine freedom might concede and affirm that the attributes of 'creator' or 'redeemer' exist within God necessarily by virtue of His divine simplicity. However, to give into this concession creates the alternative conundrum – that of contingency. If God creates *necessarily*, it will mean that there is not a possible world in which God could not have created or existed alone apart from creation.

We can find two modern expressions of this line of argumentation in the work of R.T. Mullins and Jay Wesley Richards. Mullins argues that divine simplicity should not be listed amongst the divine perfections as he thinks it is not 'metaphysically compossible with who God is.'[100] He argues this on the basis that 'the Triune God is perfectly free, and freedom … is not compossible with pure act. One should recall that as pure act God has no unactualized potential. If God has any unactualized potential, he is not simple.'[101]

Given his understanding of divine freedom, Mullins argues we should conclude that it is possible that God could have created an alternate universe from the actual one we inhabit. Seeking to ask if God could have possibly performed such an action, Mullins notes, 'the answer seems to be "yes," if God is free.' However, he continues: 'If God did *not* create a different universe, he has unactualized potential. Divine simplicity should push one to say that God *did* create another universe. In fact, simplicity should push one to say that God created an infinite number of universes.'[102] The answer, for Mullins, is to deviate from the doctrine of pure actuality, along with strong immutability and simplicity with it.

Elsewhere, Mullins argues that a classical Thomistic articulation of logical, non-real, relations simply does not solve the problem of divine freedom and contingency. Using the example of God's gracious act in the economy of redemption, he writes:

---

99. These are the problem attributes put forward by R.T. Mullins in 'Simply Impossible: A Case Against Divine Simplicity' (*JRT*, Volume 7, 2013), 191.

100. Ibid., 194.

101. Ibid., 194.

102. Ibid., 195.

Augustine and Lombard will quickly appeal to the doctrine of predestination at this point to avoid any change in God. God has, from eternity, decreed to love Peter, they will say, so God has undergone no change in his decree. Does this really solve anything? Not at all. God's eternal decree to bestow grace upon Peter is not identical to the actual manifestation of that grace upon Peter for Peter does not eternally exist. God cannot bestow grace on Peter or express his love toward Peter until the actual concrete particular that is Peter comes into existence. God can express all sorts of loving gestures toward Peter before Peter comes to exist (e.g. eternally decree to send the Son and temporally send the Son), but certain expressions of love simply cannot occur until Peter in fact exists. This involves God activating a potential that he did not previously actualize: *bestowing grace on Peter*. It also involves God coming to have an accidental property: *the bestower of grace on Peter*. God has undergone a change, and Augustine and Lombard have failed to rebut this difficulty. They might try to appeal to the denial of real relations again, but it seems difficult for any Christian to seriously maintain that God only stands in a relation of reason to creation in the economy of salvation.[103]

Jay Wesley Richards argues in a similar vein, asserting that pure actuality is a difficult doctrine to accommodate. Instead, he insists that Christian theologians ought to accept God's possessing potentiality in order to protect divine freedom. Dealing with the awkward tensions that simplicity and immutability have with divine freedom and contingency, he argues that the solution of either eternality or 'Cambridge properties' are not sufficient. Ultimately, he proposes a form of 'mutability' which might better do justice to divine freedom than a strict changelessness could account for. He writes:

> Even if from eternity God knows what he chooses to create, if God's choice to create is free in the libertarian sense, then he could have chosen differently. In that case, what God would have known from eternity as actually created would be different from what he actually has created. Therefore we should conclude that God is immutable in those respects relevant to his essential perfection and aseity but

103. R. T. Mullins, *The End of a Timeless God* (Oxford: Oxford University Press, 2016), 125. He concludes, 'The Christian God cannot be timeless, strongly immutable, and simple.' He is also worried that a notion of divine simplicity runs the risk of a 'modal collapse.' We will not treat this argument here, but interested readers can see Mullins' thought in *The End of a Timeless God*, 137-43.

'mutable' with respect to certain contingent properties because of his freedom.[104]

Conclusion

Even though the doctrine of divine immutability has enjoyed relatively unanimous affirmation throughout a majority of Christian antiquity, the last few centuries have brought about various waves of deviations and denials from a classical understanding of God's changelessness. These deviations and denials are variegated in both source and content, yet each of them predicates movement in God or presents a 'problem' in one of five ways: relational/soteriological, incarnational, creation/divine action, knowledge/will, and divine freedom/contingency. Each of these movements predicated to God – by individual theologians or groups of theologians – breaks from the working definition that began this chapter. As we turn now, in Part Two of the book, to a threefold witness for divine immutability – historical, biblical, and metaphysical – we will make use of both our working definition and outlined deviations. Responding point-by-point to each denial is not the jurisdiction of what we are after here, nevertheless it will prove helpful, as we move into a constructive articulation of the classical doctrine, to interact with these deviations and denials in order to demonstrate the superiority of the classical understanding as we move toward explicating the soteriological significance of God's inalterability.

---

104. Richards, *Untamed God*, 212. While it is not the aim of this chapter to answer these deviations and denials of divine immutability, readers interested in a counter perspective to Richards and Mullins' research project should consult Steven J. Duby, 'Divine Simplicity, Divine Freedom, and the Contingency of Creation: Dogmatic Responses to Some Analytic Questions' in (*JRT*, Volume 6, 2012), 115-42. Instead of deviating from immutability or simplicity, Duby makes use of the helpful scholastic categories of 'absolute' and 'relative' attributes (ibid., 126). Employing these categories allows Duby, and those in the classical tradition, to affirm divine simplicity, divine immutability, *actus purus*, God's freedom of indifference with respect to creation, and creation's contingency upon God.

PART TWO

A Three-Fold Witness for Divine Immutability

CHAPTER THREE

Historical Witness: Divine Immutability in the Halls of History

The history of God's people contains a rather consistent witness to the inalterability of our Triune God. From both the mouths of confessors and the pages of confessions, we hear of the immutable glory of an immutable God. Though exceptions exist, and modernity often chose to discard the doctrine that was entrusted to them, the teaching of God's changelessness has enjoyed a stable witness throughout theological antiquity that few other doctrines have.[1]

Examining this consistent witness allows us to turn our current study toward constructions. The previous two chapters set the stage for the rest of the project and were thus deconstructive in nature. We examined modernity's distaste for metaphysical intrusions into the arena of theological method in Chapter One and the consequential deviations and denial of the doctrine of divine immutability that followed in Chapter Two. Now, in Part Two of the project, 'Divine Immutability in the Halls of History,' we can move past deconstructions toward putting

---

1. It would, however, be naïve to assume that all articulations of God's changelessness were monolithic given that certain eras and certain theologians emphasized differing points within the teaching of God's changelessness. Even using a phrase like 'classical immutability,' which I have chosen to do throughout this project, is in need of some nuance because of different emphasis even amongst classic confessors of immutability. However, for meaningful theological construction and due to a strong consistency of confirmation, the language has been adapted.

together a constructive affirmation of divine immutability by examining the historical, biblical, and metaphysical witness in favor of the doctrine.

Part Two does not aim to exhaust the literature or material in any of these three fields – history, Scripture, or metaphysics. Nor will its primary aim be to respond to each point of deviation or denial from the previous chapter. However, working through pertinent literature in all three fields and utilizing the deviations as talking partners will allow us to articulate a well-rounded understanding of classical immutability. The current chapter begins this threefold journey by working through a brief history of divine immutability.

Divine Immutability in the Early Church

John Behr describes the work of the church fathers as 'continuing the task set by the apostles, that of trying to give a good account of their faith in the crucified messiah, affirming that this one who died as a man is indeed the Son of God.'[2] While this 'good account' consists of numerous doctrines, an unchanging God is surely on the list. Building off the testimony of Scripture, the firstfruits of the post-biblical Christian tradition aided in articulating God's changelessness in meaningful ways that are still utilized today. Examining the literature of the early church reveals patristic theology bears a near unanimous witness in affirmation of God's inalterability.[3]

The continuity between the fathers in their avowal of divine immutability is so consistent that in his treatment of the early church's understanding of the doctrine, Bruce Ware, making a methodological decision, stated: 'Because certain ways of talking about the divine immutability are characteristic of many of these theologians, proceeding one to another thinker would prove to be too repetitive.'[4] Ware is correct. Working one-after-another through the church fathers in hopes to demonstrate their view of immutability would indeed be repetitive, and this repetition is

---

2. John Behr, *The Case Against Diodore and Theodore: Texts and Their Contexts* (Oxford: Oxford University Press, 2011), 4.

3. I say 'near unanimous' because some scholars argue that there were orthodox theologians who held to a form of divine mutability. See Joseph M. Hallman, 'The Mutability of God: Tertullian to Lactantius,' *Theological Studies* 42.3 (1981): 373-93. Hallman claims: 'Early Christian thinkers do not generally deny immutability, but at the same time do not always feel that it should be held in the absolute monopolar sense' (ibid., 374). He then works through Tertullian's interaction with Marcion to assert that Tertullian held to mutability regarding relations and the incarnation.

4. Ware, *Evangelical Reexamination*, 38.

instructive. A refrain oft repeated throughout the halls of ecclesiastical history should cause us to pause when opting to run toward a contrary opinion. The witness of history should not act as the evangelical's final authority, but it should bear significant weight if a doctrinal judgment puts one outside of the great tradition that spans continents and centuries.

While Scripture acts, for the Protestant theologian, as the *norma normans non normata* (the norm which is not normed), nevertheless we ought to make room for lesser authorities to not *norm* but *inform* our theological endeavors. So then, the halls of history, while not having the intrinsic authority to norm Scripture, as nothing does, can still be a form of *norma normata*, or a rule that is ruled. Therefore, in this brief tracing of the patristic understanding of divine immutability, we will strive for a balance in the tension of a holy repetition and insightful early nuances regarding divine immutability.

Incomprehensibility and the Creator-Creature Distinction

At the foundation of the patristic understanding of divine immutability is both the doctrine of incomprehensibility and the Creator-creature distinction. God's lack of compounded faculties, along with His atemporal eternity, renders Him not merely grander than His creatures, as if the two are comparable by varying degrees. Rather, He is altogether different in kind. The Lord's supreme uniqueness puts Him out of reach, in a univocal sense, from finite intellectual faculties. Here we could skim the surface of the patristic literature for a swarm of affirmations, but we will instead rely on the voices of a few. Maximus the Confessor demonstrates God's uniqueness and incomprehensibility using the triad of substance, potentiality, and actuality. In each of these ways God is exceptional from the existence of His creation and the creatures who inhabit it. Maximus writes: 'God is one, without first principle, incomprehensible, throughout being the total potentiality of being; he excludes absolutely the concept of temporal or qualified existence. ... [H]e is indefinite, immobile, and infinite, since he is infinitely beyond substance, potentiality, and actuality.'[5]

---

5. Maximus the Confessor, *Two Hundred Chapters on Theology, 1.1–1.2* (New York: St. Vladimir's Seminary Press, 2015), 43.

In step with many authors of his era, Maximus concludes that God's being beyond substance, potentiality, and actuality necessitates divine accommodation as the theological life is one of attempting to describe an incomprehensible being. He concludes, 'Never can a soul reach out toward the knowledge of God if God himself does not, having condescended, lay hold of it and lead it up to himself.'[6]

Far from being insignificant from the conversation of immutability, the patristic conception of incomprehensibility and the Creator-creature distinction is directly related to God's inalterability. Irenaeus makes this point explicit in his *Against Heresies*, as he opines: 'God differs from man in this, that God makes, but man is made. Surely that which makes is always the same; but that which is made must receive a beginning, a middle, addition, and increase.'[7] A factor in the distinction between the Creator and His creatures is the reality of being created necessitates the creature has the property of beginning, middle, and the potentiality of increase. These attributes may not be properly predicated of the Creator, for He is always and ever the same.

Concluding the twenty-first chapter of his *Treatise on the Soul*, Tertullian also highlights the distinction between that which is created and that which creates by linking the former to mutability. Tertullian writes:

> Now that which has received its constitution by being made or by being born, is by nature capable of being changed, for it can be both born again and re-made; whereas that which is not made and unborn will remain forever immoveable. Since, however, this state is suited to God alone, as the only Being who is unborn and not made (and therefore immortal and unchangeable), it is absolutely certain that the nature of all other existences which are born and created is subject to modification and change.[8]

Eternal Modes of Subsistence and Trinitarian Immutability

A reappearing concern in the patristic literature is that of the eternal modes of subsistence – paternity, filiation, and spiration. This, of

---

6. Maximus the Confessor, *Two Hundred Chapters on Theology*, 61.

7. Irenaeus, *Against Heresies*, in *The Faith of the Early Fathers*, trans. William Jurgens, (Collegeville: The Liturgical Press, 1970), 1:84. Maximus uses very similar language, yet writes as God's not having a 'first principle, intermediate state, or ending' (Maximus, *Two Hundred Chapters on Theology, 1.1–1.2*, 43).

8. Tertullian, *A Treatise on the Soul* (*ANF* 3:202).

course, is no surprise given the church fathers' Trinitarian emphasis and development in the first few centuries after the conclusion of the canon. John of Damascus has the chronological benefit of constructing his theological works at the tail end of the patristic period and the beginning of the medieval era. This chronological benefit affords John of Damascus a level of precision that is hard to rival in patristic literature. Writing with conciliar conclusions in mind, John says of the Triune modes of subsistence:

> So then in the first sense of the word the three absolutely divine subsistences of the Holy Godhead agree: for they exist as one in essence .... For the Father alone is ingenerate, no other subsistence having given him being. And the Son alone is generate, for he was begotten of the Father's essence without beginning and without time. And only the Holy Spirit proceedeth from the Father's essence, not having been generated but simply proceeding.[9]

John of Damascus' articulation of the eternal modes of subsistence allows him to say two things regarding Triune immutability: (1) All that belongs to the essence of the Father belongs to the essence of the Son and Spirit, and (2) the eternality of the Son's generation means there is no change in the First or Second Persons of the Trinity. To the former point, John of Damascus writes: 'We believe, then, in One God, one beginning, uncreated, unbegotten, imperishable and immortal, everlasting, infinite, uncircumscribed, boundless, of infinite power, simple, uncompounded, incorporeal, without flux, passionless, unchangeable, inalterable.'[10] Since Jesus is consubstantial with the Father according to His divinity, John is able to predicate these attributes, and more, to the Second Person of the Trinity by virtue of generation, save unbegottenness, which alone belongs to the Father.

To the second point – that the eternality of Christ's generation prevents alterability in the Father or the Son – the theologian insists: 'There never was a time when the Father was and the Son was not, but always the Father and always the Son, who was begotten of him, existed together. For he could not have received the name Father apart from the Son.' He continues: 'for if he were without the Son, he could not be the Father: and if he thereafter had the Son, thereafter he became the Father,

---

9. John of Damascus, *Exposition of the Orthodox Faith* (*NPNF* 9:9).
10. Ibid.

not having been the Father prior to this, and he was changed from which was not the Father and became the Father.' For John of Damascus, a break from Arianism was crucial, as the co-eternal nature of generation saves change in God, 'unless we grant that the Son co-existed from the beginning with the Father, by whom he was begotten, we introduce change into the Father's subsistence.'[11]

'Unchangeably the Self-Same': Augustine on Divine Immutability

While the doctrine of divine immutability shows up often in the pages of patristic writers, arguably, it shows in no theologian more frequently than Augustine of Hippo.[12] On the notion of God being mutable, Augustine exclaims, 'a thing which far be it from us to believe of God.'[13] On the contrary, God is 'unchangeably the Self-same.'[14] In his *Confessions*, divine immutability plays an important role for Augustine as it is God's unchangeable nature that enables Him to truly and fully know Himself. He writes, 'That no one but the unchangeable light knows Himself.'[15] This fully self-aware, unchangeable light illuminates an epistemic foundation for changeable creatures. Here Augustine pulls from Psalm 36 and writes: 'That the unchangeable light knoweth itself, so should it be known by that which is enlightened and changeable. Therefore, unto thee is my soul as "land where no water is" because it cannot itself enlighten itself, so it cannot itself satisfy itself. For so is the fountain of life with thee, like as in thy light we shall see light.'[16] There is, for Augustine, a fascinating correlation between God's immutability and the intellectual joy of His creatures. Augustine worries that intellectual

---

11. John of Damascus, *Exposition of the Orthodox*, 7. Augustine argues for the Son's immutability in a similar fashion. See Augustine, *The Writings against the Manichaeans and against the Donatists*, NPNF 4:356.

12. For a fuller treatment of Augustine's doctrine of divine immutability, see: Anders Tune, 'Immutable, Saving God: The Import of the Doctrine of Divine Immutability for Soteriology in Augustine's Theology' (PhD diss., The Catholic University of America, 1994), and Craig A. Hefner, '"In God's Changelessness there is Rest": The Existential doctrine of God's Immutability in Augustine and Kierkegaard,' *IJST* 20 (2018): 65-83.

13. Augustine, *On the Trinity* (*NPNF* 3:220).

14. Augustine, *Confessions* (*NPNF* 1:194-94).

15. Ibid., 196.

16. Ibid., 196.

delight that is 'elated with joy in itself' is bound to be disappointed because the self is utterly mutable (a fact he finds self-evident because creatures move from ignorance to knowledge). Yet, when the creature's mind turns to the unchangeable Wisdom, it will find a subject truly worthy of intellectual delight. Augustine writes, 'desisting and subsiding from boasting and self-conceit, it strives to cling to God, and to be recruited and reformed by him who is unchangeable.'[17]

Furthermore, in his *Confessions* Augustine explicitly predicates inalterability to God with a trifold formula. Numerous times Augustine writes of God's immutable being, knowledge, and will.[18] He states: 'But when he discovers and can say anything of these, let him not then think that he has discovered that which is above these Unchangeable, which Is unchangeably, and Knows unchangeably, and Wills unchangeably.' And again, 'For altogether as Thou art, Thou only knowest, Who art unchangeably, and knowest unchangeably, and willest unchangeably. And Thy Essence Knoweth and Willeth unchangeably; and Thy Knowledge Is, and Willeth unchangeably; and Thy Will Is, and Knoweth unchangeably.'[19]

This trifold immutable formula is carried over in Augustine's *On the Trinity*. In what Anders Svendsen Tune calls 'the closest Augustine comes to defining the immutable essence that is God,'[20] Augustine writes, 'the essence of God, whereby he is, has altogether nothing changeable, neither in eternity, nor in truth, nor in will.'[21] Ascribing immutability to God's being, knowledge, and will means, for Augustine, that there is never a time when we can properly ascribe accidents in God. This is a major concern in the first five books of his *On the Trinity*. Augustine is right to put in diligent work against the propensity to ascribe accidents to God and this theological conviction and method will prove to be important throughout this project. Against accidents in God, Augustine writes:

> Other things that are called essences or substances admit of accidents, whereby a change, whether great or small, is produced in them. But there

---

17. Augustine, *Letter to Dioscorus* (*NPNF* 1:443).
18. Augustine, *Confessions* (*NPNF* 1:193).
19. Ibid., 190-200.
20. Tune, *Immutable, Saving God*, 170.
21. Augustine, *On the Trinity* (*NPNF* 3:70).

can be no accident of this kind in respect to God; and therefore he who is God is the only unchangeable substance or essence, to whom certainly being itself, whence comes the name of essence, most especially and most truly belongs.[22]

To explain what he means by 'accidents in God,' Augustine uses two examples – the feathers of a raven and the hair of a man. As for the raven, we can predicate the color black to the bird's feathers only as an accidental property. If the feather is *separated* from the bird, or the bird ceases to be and 'turned into earth' the blackness of the feather will fade and disappear. The bird merely possessed the property of black accidently. Separation is not the only manner by which accidental properties are revealed, as Augustine points out in his second example of a man's hair. While full-bodied hair may stay atop a man's head and never face separation, it nevertheless loses its accidental property of being black as it transitions to gray in his aging years.

Augustine juxtaposes these two forms of accidental properties with God's essence to demonstrate that, in God, there is no increase nor decrease. In God's being, wisdom, and volition, there are no accidental properties that may come or go.[23]

Soteriology and the Immutability of the Son in Athanasius

Arguably, the theologian who most embodies the spirit of the thesis of this book is the Bishop of Alexandria, Athanasius. This is due to Athanasius not only defending the doctrine of divine immutability but doing so with an eye toward soteriology. For, Athanasius understood that a deviation or denial of divine immutability would never be satisfied by being an alteration to theology proper alone. Rather, altering an understanding of God's changelessness would inevitably find a way to seep into corollary doctrinal fields, especially soteriology.

In the day of Arianism, and even post-Nicene Christological discourse, there persisted much theological error regarding Christ's nature.

---

22. Ibid., 3:88.

23. Ibid., 3:88-89. Hilary of Poitiers deals with the similar worry against God's gaining or losing: 'I believe that God is unchangeable and that neither defect or improvement nor gain or loss affect His eternity, but what He is He always is, for this is peculiar to God.' Hilary of Poitiers, *The Trinity*, TFC (Washington: Catholic University of America Press, 1954), 25:75.

While Athanasius' rebuttals against Arianism came in many forms, divine immutability played a major role. Athanasius saw that Christological immutability protected the economy of redemption and was necessary in doing justice to both Christ's divine *and* human natures.

Dealing first with Athanasius' concern for the relationship between Christological immutability and the divine nature of the Son, two words prove very important in tracing Athanasius' argument – 'image' and 'generation.' Simply put, Athanasius is concerned that to make good on the consubstantiality between the Father and Son we must do doctrinal justice for what it means for Jesus to be generated of the Father's essence and to be the Father's image on earth.

Athanasius writes: 'the Son, being from the Father, and proper to his essence, is unchangeable and unalterable as the Father himself.'[24] Given that the Son is properly of the Father's essence, the Arian slogan – 'there was a time when he was not' – must be seen as false and anathematized by the orthodox councils. Rather, as the Father is eternal, and the Son is of the Father's essence, the Son is inalterably eternal as well. As Athanasius writes:

> But such heretics no Christian would bear; it belongs to Greeks, to introduce an originated Triad, and to level it with things originate; for these do admit of deficiencies and additions; but the faith of Christians acknowledges the blessed Triad as unalterable and perfect and ever what It was, neither adding to It what is more, not imputing to It any loss (for both ideas are irreligious), and therefore it dissociates It from all things generated, and it guards as indivisible and worships the unity of the Godhead Itself; and shuns the Arian blasphemies, and confesses and acknowledges that the Son was ever; for he is eternal, as is the Father, of whom he is the Eternal Word.[25]

Denouncing the eternality of the Son was of the severest renouncements for Athanasius. He met such denouncements with serious language and tone. 'O ye enemies of God,' says Athanasius, 'that the Son did not come out of nothing, nor is in the number of originated things at all, but is the Father's Image and Word eternal, never having not been, but being ever, as the eternal Radiance of a light which is eternal.'[26] This line of

---

24. Athanasius, *Four Discourses Against The Arians*, (*NPNF* 4:327).
25. Ibid., 4.316.
26. Ibid., 4:314.

argumentation is not confined to his work against the Arians alone. In Athanasius' *Statement of Faith*, he makes a similar argument, saying:

> He is then by nature an Offspring, perfect from the Perfect, begotten before all the hills (Prov. 8:25), that is before every rational and intelligent essence, as Paul also in another place calls him 'first-born of all creation' (Col. 1:15). But by calling him First-born, he shews that he is not a Creature, but Offspring of the Father. For it would be inconsistent with his deity for him to be called a creature. For all things were created by the Father through the Son, but the Son alone was eternally begotten from the Father, whence God the Word is 'first-born of all creation,' unchangeable from unchangeable.[27]

If we move to Athanasius' argument for Christological immutability by virtue of 'image,' the Bishop employed John 14 and Hebrews 1. In John 14, Jesus declares that He is the truth, the way, and the life and, 'If you know me, you will also know my Father. From now on you do know him and have seen him.' To this declaration, Philip asks Jesus, 'show us the Father, and that's enough for us.' Jesus' response is what becomes important for Athanasius' argument, for Jesus replies, 'Have I been among you all this time and you do not know me, Philip? The one who has seen me has seen the Father. How can you say, "Show us the Father"? Don't you believe that I am in the Father and the Father is in me? The words I speak to you I do not speak on my own. The Father who lives in me does his works. Believe me that I am in the Father and the Father is in me.' In the opening chapter of Hebrews, the author claims that Jesus is a better revelation of God. The third verse states that Jesus 'is the radiance of the glory of God and the exact imprint of his nature, and he upholds the universe by the word of his power.'

Both of these chapters are important for Athanasius' argument of Christological immutability; for if Christ is to be the true and better revelation of the Father, how could something that is essentially alterable image that which is eternally inalterable? Athanasius writes, regarding the relationship between the Father and the Father's image: 'Proceed we then to consider the attributes of the Father, and we shall come to know whether this Image is really his. The Father is eternal, immortal, powerful, light, King, Sovereign, God, Lord, Creation, and Maker.' Athanasius continues: 'These attributes must be in the Image, to make

---

27. Athanasius, *Statement of Faith* (*NPNF* 4:85).

it true that he "that hath seen" the Son "hath seen the Father".[28] For Athanasius, it would be disingenuous at best to state that Jesus is the 'image of the invisible God' if He be completely mutable, and the Father be immutable. In his conclusion to the argument based on 'image,' Athanasius focuses specifically on changelessness, saying:

> He is shewn to be the Father's Expression and Image, remaining what he is and not changing, but thus receiving from the Father to be one and the same. If then the Father change, let the Image change; for so is the Image and Radiance in its relation towards him who begat It. But if the Father is unalterable, and what he is that he continues, necessarily does the Image also continue what he is, and will not alter. Now he is Son from the Father; therefore, he will not become other than is proper to the Father's essence.[29]

Not only for the purposes of establishing the divine nature does Athanasius argue in favor of Christological immutability, but also for establishing the genuine reality of Christ's human nature. In a personal letter to Epictetus, Athanasius argues that like how divine immutability protects against the idea of Christ being created from naught, it also protects against the idea of the eternal divine Word *changing* into flesh. Rather, it was a genuine flesh which Christ assumed, which did not pre-exist the incarnation of Christ. In his letter, Athanasius writes: 'If the Word is coessential with the body which is of earthly nature, while the Word is, by your own confession, coessential with the Father, it will follow that even the Father himself is coessential with the body produced from the earth. And why any longer blame the Arians for calling the Son a creature ...'[30] He continues:

> ... when you go off to another form of impiety, saying that the Word was changed into flesh and bones and hair and muscles and all the body, and

---

28. Athanasius, *Four Discourses Against the Arians* (*NPNF* 4:318).

29. Ibid. 4:319. In another volume, Athanasius states the important point again, 'But though he is Word, he is not, as we said, after the likeness of human words, composed of syllables; but he is the unchanging Image of His own Father. For men, composed of parts and made out of nothing, have their discourse composite and divisible. But God possesses true existence and is not composite, wherefore His Word also has true Existence and is not composite, but is the one and only-begotten God, Who proceeds in His goodness from the Father as from a good Fountain, and orders all things and holds them together.' Athanasius, *Against the Heathen* (*NPNF* 4:26).

30. Athanasius, *Personal Letters* (*NPNF* 4:571).

was altered from its own nature? For it is time for you to say openly that he was born of earth; for from earth is the nature of the bones and of all the body. What then is this great folly of yours, that you fight even with one another? For in saying that the Word is coessential with the Body, you distinguish the one from the other, while in saying that he has been changed into flesh, you imagine a change of the Word himself. And who will tolerate you any longer if you so much as utter these opinions? For you have gone further in impiety than any heresy. For if the Word is coessential with the Body, the commemoration and the work of Mary are superfluous, inasmuch as the body could have existed before Mary, just as the Word also is eternal: if, that is, it is as you say coessential with the Body. Or what need was there even of the Word coming among us, to put on what was coessential with himself, or to change his own nature and become a body? For the Deity does not take hold of itself, so as to put on what is of its own Essence, any more than the Word sinned, in that it ransoms the sins of others, in order that changing into a body it should offer itself a sacrifice for itself, and ransom itself.[31]

We bring our section on Athanasius to a close by showing that the Bishop's attention to Christological immutability, as seen above, had a soteriological concern. It was not to simply defend the doctrine of divine immutability in the divine nature of the Son that Athanasius spent so much ink on the doctrine. Rather, for Athanasius – as it should be for us – there was an undeniable link between God's changelessness and what He might accomplish in the economy of redemption. Returning to Athanasius' work *Against the Arians*, Athanasius turns to this concern in his second discourse. He writes, 'For he is faithful as not changing, but abiding ever, and rendering what he has promised.' Athanasius uses this line of argumentation to differentiate the God of Christianity from the gods of the Greeks, saying:

> Now the so-called gods of the Greeks, unworthy the name, are faithful neither in their essence nor in their promises; for the same are not everywhere, nay, the local deities come to naught in course of time, and undergo a natural dissolution; wherefore the Word cries out against them that 'faith is now strong in them,' but they are 'waters that fail,' and 'there is no faith in them.' But the God of all, being one really and indeed and true, is faithful, who is ever the same, and says, 'see now, that I, even I am

---

31. Athanasius, *Personal Letters* (*NPNF* 4:571-72).

he,' and I 'change not;' and therefore his Son is 'faithful' being ever the same and unchanging, deceiving neither in his essence nor in his promise.[32] Christ's divine and immutable nature render Him capable of being faithful both to the divine essence and to His covenantal promises in the economy of redemption. Athanasius ought to be a model for what it looks like to root the Trinitarian work *ad extra* in God's life *in se*.

Divine Immutability in Medieval Theology

The patristic era does not monopolize doctrinal development and dedication to divine immutability. On the contrary, as the church moved into the Middle Ages, so too did the teaching of divine immutability. It would, no doubt, be profitable to examine dozens of medieval theologians at length; however, we will instead focus our time on two chief theologians who taught explicitly about God's unchanging essence – Anselm of Canterbury (1033–1109) and Thomas Aquinas (1225–1274).

Immutability in Anselm's Monologion and Proslogion

Thanks to the consistent pleas and begging of his students, Anselm of Canterbury put pen to paper and produced his famed *Monologion* and its subsequent *Proslogion*.[33] Of the former work, Anselm himself characterized the eighty-chapter piece as 'an example of meditation on the meaning of faith.' Anselm followed up this 'example of meditation' with the *Proslogion*, which he described as 'faith in quest of understanding.'[34]

In both the *Monologion* and the *Proslogion*, divine immutability has a part to play. In the *Monologion* Anselm works through the 'supreme essence' and details the goodness of God and that which comes from God. After navigating aspects of the *creatio ex nihilo* and participation in God's goodness, Anselm turns to address a number of divine perfections – including immutability. Key to Anselm's brief discussion of immutability in *Monologion* is the denial – at least of a certain kind –

---

32. Athanasius, *Four Discourses Against the Arians* (*NPNF* 4:352-53).

33. For an introduction to both works, along with *Why God Became Man*, see Brian Davies and G. R. Evans, *Introduction* in *Anselm of Canterbury: The Major Works* (Oxford: Oxford University Press, 2008), vii-xxiii. For a broader introduction to the life and work of Anselm, see Brian Davies and Brian Leftow, *The Cambridge Companion to Anselm* (Cambridge: Cambridge University Press, 2005); Sandra Visser and Thomas Williams, *Anselm* (Oxford: Oxford University Press, 2008).

34. Anselm, *Proslogion*, 83.

of accidents in God.[35] Anselm denounces any accidents which predicate mutability. However, he nuances his position and opines that not all accidents entail such mutability, such as 'some relations.' To explain, he uses the example of someone being born:

> Take someone who is going to be born next year. At the moment I am not taller than him, or smaller than him; nor the same height as, or similar to, him. When he is born, however, I will be able to have, and to lose, all these relations, without my changing at all, insofar as he grows and changes through different qualities. Some accidents, then, bring alterability with them in some respect. And other accidents do not take away inalterability in any respect whatsoever.[36]

This example of accidental relations in flux leads Anselm to the conclusion that, 'There is nothing, therefore, that can be accidental to the essence of the supreme nature so as to allow us to infer mutability.'[37] In the hypothetical, the figure brought into existence by birth now has accidental properties that begin to alter. Height, weight, age, and the like begin to fluctuate in the fictitious figure, yet these accidental properties are merely relational accidents and bear no change to the one relating to them. In this way, accidents entailing mutability may not properly be predicated of God. Anselm concludes this section by saying, 'The supreme essence is, therefore, never different from itself, not even accidentally. ... Whatever the rules are for using the term "accident" properly, this is true and beyond doubt: nothing may be predicated of the supreme and immutable nature which might suggest that it is mutable.'[38]

While Anselm did not intend for this hypothetical to be a lesson in atemporality, it is instructive in demonstrating the relationship between mutability and time, for it is the figure's passing through a succession of moments which brings about the growth and each accidental property. Chapter 25 of the *Monologion* clarifies immutability in two ways then:

---

35. I say 'at least of a certain kind' because Anselm is happy to distinguish between two types of accidents. He distinguishes between those accidents 'whose presence or absence implies some change in the subject: e.g. all colors. [and] others cause no change in that of which they are predicated: e.g. some relations' (Anselm, *Monologion*, 41). For more on varying types of accidents, see Pasnau, *Metaphysical Themes*, 191-94.

36. Anselm, *Monologion*, in *Major Works*, 41-42.

37. Ibid., 42.

38. Ibid., 42.

(1) by showing that not all accidents are created equal and any accident which predicates mutability may not be ascribed to the supreme essence; and (2) demonstrating that temporality breeds mutability.

Written one year after *Monologion*, *Proslogion* is a result of Anselm's desire to press deeper into the logic behind affirming God's existence. The eighty chapters that make up *Monologion* entail variegated lines of reasoning God's existence. However, after crafting the arguments which make up *Monologion*, Anselm was plagued with the challenge of distilling all the arguments of his previous work into 'one single argument that for its proof required no other save itself.'[39]

Constructed in 1077, the *Proslogion* to this day is largely synonymous with what came to be known as 'the ontological argument' for God's existence. However, readers will note that the formal portions of the ontological argument conclude in chapter three of this twenty-six-chapter treatise. While a singular, rational argument for God's existence was Anselm's goal, he gave readers more than that. We find in the *Proslogion* an informed prayer of intellectual power that demonstrates the proper movement from doctrine to doxology.[40] Anselm moves from attempting to articulate the incomprehensible divine essence to the worship that such an essence induces. Characterizing the *Proslogion*, Rik van Nieuwenhove writes that 'By pondering the mysteries of faith he draws closer to God; theological thinking is a foretaste, however inadequate, and inchoative participation in the vision of God.'[41]

While divine immutability is nowhere named in the *Proslogion*, it is everywhere assumed. Developing the argument that God is 'something-than-which-nothing-greater-can-be-thought,' Anselm directly deals with divine perfections throughout the work. In various chapters Anselm lists attributes such as 'perceptive, omnipotent, merciful, impassible ... living, wise, good, blessed, eternal.'[42] In chapters six

---

39. Anselm, *Preface to Proslogion*, in *Major Works*, 82.

40. For more on Anselm's *Proslogion*, see: Marilyn McCord Adams, 'Praying the Proslogion' in *The Rationality of Belief and the Plurality of Faith*. Ed. Thomas Senor (Ithaca: Cornell University Press, 1995); and Gavin R. Ortlund, *Anselm's Pursuit of Joy: A Commentary on the Proslogion* (Washington: Catholic University of American Press, 2020).

41. Rik van Nieuwenhove, *An Introduction to Medieval Theology* (Cambridge: Cambridge University Press, 2012), 87.

42. Anselm, *Proslogion*, 94.

through ten Anselm seeks to synthesize seemingly contradictory attributes such as God's being perceptive while not possessing a body (ch. 6), His being omnipotent while having inability to do certain tasks (ch. 7), His being simultaneously merciful and impassible (ch. 8), His being supremely just to the wicked and one who spares the righteous (chs. 9–10). Of all the attributes, he arguably discusses divine simplicity with the greatest length. In chapter eighteen Anselm writes: 'For whatever is made up of parts is not absolutely one, but in a sense many and other than itself, and it can be broken up either actually or by the mind – all of which things are foreign to You. … Therefore there are no parts in You, Lord; neither are You many.'[43]

The significance of immutability becomes apparent in Anselm's treatment of attributes. For example, he writes of God's atemporality: 'you were not, therefore, yesterday, nor will you be tomorrow, but yesterday and today and tomorrow You *are*.'[44] As in *Monologion*, Anselm denies God's experiencing a change in succession of moments such that neither yesterday nor tomorrow may be predicated of God's experience. A similar strategy is taken regarding God's omnipresence. Anselm notes, 'All that which is enclosed in any way by place or time is less than that which no law of place or time constrains. Since nothing is greater than You, no place or time confines You but You exist everywhere and always.'[45]

In one of his lists of divine perfection, Anselm concludes that God is 'whatever it is better to be rather than not to be.'[46] Though Anselm never treats divine immutability in *Proslogion*, his treatment of corollary divine perfections necessitates God's inalterability and we can conclude, with Anselm, that it is better for God to be unchanging rather than not.

Thomas Aquinas on the Unmoved Mover

In the *Prima Pars* of *Summa Theologica*, Aquinas says of divine simplicity: 'when the existence of a thing has been ascertained there remains the further question of the manner of its existence.'[47] Question three of the *Summa* is an appropriate place for the Italian theologian to assert this

43. Ibid., 98.
44. Ibid., 98, emphasis original.
45. Ibid., 94.
46. Ibid., 94.
47. Aquinas, *ST*, Ia3.2.

proposition as the previous question deals with Aquinas' five proofs for the existence of God. Brian Davies notes that these five proofs 'are famous and have given rise to a huge amount of literature both expository and critical.'[48] Summarizing the 'famous' five arguments, Michael Dodds says they can be categorized as: '(1) motion; (2) efficient causality; (3) contingency and necessity in beings; (4) grades of perfection in beings; and (5) finality in nature.'[49]

The first of Aquinas' five proofs is pertinent to our discussion here as it pertains to motion. Aquinas argues that 'in the world some things are in motion.'[50] This is evident to us, as we perceive our creaturely surroundings and see change and motion everywhere – time, space, matter, etc. If it is true that much is in motion around us, it also must be true that something set these items in motion. Aquinas argues that recounting the causative effect of motion back to its source will run into an abundance of causes until one arrives at the first mover – God Himself.

Aquinas describes the type of motion he has in mind here by utilizing the language of potency and act. He argues that nothing can be in motion except that which poses potentiality, for change is simply the motion from potency to actuality. For explanatory purposes, Aquinas draws to the mind the example of a fire and the logs that make up the fire. 'Thus, that which is actually hot, as fire, makes wood, which is potentially hot, to be actually hot, and thereby moves and changes it.'[51] The flames no longer have the potentiality of heat – as it is an actualized property – and it is those flames that actualize the potential property of heat within the logs. This is the exact kind of motion that may not be predicated of God as this form of motion entails potentiality.

Aquinas is building on Aristotle's argument of a first mover,[52] yet he is forced to nuance Aristotle's position for theological purposes, for, in Aristotle's articulation, the first mover inaugurates the chain of motion

48. Brian Davies, *Thomas Aquinas's Summa Theologiae: A Guide and Commentary* (Oxford: Oxford University Press, 2014), 34.

49. Dodds, *The Unchanging God of Love*, 94.

50. Aquinas, *ST*, Ia2.3.

51. Aquinas, *ST*, Ia2.2.

52. Aristotle, *Metaphysics*, in *Metaphysics, Books X-XIV: The Oeconomica, Magna Moralia*, Trans. Hugh Tredennick and G. Cyril Armstrong (Cambridge: Harvard University Press, 1935), 150.

with a first act of self-motion. However, Aquinas denounces this view on two grounds: first, he writes that it is impossible for an object to both have potentiality and actuality in the same respect. Second, the idea that the first mover must move himself would entail complexity of being. There must be composition such that an actualized part could move a part that possesses potentiality. As Aquinas moves toward question three and addresses divine simplicity, it becomes evident that this cannot be said of God.[53] On the contrary, God is the unmoved first mover who lacks potentiality, parts, and accidental qualities.

The concept of an unmoved mover is an important element of Aquinas' *Summa Contra Gentiles* as well. In *Summa Contra Gentiles*, readers might be surprised to find that Aquinas does not treat the doctrine of divine immutability in a stand-alone article or chapter like he does with the ninth question of *Prima Pars*. However, while not receiving a stand-alone chapter, Thomas' argument and the development therein depend on divine immutability. This is why, for example, he can say in the fourteenth chapter of Book One, which treats predication by way of remotion: 'As a principle of procedure in knowing God by way of remotion, therefore, let us adopt the proposition which, from what we have said, is now manifest, namely, that God is absolutely unmoved.'[54] And again, when Thomas treats divine eternality in *Summa Contra Gentiles*, he can say without hesitation: 'Since, however, we have shown that God is absolutely immutable, he is eternal, lacking all beginning or end.'[55]

While he never addresses immutability explicitly, Aquinas can begin both chapters fourteen and fifteen with this assumed acceptance of God's changelessness due to his work in demonstrating the necessity of God's immutability by His virtue of being the unmoved mover in the previous chapter. Chapter thirteen is a series of proofs for God's existence, and again, Michael Dodds is helpful to summarize these proofs: (1) motion, (2) efficient causality, (3) perfection in being and truth, and (4) the government of the world.[56] In his argument of the unmoved mover, Aquinas builds again off Aristotle to show that (1) 'everything that is

---

53. Aquinas, *ST*, Ia2-3.

54. Aquinas, *Summa Contra Gentiles*, Book I (Indiana: University of Notre Dame Press, 1975), 97.

55. Aquinas, *SCG* I, c15.1.

56. Dodds, 86.

moved is moved by another' and (2) 'that in movers and things moved one cannot proceed to infinity.'[57]

After working through two differing views of how to understand motion, as seen in Aristotle vs. Plato, Aquinas comes to the conclusion: 'Therefore, some self-moving being must have a mover that is moved neither through itself nor by accident.'[58] Similar to his conclusion in *Summa Theologica*, ultimately, Aquinas resolves the conversation of the unmoved first mover which must not regress into infinity, nor move itself, nor be moved by an accident by stating, 'there must, therefore, be an absolutely unmoved separate first mover. This is God.'[59] This theological reasoning on the unmoved mover allows Aquinas to pick up after the proofs of God's existence on the foundation that God *must* be immutable.

While we saw Aquinas indirectly treat immutability through the argument of the unmoved mover in *Summa Contra Gentiles,* he does address the doctrine head on in *Summa Theologica.* As Aquinas turns to address divine immutability explicitly in Ia9, he builds his case for immutability 'from what precedes,' meaning he constructs his understanding of immutability on the foundation of God's existence, divine simplicity, perfections, goodness, and infinity – as these are the topics of questions one through eight. Aquinas provides three arguments for divine immutability, all of which are intricately related to another aspect of the divine life. In his first argument he insists that the first mover 'must be pure act, without admixture of any potentiality.' He continues, 'Everything which is in any way changed, is in some way in potentiality. Hence it is evident that it is impossible for God to be in any way changeable.'[60]

His second argument is concerned again with divine simplicity. Aquinas writes that whatever changes 'remains as it was in part, and passes away in part.' This would necessitate composition, which cannot be properly predicated to God for He has been shown – in Ia3 – to be

---

57. Aquinas, *SCG* I, c13.4. Aquinas defends both of these points with three subpoints each. For the first proposition, see *SCG* I, c13.5-10 and for the second proposition, see *SCG* I, c13.12-16.

58. Aquinas, *SCG* I, c13.24. cf. also, *SCG* I, c13.10.

59. Aquinas, *SCG* I, c13.28.

60. Aquinas, *ST*, Ia9.1.

'altogether simple.'[61] His third and final argument deals with divine infinitude; Aquinas writes that 'everything which is moved acquires something by its movement, and attains what it had not attained previously.' Of course, this means that God must not be moved as 'God is infinite, comprehending in himself all the plenitude of perfection of all being, he cannot acquire anything new, nor extend himself to anything whereto he was not extended previously.'[62]

In question nine, then, Aquinas concludes that God is altogether unmovable. His lack of potentiality, together with His simplicity and His infinitude, means He may not be said to move into any greater actuality, move in any part, nor move into acquiring anything new.

Thomas' writings concerning immutability are not confined to *Summa Theologica* and *Summa Contra Gentiles*. On the contrary, Aquinas explicitly refers to or alludes to the doctrine of divine immutability in nearly all his published work.[63] In his commentary on Lombard's *Sentences*, Aquinas echoes a similar argument to his first of three in *Summa Theologica*: 'One ought to say that Every motion or mutation, howsoever it be said, follows upon some possibility, since motion is an act of an existent in potency. Hence, since God is pure act, having nothing of potency admixed, there can be no mutation in him.'[64] Relating this conception of God's pure actuality to that of temporal creation and divine action, Dodds helpfully summarizes one of Aquinas' responses to objectors of divine inalterability:

> Thomas shows how God's 'transient action' in the production of creatures is directed by his immanent activity of knowing and willing. God's operation is unlike that of creatures since it is his very substance. Things whose operation is different from substance must be moved to action since in acting they acquire a new actuality they cannot give themselves. Since God's operation is his substance, he does not need to be moved by another

---

61. Ibid., *ST*, Ia9.1, cf. Ia3.

62. Ibid., *ST*, Ia9.1, cf. Ia7.

63. Dodds, *The Unchanging God of Love*, 46. Dodds says this nearly verbatim: 'Thomas refers to the immutability of God in almost all his major works.' Dodds then proceeds to work through most of Aquinas' major publications detailing the role of immutability throughout his corpus (pp. 46-105).

64. Aquinas, *Thomas Aquinas's Earliest Treatment of the Divine Essence: Scriptum super libros Sententiarum, Book 1 Distinction 8*, trans. E. M. Macierowski (New York: University of New York Press, 1997), 75.

to operate. As his substance is eternal, so is his operation. The effect of his operation, however, need not be eternal. It proceeds from him not eternally, but according to the order of wisdom in God's immanent activity of knowing and loving.[65]

It is not without reason that most articulations of divine immutability make reference to the great medieval Italian theologian. Aquinas aids readers in articulating God's unchanging essence as it relates to philosophical inquiry and other divine corollaries of being.

Divine Immutability in the Confessions and Confessors of the Reformation and Post-Reformation

Theological retrieval was in the air during the era of the Reformation. The Reformers' *ad fontes* posture led them to reexamine the Scriptures not for novelty but for reclamation of the doctrines of old. The schism that was the Reformation happened, at least in part, due to soteriological and bibliological concern. However, theology proper and divine ontology was – and is today – a point in which Catholics and Protestants can hold the line arm and arm. Thomistic and Augustinian presuppositions pervade both Vatican City and Geneva.

Reformation and Post-Reformation Confessions

The legacy of the Reformers regarding theology proper manifests in many ways and places; one such way is via the creeds and confessions of the Reformation.[66] While theology proper in the Reformation creeds and confessions is a more than worthwhile topic of exploration, we will here focus on the emphasis of divine immutability found on the pages of Reformation and post-Reformation confessions. Using the confessions as a window into the theology of the Reformation and post-Reformation movement is a helpful venture, for as Fairbairn

---

65. Dodds, *The Unchanging God of Love*, 49.

66. Though not restricted to the Reformation and the Reformers alone, Jaroslav Pelikan identified no less that fifty formal creeds that explicitly confess divine perfections. This is again a testimony to the unified witness of the Christian church regarding theology proper. See Jaroslav Pelikan, *Credo: Historical and Theological Guide to Creeds and Confessions of Faith in the Christian Tradition* (New Haven: Yale University Press, 2003), 545.

and Reeves point out, 'The leaders of the early Reformation created many confessions, more than were produced in any other period in church history until the rise of global confessions in the modern church.'[67] Making a similar point, Jaroslav Pelikan notes that three documents chronicling the proliferation of Reformation creeds – *Collectio Confessionum in Ecclesiis Reformatis Publicatarum*,[68] *Die Bekenntnisschriften der evangelish-lutherischen Kirche*,[69] and *Documents of the English Reformation*[70] – make up 'with few overlapping documents between the three volumes, to almost three thousand pages.'[71] Simply put, addressing Reformation theology through the means of confessions and creeds provides ample material in articulating doctrinal positions.

Though we can read of God's unchanging nature in a good number of confessions from the fifteenth through seventeenth centuries, it would be revisionist history to insinuate it had unanimous representation. On the contrary, a number of important historic creeds leave out the vital doctrine as it was not under contest as other points of doctrinal disagreements of the era. For some of these creeds, theology proper is left out altogether;[72] for others, while there is a section dealing with Trinitarianism or the doctrine of God, immutability is not listed among the treated theological positions. For example, talk of broader theology proper is absent from the early Reformation documents such

---

67. Donald Fairbairn and Ryan Reeves, *The Story of Creeds and Confessions: Tracing the Development of the Christian Faith* (Grand Rapids: Baker Academic, 2019), 247. For a brief account of how the Reformation and post-Reformation confessions relate to one another, see J. V. Fesko, *The Need for Creeds Today: Confessional Faith in a Faithless Age* (Grand Rapids: Baker Academic, 2020), 19-41.

68. H. A. Niemeyer, *Collectio Confessionum in Ecclesiis Reformatis Publicatarum* (Leipzig: Sumptibus Lulii Klinkhardti, 1840).

69. Irene Dingel, *Die Bekenntnisschriften der evangelish-lutherischen Kirche* (Göttingen: Vandenhoeck & Ruprecht, 2014).

70. Gerald Bray, *Documents of the English Reformation*, 3rd ed. (Cambridge: James Clarke Company, 2020).

71. Pelikan, *Credo*, 460.

72. As Scott Swain notes, 'The doctrine of God's being and attributes was not a disputed article at the time of the Reformation. It was not for that reason a neglected topic.' See Scott Swain, 'The Being and Attributes of God,' in *Reformation Theology*, ed. Matthew Barrett (Wheaton: Crossway, 2017), 218. While the doctrine of God was not neglected, as Swain says, it did not have the place of primacy by way of debate in the era of Reformation which necessitated a lack of need to address it in some confessions.

as Zwingli's *Sixty-Seven Theses*[73] as well as the *Bern Theses*.[74] Others, however, might mention broader theology proper, yet still explicit talk of divine immutability is absent. For example, the *Augsburg Confession* builds off the witness of the Nicene divines and condemns the heresies of the Manichees, Valentinians, Arians, Eunomians, Mohammedans, and Samosatenes. However, this is as specific as the first article, dealing with Trinitarianism, gets.[75] The same could be said for the *First Confession of Basel*, which has the 'unique feature' of 'connect[ing] the doctrine of election to the doctrine of God' yet does so without explicit mention of God's inalterability.[76]

Turning to confessions that deal directly with divine immutability, the middle of the 1500s proved important. The thirty-five-article French Confession (1559), penned largely by the Genevan Reformers including Calvin and Theodore Beza, makes explicit mention of divine ontology and theology proper, including the doctrine of divine immutability. This 1559 confession, along with others, instructs us by way of theological method as the prolegomenous nature of theology proper. In article one, preceding any confession regarding divine revelation, the French confession declares, 'We believe and confess that there is but one God, whose Being only is simple, spiritual, eternal, invisible, immutable, infinite, incomprehensible, ineffable, who can do all things, who is all-wise, all good, most just, and most merciful.'[77]

Just two years later, in the lowlands of the Netherlands and Belgium, the famous Belgic Confession was birthed. Arriving in 1561, largely by the pen of Guido de Brès, the Belgic Confession stands as one of the more influential confessions even to this day. Heavily influenced by the French Confession, the Belgic Confession begins its first article laying ground in theology proper. The first article reads: 'We all believe with the heart and confess with the mouth that there is one only simple and spiritual

---

73. James T. Dennison, Jr., *Reformed Confessions of the 16ᵗʰ and 17ᵗʰ Centuries in English Translations* (Grand Rapids: Reformation Heritage, 2008), 1:1-8.

74. Ibid., *RCC*, 1:40.

75. Schaff, *CoC*, 3:7-8. For more on the significance of the Augsburg Confession, see Leif Grane, *The Augsburg Confession: A Commentary*, trans. by John H. Rasmussen (Minneapolis: Augsburg, 1987); and Fairbairn and Reeves, *The Story of Creeds and Confessions*, 261-65.

76. Fairbairn and Reeves, *The Story of Creeds and Confessions*, 285.

77. Dennison, *RCC*, 2:141.

Being, which we call God; and that he is eternal, incomprehensible invisible, immutable, infinite, almighty, perfectly wise, just, good, and the overflowing fountain of all good.'[78]

Again, the reader can see the unchangeable character of God emphasized alongside other divine perfections in the Belgic Confession. This trend continues in the heritage of Reformation creeds with the Canons of Dort and ultimately with the Westminster Confession of Faith. As for the Canons of Dort, the eleventh article reads: 'And as God himself is most wise, unchangeable, omniscient, and omnipotent, so the election made by him can neither be interrupted nor changed, recalled nor annulled; neither can the elect be cast away, nor their number diminished.'[79]

Though the Westminster Confession breaks tradition with these former three by way of method – putting first the doctrine of revelation in chapter one, then moving to 'of God, and the Holy Trinity' in chapter two – it nevertheless remains consistent in stringing together the divine perfections, including immutability. The first article of the second chapter reads:

> There is but one only, living, and true God, who is infinite in being and perfection, a most pure spirit, invisible, without body, parts, or passions; immutable, immense, eternal, incomprehensible, almighty, most wise, most holy, most free, most absolute, working all things according to the counsel of his own immutable and most righteous will, for his own glory; most loving, gracious, merciful, long-suffering, abundant in goodness and truth, forgiving iniquity, transgression, and sin; the rewarder of them that diligently seek him; and withal, most just, and terrible in his judgments, hating all sin, and who will by no means clear the guilty.[80]

Along with noticing the doubly mentioned immutable character of God in this article of the Westminster Confession, readers should also notice the proximity of divine ontology and soteriology in this single article. The Westminster divines saw no issue with moving immediately from divine perfections such as simplicity, impassibility, and immutability to clauses regarding God's unchanging will which has set its course on the redemption of sinners in the gospel of Jesus Christ.

---

78. Ibid., 2:425.
79. Schaff, *CoC*, 3:583.
80. Schaff, *CoC*, 3:606-07.

Post-Reformation Confessors

In his magnificent four-volume study of Reformation and post-Reformation theology, Richard Muller notes: 'The conception of divine immutability is certainly a mark of continuity between the Reformers and the Protestant orthodox – indeed, it is a mark of continuity in the thought of the church from the time of the fathers through the seventeenth century.'[81] Muller is correct, for consistent is the Christian witness for divine immutability in both the confessions of the Reformation and the confessors of the post-Reformation. This brief section examines five such confessors – Francis Turretin, Stephen Charnock, John Owen, Petrus van Mastricht, and John Gill. Given the wide acceptance of the doctrine of divine immutability during the post-reformation era, there are a fair number of representatives to choose from whose voice could prove helpful in fleshing out the doctrine of divine immutability from the sixteenth to eighteenth centuries. However, these five – Turretin, Charnock, Owen, Mastricht, and Gill – give a good sampling of the key components of the post-reformation articulation of divine changelessness from key theologians who span countries and years.

Francis Turretin (1623–1687)

To exaggerate the influence of Francis Turretin's masterpiece, *Institutes of Elenctic Theology* would be difficult. Just as a demonstration of the work's influence on English-speaking systematicians, Charles Hodge's biographer, Paul Gutjahr, wrote: 'Turretin's massive, multivolume *Institutes of Elenctic Theology* stood as one of the most respected systematic theologies in the Reformed tradition. ... [It] remained *the* primary textbook at Princeton Seminary until the early 1870s, when it was finally replaced with Hodge's own *Systematic Theology*.'[82] Hodge himself said of Turretin, '[he is] the best systematic theological writer with whom we are acquainted.'[83]

---

81. Muller, *PRRD*, 3:308.

82. Paul C. Gutjahr, *Charles Hodge: Guardian of American Orthodoxy* (Oxford: Oxford University Press, 2011), 70, emphasis original.

83. Charles Hodge, 'Short Notices,' *Biblical Repertory and Princeton Review* 17 (1845): 190. For more on the biography and background of Turretin, see: Nicholas A. Cumming, *Francis Turretin (1623–87) and the Reformed Tradition* (Leiden: Brill, 2020).

With the eleventh question under the third topic – The One and Triune God – Turretin treats the inquiry, 'Is God immutable both in essence and will?' Again, as we have seen, Turretin answers in the strong affirmative: 'We affirm: Immutability is an incommunicable attribute of God by which is denied him not only all change, but also all possibility of change, as much with respect to existence as to will.'[84]

Building off John of Damascus, Turretin ties divine immutability closely with divine aseity. As John of Damascus affirmed, all created beings are mutable because they have 'taken their being from some other than themselves.' God, on the contrary, is immutable because 'he is from himself and recognizes no cause above himself.'[85] It is due to His *a se* essence that all change is removed from Him, as Turretin notes, 'dependence *a priori;* passive power, error of mind, inconstancy of will' are unthinkable for a being who has the fullness of life in Himself.[86]

After dealing with common objections to divine immutability – creation, incarnation, divine freedom, biblical images of divine repentance – Turretin concludes his treatment of divine immutability by affirming that the Church's affirmation of an immovable God must not be confused for a heterodox Stoic idea of an immobile God. He writes, 'The necessity of the immutability we ascribe to God does not infer Stoic fate. It is only an extrinsic necessity and from the hypothesis of the divine will, without interference with the liberty and contingency of things.'[87]

Stephen Charnock (1628–1680)

While there are other Puritans who published more than Stephen Charnock, few – if any – wrote with the depth of wisdom and insight on the divine life as the Englishman. Though he died at the all-too-early age of fifty-two, Charnock managed to write a number of volumes before his death. Many of these writings, a majority in fact, were published

---

84. Turretin, *IET,* III.XI.1.

85. Ibid., *IET,* III.XI.4.

86. Ibid., *IET,* III.XI.4.

87. Ibid., *IET,* III.XI.14. While not in reference to Turretin explicitly, Richard Muller, *PRRD,* 3:310, puts an exclamation point on this false narrative: 'The modern writers who argue against the doctrine of divine impassibility as if it were little more than the uncritical importation of a Stoic concept are beating, not a dead, but a nonexistent horse.'

postmortem.[88] One such work is his *Discourse on the Existence and Attributes of God*. In this collection of writings, Charnock deals with subjects ranging from epistemology to atheism, divine perfections, and more. Within its pages readers find a sharp and profound articulation of theology proper and the doctrine of God.

One of the many divine perfections that Charnock addressed in this volume is divine immutability. As we have seen in the previous chapter, Charnock defined immutability as 'The essence of God, with all the perfections of his nature, are pronounced the same, without any variation from eternity to eternity.' Charnock expounds on this, expanding the definition beyond essence and nature. Ultimately, he applies divine immutability to four particulars. He says God is unchangeable: (1) 'in his essence,' (2) 'in regard of knowledge,' (3) 'in regard of his will and purpose,' and finally (4) 'in regard of place.'[89]

For Charnock, immutability was of utmost importance since 'immutability is a glory belonging to all the attributes of God.'[90] This point will come into play as we dissect the soteriological implications of immutability in relation to corollary divine perfections, but it is not to be missed here either. Charnock knew that if immutability is taken away, so too must all the attributes of our God. He was chiefly concerned, like van Mastricht, with divine simplicity. In axiomatic fashion, he argued that 'mutability belongs to contingency':

> Mutability is absolutely inconsistent with simplicity, whether the change come from an internal or external principle. If a change be wrought by something without, it supposeth either contrary or various parts in the thing so changed, whereof it doth consist; if it be wrought by anything within, it supposeth that the thing so changed doth consist of one part that doth change it, and another part that is changed, and so it would not be a simple being.[91]

Charnock here demonstrates the reliability of his axiom on complexity of being necessitating mutability by explaining that alteration to any

---

88. James M'Cosh, 'Introduction to Charnock's Life and Work,' in *The Works of Stephen Charnock*, XX vols. (Edinburgh: Banner of Truth, 1865), 1:vii-xlvii.

89. Stephen Charnock, *Discourse on the Existence and Attributes of God*, in *The Works of Stephen Charnock*, 1:382-90.

90. Ibid., 1:381.

91. Ibid., 1:393.

of the divine essence would necessitate composition since God would need both parts of potency and parts of actuality. This line of reasoning runs through the halls of history, especially in medieval theologians such as Aquinas.

Using an agricultural metaphor, Charnock explains an underdeveloped benefit of classical immutability. He writes that similar to how the root of a plant 'lies firmly in the earth' while its branches 'are shaken with the wind,' so too is the divine essence firmly immutable while the cultural gusts move God's people to and fro.[92] Charnock here is of course describing God's providence and sovereign activity. More specifically, Charnock means to depict the nature of God's 'ordering and governing' all things. God's inalterability uniquely qualifies Him to providentially order that which is in constant flux.[93] In conclusion he writes, 'the principle of all things must be immutable.'[94]

John Owen (1616–1683)

We turn our attention to another English Puritan, John Owen. Owen's work is worth considering regarding divine immutability in that it demonstrates well aspects of post-Reformation theological method as well as demonstrating what a soteriological concern for divine immutability can look like. We will see both of these aspects in John Owen by examining two of his polemical writings, his works against Socinianism and Arminianism.

In and out of varying jails and prisons in the first half of the 1600s was a theologian by the name of John Biddle. He was a theologian of the Socinian order and, through a series of publications, his views arguing against the deity of the Son and the Spirit became widely read. Eventually, Biddle's work, along with the work of others, necessitated a formal response. The task of preparing a formal response was given to Oxford theologian, John Owen. Given that Biddle's work deals directly with Trinitarianism and theology proper, Owen's multi-hundred-page response touches on a number of important points – especially divine simplicity, pure actuality, and theological method.

---

92. Ibid., 1:395.

93. On top of his agricultural metaphor, Charnock also employs a mathematical metaphor to describe his point. 1:395.

94. Ibid., 1:395.

Responding to Biddle's catechism, Owen says of Biddle's doctrine of God that 'his second chapter, which is concerning God, his *essence, nature,* and *properties,* is second to none in his whole book for blasphemies and reproaches of God and his word.'[95] Owen lists out the features of Biddle's doctrine of God which features 'one person, of a visible shape and similitude, finite, limited to a certain place, mutable, comprehensible, and obnoxious to turbulent passions, not knowing the things that are future and which shall be done by the sons of men.'[96] This is, of course, a far cry from Owen's articulation of God's perfections within his own catechism. In answering the question, 'What are the attributes of God?', Owen writes, 'Eternity, infiniteness, simplicity or purity, all-sufficiency, perfectness, immutability, life, will, and understanding.'[97]

Between Owen and Biddle is a substantial difference of opinion regarding theological method. Owen quotes Biddle in the preface to his catechism in which Biddle describes his method by saying that he intends to 'assert nothing' and on the contrary plans to introduce the Scripture and allow the Scriptures to speak for themselves. On the contrary, Owen sees the futility in such a biblicism and argues that while this is what Biddle fancies himself doing, he nevertheless fails in his project.[98] Rather than a mere biblicism, Owen argues that certain metaphysical and essential assumptions are not only helpful, but necessary in making true sense of the biblical data.[99] He particularly makes use of divine simplicity and omnipresence.

Of divine simplicity, Owen notes, 'God says of himself that his name is *Ehejeh,* and he is I AM – that is, a simple being, existing in and of itself; and this is that which is intended by the simplicity of the nature of God, and his being a simple act.' (Exod. 3:14) Owen goes on to elaborate, 'though simplicity seems to be a positive term, or to denote something positively, yet indeed it is a pure negation, and formally,

---

95. John Owen, *The Mystery of the Gospel Vindicated* in *The Works of John Owen* (Edinburgh: Banner of Truth Trust, 1966), XII:86.

96. Ibid., XII:86. Emphasis original.

97. Owen, *The Great Catechism,* I:471.

98. See Owen, *Gospel Vindicated,* XII:61-70, for his critique of Biddle's theological method.

99. Biddle becomes a helpful example – along with much Socinian theology – of how we might use the language of Scripture while failing to preserve the meaning of Scripture.

immediately, and properly, denies multiplication, composition, and the like.'[100] Owen's denying any composition in God relates directly with divine immutability in his argument against Biddle. Owen writes:

> Yeah, that God is, and must needs be, a simple act ... is evident from this one consideration, which was mentioned before: if he be not so, *there must be some potentiality in God*. Whatever is, and is not a simple act, hath a possibility to be perfected by act; if this be in God, he is not perfect, nor all-sufficient. Every composition whatever is of power and act; which if it be, or might have been in God, he could not be said to be immutable, which the Scripture plentifully witnesseth that he is.[101]

In another polemical work, *A Display of Arminianism*, Owen makes use of the category of *actus purus*. Owen's articulation and utilization of pure act is closely related to divine immutability, and he brings out the category with soteriological concern. Dealing with the Arminian notions of the freedom of the will, Owen writes that the creature's will must not be understood to be independent in totality, for to do so would necessitate pure actuality – which we cannot predicate to creatures. Owen argues, 'Everything that is independent to any else in operation is purely active, and so consequently a god; for nothing but a divine will can be a pure act, possessing such a liberty by virtue of its own essence.'[102]

In this argument against the total independence of the creature's will, Owen utilizes Thomistic categories of potency and actualization. Carl Trueman, writing on Owen's Trinitarian theology, shows the soteriological concern of what Owen is up to at this point in his argumentation against Arminianism:

> As God, therefore, is fully actualized being, with no potential to change whatsoever, one obvious inference is that, if creation is to stand in any relation to God at all, it must be in a position of strict ontological and causal

---

100. Owen, *Gospel Vindicated*, XXII: 71.

101. Ibid., XXII:72. This quote also shows the methodological difference between Owen and Biddle. For, as we see in this block quote, Owen's method allows him to reason toward divine simplicity from divine immutability. Furthermore, in *no way* is this seen as a deviation from the truthfulness of the Scriptures on Owen's part either. Owen makes a similar theological move thirty pages later when he builds from divine immutability toward incorporeality, infinitude, omnipresence, and ubiquity. Owen writes, 'If he be immutable, then he is also incorporeal, and consequently without shape' (*Gospel Vindicated*, XXII:105).

102. Owen, *A Display of Arminianism*, X:119-20.

subordination. If there were not the case, then God would be mutable and thus not Pure Act. It is this thought, combined with the rejection of the possibility of an infinite change of causal regression, which lies at the heart of Aquinas's famous 'Five Ways' to prove God's existence. Owen, however, does not use the argument here as a way of proving that God exists, but applies it instead to the problem of providence and, in a more strictly soteriological sphere, to the relation between human acts and God's grace.[103]

In these two polemical works – one on Socinianism and one on Arminianism – Owen is a great model of demonstrating how divine immutability should not only be affirmed, but how the doctrine of God's changelessness has dogmatic implication in both methodology and soteriology.

Petrus van Mastricht (1630–1706)

Petrus van Mastricht composed many pages on the divine essence. Among the many contributions van Mastricht made to the discussion was his articulation of proper methods of predicating attributes or properties to God.[104] Two important ingredients to van Mastricht's method of predication were the doctrines of divine simplicity and pure actuality. The Dutch theologian wrote, 'above all this must be laid as a foundation: all the attributes together in God are nothing but one certain most simple and most pure act, his very essence, and his infinite perfection.'[105]Building off Augustine's De Trinitate, van Mastricht argues that we must not only deny change in God but even the possibility of 'different types of change.'[106] He continues to opine that God is immutable (1) with respect to His essence; (2) with respect to accidents; (3) with respect to His knowledge; (4) with

---

103. Carl Trueman, *The Claims of Truth: John Owen's Trinitarian Theology* (Bletchley: Authentic Media Publishers, 2002), 119-20. Christopher Cleveland further points out the soteriological concern undergirding Owen's words here. See Cleveland, *Thomism in John Owen* (London: Routledge, 2013), 39.

104. See van Mastricht's discussion in *TPT* 2:116-21. For a longer discussion of post-Reformation methodology in predicating attributes, see Muller, *PRRD*, 3:195-205. Muller, *PRRD*, 3:201, makes a helpful observation, beyond predication, about the post-Reformation theological method concerning divine attributes and the relationship between exegesis and theological reasoning.

105. Ibid., *TPT*, 2:117.

106. Ibid., *TPT*, 2:156.

respect to His will and decree; (5) with respect to His words; and (6) with respect to place.[107]

With item five – that God does not change 'with respect to his words' – van Mastricht expounds the idea by showing that God's Word does not change, for one with an altered word is one with an altered will, but this cannot be with God, for His will is His very essence. It is no surprise, then, to see the Reformed theologian demonstrate the soteriological import of this notion by implying that a synergistic model of soteriology implies a version of mutability. He writes that the 'semi-Pelagians, Jesuits, Remonstrants, Anabaptists, and indeed even the Lutherans, acknowledge a sort of divine will that depends on a condition to be supplied by man.'[108] Mastricht says in this form of back-and-forth between the Creator and the creature, God's will – dependent on man's choice – must change 'hour by hour.'

While we will not treat it here, as it will be more apropos later, Mastricht ends his treatment of divine immutability with six practical implications of the doctrine. Mastricht states that divine immutability 'is profitable' for: (1) God's glory, (2) For the despising of the creatures, (3) For the detestation of sin, (4) For confidence and comfort in any circumstance, (5) For fleeing inconstancy and fickleness, and (6) For the study of constancy.[109]

John Gill (1697–1771)

Baptist theologian, John Gill, had much to say regarding the perfection of divine immutability. His longest treatment of the doctrine comes in his *Body of Divinity*. In Gill's treatment of divine immutability, he first works through the way in which divine changelessness is another point which distinguishes the Creator from the creatures and then turns to showing the ways in which the Creator is inalterable.

'Mutability belongs to creatures, immutability to God only; creatures change, but he does not.'[110] This quote serves as a summary for the first portion of Gill's treatment of immutability. To prove this thesis, Gill

---

107. Ibid., *TPT*, 2:156.

108. Ibid., *TPT*, 2:157.

109. Ibid., *TPT*, 2:161-63.

110. John Gill, *A Complete Body of Doctrinal and Practical Divinity* (Paris: Baptist Standard Bearer, 2007), 35.

works through different aspects of creation to demonstrate that God alone is immutable, and therefore is distinct from that which He made.

The Heavens and Earth: God created the heavens and earth, and as creatures, both change. Gill wrote, 'The visible heavens are often changing; they are sometimes serene and clear, at other times covered with clouds and darkness, and filled with meteors, snow, rain, hail, etc ... it has undergone one great change by a flood and will undergo another by fire.'[111]

The luminaries: Gill referred to the sun as 'that great luminary, and fountain of light and heat,' yet he notes that even the sun alters. The sun 'has its parallaxes, or various appearances, at morning, noon, and evening; it has its risings and settings; and never rises and sets at the same point in the heavens one day in the year, but always varies a little.'[112] Yet, using James 1:17, Gill shows that there is no such variableness in the Creator.

Angels: Gill notes that angels, 'even the most excellent of them' are capable of change.[113] He points to the angels' ability to fall as a demonstration of the fact that angels are not immutable. Their being cast down to hell and delivered into the chains of darkness (Jude 1:6) demonstrates their alterability.

Mankind: Even in man's most excellent state, Adam in the garden, showed that sinlessness was not enough to obtain any kind of immutability. Gill noted: 'Man, at his best estate, his estate of innocence ... was altogether vanity.' He continued: 'For though not sinful, yet being mutable, and left to the mutability of his will, which was his vanity, when tempted fell into sin.'[114]

After treating these created beings – the heavens and earth, the great luminaries, the angels, and mankind, Gill moves on to show in what ways God is immutable. He lists at least five ways which we should predicate immutability to God. Gill wrote that God is immutable in His (1) nature and essence, (2) perfections or attributes, (3) purposes and decrees, (4) love and affections to His people, and (5) covenant of grace.[115]

---

111. Ibid., 35.
112. Ibid., 36.
113. Ibid., 36.
114. Ibid., 36.
115. Ibid., 36-40.

Divine Immutability in the Modern Era

What precedes in this chapter attests to the reality that, as we have noted, the doctrine of divine immutability enjoyed a near unanimous affirmation through the history of the church. However, as we saw in Chapter Two, this largely changed in the modern era. As *being* gave way to *becoming* in Christian theology proper, post-Enlightenment theologians increasingly denied divine immutability. The streams of denials and deviations flowed from variegated sources as theologians in the modern era denounce an unchanging God for reasons spanning soteriology, anthropology, and metaphysics.

However, since the focus of Chapter Two was deviations and denials, we will keep the treatment here to affirmations of a classical expression of divine immutability. More specifically, we use Herman Bavinck as our primary example and briefly turn to contemporary expressions toward the end of this section.

Herman Bavinck (1854–1921)

Born in the Netherlands on December 14, 1854, Bavinck would age to become one of Holland's most prolific theologians.[116] For Bavinck, immutability is of the utmost theological importance. In fact, he once wrote, 'The doctrine of God's immutability is of the highest significance for religion.'[117]

For Bavinck's account of God's unchanging nature, the distinction between *being* and *becoming* was significant. He wrote:

> The difference between the Creator and the creature hinges on the contrast between being and becoming. All that is creaturely is in process of becoming. It is changeable, constantly striving, in search of rest and satisfaction, and finds this rest only in him who is pure being without becoming. This is why, in Scripture, God is so often called the Rock (Deut. 32:4, 15, 18, 30, 31, 37; 1 Sam. 2:2; 2 Sam. 22:3, 32; Pss. 19:14; 31:3; 62:2, 7; 73:26; etc.). We humans can rely on him; he does not change in his being, knowing, or willing. he eternally remains who he is. Every change is foreign to God. In

---

116. For a biographical account of Herman Bavinck, see James Eglinton, *Bavinck: A Critical Biography* (Grand Rapids: Baker, 2020); and Ron Gleason, *Herman Bavinck: Pastor, Churchman, Statesman* (Phillipsburg: P&R Publishing, 2010).

117. Herman Bavinck, *The Doctrine of God* (Edinburgh: Banner of Truth, 1977), 149. Bavinck's emphasis on divine immutability makes him a strong and justifiable candidate to bring our treatment of the modern era to a close.

him there is no change in time, for he is eternal; nor in location, for he is omnipresent; nor in essence, for he is pure being.[118]

This lengthy quote is instructive for Bavinck's understanding of immutability for a number of reasons: first, as mentioned, the significance of negating *becoming* in God is vital for the Dutch theologian. As Bavinck traverses the history of literature regarding immutability, he notes a number of ways in which theologians have abandoned a faithful teaching of immutability yet argues this issue of becoming is at the root of them all. He espouses, 'However variously it may be elaborated, the basic idea is the same: God *is* not, but *becomes*.'[119] For Bavinck, alteration causes a cessation of what once was. However, this is unthinkable for the divine life, as 'true being belongs to him who does not change' and God is the only being who truly *is*.[120]

Second, in this quote Bavinck relates immutability to God's other divine perfections. Bavinck relates immutability to God's atemporality, omnipresence, and divine essence, noting that He has no change in time, no change in location, and is pure in being. In his *Reformed Dogmatics*, Bavinck brings special attention to the relationship between immutability and divine aseity. He begins his treatment of God's inalterability by saying, 'a natural implication of God's aseity is his immutability.'[121] This makes sense, given the previous emphasis on God who *is*, as Bavinck roots God's *is-ness* in His aseity: 'Now when God ascribes this aseity to himself in Scripture, he makes himself known as absolute being, as the one who *is* in an absolute sense.'[122] We can also see Bavinck's proclivity to connect divine immutability to corollary perfections as he works through his arguments for why one should affirm the classical articulation of God's unchanging nature.

His third reason is 'that the rejection of the doctrine of God's immutability implies the rejection of all God's attributes: if God is changeable, he cannot be eternal, omniscient, etc.'[123]

---

118. Bavinck, *RD*, 2:156.
119. Ibid., emphasis original.
120. Ibid., 2:154.
121. Ibid., 2:153.
122. Ibid., 2:152, emphasis original.
123. Bavinck, *Doctrine of God*, 147.

Bavinck concludes his section on immutability, like many before him, demonstrating that immutability and immobility are not synonymous. This point will of course be vital as this project moves to connecting theology proper and soteriology. Yet, Bavinck gives us a foretaste as he articulates a proper understanding of immutability that still affords meaningful relationships between the Creator and His creatures.[124]

Contemporary Theologies

With Bavinck as our primary example of a modern affirmation of classical immutability, we can now briefly turn to a number of contemporary theologians. While Chapter Two noted an alarming number of modern-era theologians who deviate from or outright deny classical immutability, this does not mean that the modern era – specifically, contemporary theologians – unanimously abandoned the vital doctrine. On the contrary, there is a growing interest in 'retrieving' classical doctrines in our day, and divine immutability is among those doctrines that need to be – and is being – retrieved.[125]

Moreover, it is an encouragement to see that contemporary publications dealing with divine immutability come from both Protestant and Roman Catholic authors and presses. On the Catholic side, Thomas Weinandy's *Does God Change?*[126] and Michael Dodds' *The Unchanging God of Love: Thomas Aquinas and Contemporary Theology on Divine Immutability*[127] have both proven to be formidable volumes on divine inalterability composed in the last few decades.

The contemporary attestation of divine immutability flows from Protestant ink as well as Catholic. For example, Steven Duby, while focusing primarily on divine simplicity, has produced important scholarship

---

124. Bavinck, *RD*, 2:158-59.

125. On theological retrieval, see Michael Allen and Scott Swain, *Reformed Catholicity: The Promise of Retrieval for Theology and Biblical Interpretation* (Grand Rapids: Baker, 2015), 1-17; Gavin Ortlund, *Theological Retrieval for Evangelicals: Why We Need Our Past to Have a Future* (Wheaton, IL: Crossway, 2019). For a test case on theological retrieval, see *Retrieving Eternal Generation*, ed. Fred Sanders and Scott Swain (Grand Rapids: Zondervan, 2017).

126. Thomas G. Weinandy, *Does God Change?* (Still River, Mass: St. Bede's Publications, 1985).

127. Michael J. Dodds, *The Unchanging God of Love: Thomas Aquinas and Contemporary Theology on Divine Immutability* (Washington D.C.: Catholic University of America Press, 2008).

for students of divine simplicity. James Dolezal has devoted many pages to articulating a modern articulation of classical theism. In his volume, *All That Is in God: Evangelical Theology and the Challenge of Classical Theism*, Dolezal writes: 'Classical Christian Theism is deeply devoted to the absoluteness of God with respect to his existence, essence, and activity. Nothing about God's being is derived or caused to be.'[128] This quote is an accurate summary of Dolezal's writing ministry as he has worked to show God's absoluteness through theology proper, including divine immutability.

We can see the emphasis on divine immutability from Craig Carter as well. Carter's research program is one marked by similarities in both method and content as many proponents of divine immutability in theological antiquity. In his latest book, *Contemplating God with the Great Tradition*, Carter writes: 'The purpose of this book is to establish congruence between the classical Nicene doctrine of God and the teaching of Holy Scripture.'[129] In his understanding of what constitutes a Nicene doctrine of God is divine immutability, for which Carter makes the case throughout his work.[130]

Matthew Barrett is another Protestant theologian who has written explicitly on the classical articulation of divine immutability.[131] While published for the trade audience, Barrett brings classical inalterability to the everyday churchman. Using the 'A-team' of Augustine, Anselm, and Aquinas, Barrett discusses pure act, passive potency, and the connection to God's divine essence and attributes to show the significance of divine immutability.[132]

While it is easy for readers to view Richard Muller's *Post-Reformation Reformed Dogmatics* as a work of historical synthesis bringing together

---

128. Dolezal, *All That Is in God*, 10. See also Dolezal, *God without Parts: Divine Simplicity and the Metaphysics of God's Absoluteness* (Eugene, OR: Pickwick Publications, 2011).

129. Carter, *Contemplating God With the Great Tradition: Recovering Trinitarian Classical Theism* (Grand Rapids: Baker Academic, 2021), 44.

130. Carter writes, 'I am arguing that the Nicene doctrine of God consists of joining together a philosophical understanding of God as the simple, immutable, eternal, First Cause of the universe with the biblical understanding of the God who reveals himself in history as Father, Son, and Holy Spirit' (Carter, *Contemplating God*, 44).

131. Matthew Barrett, *None Greater: The Undomesticated Attributes of God* (Grand Rapids: Baker, 2019). See also Matthew Barrett's forthcoming volume on the doctrine of God with Baker Academic.

132. Ibid., 89-111.

the various voices of the seventeenth-century Reformed Orthodox, it should not be missed that Muller's work is still a contemporary beacon of light in modern theology. Muller's brilliance is on display throughout his four-volume work, yet his section on divine immutability is especially helpful in navigating the complexities of the conversation.[133]

These are but a few voices in the chorus of theologians singing God's unchanging nature.[134] While we should be thankful for the growing number of efforts aimed at retrieving divine immutability, we can see that the job is far from over as we bear witness to the alarming lack of book-length publications from Protestant evangelicals defending a classical understanding of God's immutability.

Conclusion

A few final remarks are in order to bring the variegated themes of this brief historical survey to bear on our present discussion of God's immutability in relation to the salvation of His people. The halls of history teach an immutable God. As we traverse these halls and enter into the unique rooms of each era, nuances become clearer, as does the church's articulation of God's unchangeableness. In the school of history we learn about the immutable Triune God of the patristic fathers, the medieval God as something-than-which-nothing-greater-can-be-thought, the eternally unwavering God of the Reformed confessions, the purely actualized Lord of the post-Reformation confessors, and the unaltering *a se* God of modernity.

These historic articulations of predicating divine immutability will prove instructive as we make our way toward soteriological implications. We will need these theological forebearers to remind us again of pure actuality, eternal modes of subsistence, negation, causality, eminence, potentiality, and the like. Moreover, many names will reappear as we turn our attention from the historical witness to divine immutability to the biblical and exegetical witness. In the halls of history, we are educated of the God in whom there is '*no shadow of turning*' (James 1:17).

---

133. Muller, *PRRD*, 3:308-20.

134. See also some of the works previously sighted in this project such as Steven Duby, *God in Himself*, and Eleonore Stump, *The God of the Bible and the God of the Philosophers*.

CHAPTER FOUR

Biblical Witness: Divine Immutability in the Pages of Scripture

Exegesis in Relation to Christian Dogmatics and the Search of a Biblical Articulation of Divine Immutability

In the divine discourse of sacred Scripture, God is the first and foremost actor. From the opening act of creation to the concluding drama of new creation, the Lord is pre-eminent. While the pre-eminence of our Triune God is relatively non-controversial, how to articulate matters concerning the divine being from the biblical data proves to be shakier ground. Therefore, a few notes on exegetical method and biblical-theological reasoning are in order as we search for a biblical articulation of divine immutability.

As we examine the passages that detail a robust doctrine of God, it becomes evident that divine immutability is a concern for the biblical authors. The problem, however, is those interested in demonstrating a biblical affirmation of divine immutability and those wishing to demonstrate a biblical affirmation of divine mutability have an equally easy task, for it is not a difficult task to pull proof texts that seem to indicate either change or changelessness in the divine life.

For example, those aiming at indicating changelessness might make use of a verse like Malachi 3:6: 'For I the LORD do not change; therefore you, O children of Jacob, are not consumed.' The first seven words of this single verse seem to be an undeniable affirmation of God's inalterability. On the contrary, proponents of movement in God might bring forth a passage such as Exodus 32 in which Moses and the Lord have a back-and-forth about the punishment to befall those who constructed the golden calf. In anger, the Lord promises destruction and Moses intercedes on behalf of the people, calling to mind what the Egyptians might conclude if YHWH was to destroy His people, and the promises made to Abraham, Isaac, and Israel. The conclusion of the story – which we will revisit later – comes in the fourteenth verse as God is said to 'relent from the disaster that he had spoken of bringing on the people' (Exod. 32:14).

These two verses are but a few examples that instruct us that a naïve biblicism will not be enough in our task of articulating a biblical understanding of divine immutability. The debate of divine changelessness is a grander discussion than which side can cull the most biblical passages. Rather, this discussion requires faithful exegesis wedded with appropriate Christian theological reasoning. Theological reasoning aids the exegetical task by utilizing Christian wisdom to bring all relevant sources together in hopes to articulate biblically faithful truths about God. In doing so, we will see, as Richard Muller notes, 'the argument for divine immutability does not rest merely on the several texts that deny change in God, but on a broad grouping of texts that not only deny change in the most basic sense, but that also speak of the stability or changelessness of God's knowledge, counsel, will, purpose, and promises.'[1]

Instead, a faithful articulation of divine immutability calls for a more robust theological method. More than *mere* biblicism, a robust understanding of the biblical foundation for divine immutability contains three elements: first, one should consider the covenantal faithfulness of the Lord on display from the beginning to end of Scripture; second, we still ought to examine individual pericopes and passages in hopes to hear what the text has to explicitly say about the doctrine; third, and finally, the Christian theologian cannot afford to neglect theological reasoning and consider what must be true about God given *what else* the Bible says about God. In short:

---

1. Muller, *PRRD*, 3:314.

(1) God's covenant faithfulness through the ages *demonstrates* divine immutability;

(2) Particular pericopes and passages *teach* divine immutability;

(3) Theology reasoning given what else is true of God *demands* divine immutability.[2]

This threefold method for arriving at a biblical understanding of God's changelessness provides a sturdy foundation and contains the theological tools needed to make sense of detracting passages. A quick word is in order for each element of this method of theology:

First, one should consider the covenantal faithfulness of the Lord on display from the beginning to end of Scripture. From the opening tragedy of the garden in which we read of the fall of man; the Lord is already demonstrating covenantal faithfulness. In the Protoevangelium we see what the Israelite people will experience for centuries to come – this God is faithful to His covenant. While not sufficient in itself, the argument toward immutability as seen in God's covenant faithfulness – when taken with the other portions of the argument – is a strong one. With a mutable God, we would expect to see ebbs and flows with regard to the covenants.

Second, we still ought to examine individual pericopes and passages in hopes to hear what the text has to explicitly say about the doctrine. While a *mere* biblicism is too shallow a theological method for sustained theological contemplation, this does not mean it is unimportant to consider individual texts. Any theological commitment to the Scripture's authority entails that we ought to hear the text and give consistent attention to our exegetical tools. Regarding the doctrine of divine immutability, there are a significant number of texts that contain either explicit or implicit witness to God's inalterability. In fact, the remainder of this chapter is a treatment of such texts.

Third, and finally, the Christian theologian cannot afford to neglect theological reasoning and consider what must be true about God given what else the Bible says about God. For a treatment of divine immutability to trend toward constructive and dogmatic theology, as well as a biblical faithful treatment, Christian thinkers ought to consider what *else* the Bible says to be true of God's being. For example, as we will see in the

---

2. See this three-fold method for articulating a biblical doctrine of divine immutability in chart form in Table Four in the *Tables and Figures* section at the back of this book.

following chapter, the Scripture proclaims a God who is *a se*, atemporal, without composition, omniscient, omnipresent, etc. For these perfections to be predicated to God in any meaningful way, they would necessarily entail the divine perfection of immutability. Therefore, one can *reason* toward the doctrine of divine immutability from the corollary biblical data concerning God's ontology.

Three more nuances for dogmatically informed exegesis

Steven Duby articulates a few nuances needed for a dogmatically informed exegetical method; while his writing was in the context of divine simplicity, his three principles prove helpful in our conversation as well. First, he notes the 'communicative *concursus*' in the biblical text means we ought to presuppose 'that the Bible is divine speech,' and since God is the God of 'truth and order' (Titus 1:2, 1 Cor. 14:33) we ought also to presuppose theological coherence.[3] In this first principle we already see hermeneutical consequence since theological reasoning will not allow us to simply interpret the previous examples of Malachi 3 and Exodus 32 as categorically contradictory. Instead, the divine authorship of the canon entails a unified story that the powerful coupling of careful exegesis and faithful theological reasoning show forth.

Second, Duby argues that dogmatically informed exegesis 'is not reducible to the plane of history.'[4] This means that at times – and with 'caution' and 'only momentarily' – Scripture moves into the conversation of the divine being. In other words, while much of the text of Scripture focuses on the economy of our Triune God, this does not mean passages pertaining to divine ontology are nonexistent. Moreover, proper reflection on the economy reveals to readers the being of God, and the being of God informs God's economy. In this way, scriptural pericopes pertaining to the divine life *ad extra* and the divine life *ad intra* maintain a reciprocal relationship that bears exegetical significance. As Duby argues, while Scripture's insistence to touch on matters of divine being do not negate divine incomprehensibility, they do indeed 'call into question the assumption that all talk of God *in se* is exegetically unwarranted, idle speculation.'[5]

---

3. Steven Duby, *Divine Simplicity: A Dogmatic Account* (London: T&T Clark, 2018), 57.

4. Ibid., 57.

5. Ibid., 57.

Third, Duby stresses the reality that a passage can make a theological point without being the primary point under consideration in that passage. Duby uses 1 Samuel 15, God's rejection of Saul, as an example and does so with an eye toward divine immutability. He writes: 'It is entirely appropriate in the light of the text (and others) both to reason about God's immutability and to acknowledge that the development of the relationship between God and his people is central in 1 Samuel.' He continues, 'The theologian need not choose between taking theology seriously (in the strict sense, as pertaining to God himself) and taking history seriously.'[6]

Our study will show that divine immutability is indeed explicitly in the text, yet these exegetical nuances allow us to bring dogmatics and hermeneutics together in a way that promotes Christian wisdom and theological reasoning. We proceed to look at Scripture by first examining pertinent passages in the Old Testament before giving attention to the New Testament. We conclude the chapter by bringing together the biblical witness to divine immutability and answering a few critiques and questions raised against the notion of divine changelessness.

'From Everlasting to Everlasting': Divine Immutability in the Old Testament

The God of Abraham, Isaac, and Jacob is unchanging. From the opening pages of the Pentateuch to the closing chapters of the Minor Prophets, God is the same 'from everlasting to everlasting' (Pss. 90:2; 103:17). The strands of God's immutability are variegated as we see His glorious inalterability in areas such as His essence, will, and knowledge, and – vital for this project – in His covenant faithfulness to the people of Israel. Here we give a brief biblical theology of divine immutability in the Old Testament by working through major divisions of the Old Testament. Of course, brevity limits the depth with which we can treat each passage. The aim here is to simply survey the text of the Old Testament with an eye toward articulating an Old Testament understanding of divine immutability.

Scripture's case for divine immutability begins in its first clause. The opening salvo testifies that 'in the beginning' (Gen. 1:1) God

---

6. Ibid., 58.

created. We saw in Bavinck's depiction of divine immutability a strong relationship between immutability and aseity. God's being *a se* uniquely qualifies Him to be present 'in the beginning.' Before earth's genesis, God was there in His self-sufficiency. Divine aseity necessitates divine atemporality in His pre-existence, and both, as we will see, demand the divine perfection of immutability. If the ultimate fountain of life, on which every contingency is built, ever ceases speaking or holding the cosmos together by the word of His power, the consequence would be catastrophic.

Yet, does not this very clause indicate change in God? After all, at one point God was not a Creator, and then after this act in the economy, He was. Does not the very operation of creation – even creation *ex nihilo* – produce new properties in the divine life? While the purpose of this project is not to answer objections to divine immutability (see Chapter Two), a few brief notes could prove helpful in a theological understanding of Genesis 1.

Charnock spends a good bit of ink answering the objection to immutability built on the economic activity of creation. In a summary of his elaborated points, he writes:

> There was no change in God when he began to create the world in time. The creation was a real change, but the change was not subjectively in God, but in the creature; the creature began to be what it was not before. Creation is considered as active or passive; active creation is the will and power of God to create; this is from eternity, because God willed from eternity to create in time. This never had beginning, for God never began in time to understand anything, to will anything, or to be able to do anything; but he always understood, and always willed, those things which he determined from eternity to produce in time. The decree of God may be taken for the act decreeing, that is eternal and the same; or for the object decreed, that is in time; so that there may be a change in the object, but not in the will whereby the object doth exist.[7]

Charnock elaborates on this point with three subpoints: (1) 'There was no change in God by the act of creation because there was no new will in him'; (2) 'There is no change in God by the act of creation because there was no new power in God'; (3) 'Nor is there any new relation

---

7. Charnock, *Discourse on the Existence and Attributes of God*, in *The Works of Stephen Charnock*, 1:397.

acquired by God by the creation of the world.'[8] If the purpose of this study was to defend the doctrine of divine immutability, we would spend a substantial amount of time on each of these points. However, on the third point – dealing with relations – given that it is an important conversation in relating divine immutability to creation *ex nihilo*, a brief comment is worth noting. The classical Thomistic model of dealing with potential relations between God and creatures in the divine act of creation is asymmetrical. Given God's essence is non-compositional and unified, it is not proper to predicate accidents to Him, including the accident of real relations. As we saw previously, there *are* those – like Anselm – who are happy to predicate accidents of relations to God so long as the predications need not imply mutability.[9] Thomas, by virtue of metaphysical commitments and theological reasoning, argues for an asymmetrical relationship in which the change and real relation belongs to the creature while immutability and a logical relation belongs to God.[10]

Tyler Wittman is helpful to summarize this point. Describing a Thomistic understanding of relations, Wittman writes:

> In other words, there is no accident in God grounding a real relation to creation because God's creative act is not the kind of transitive action perfected in its effect, nor is creation a benefit to God that might move him as a good he desires to acquire. Since there is no ontological foundation in God to ground a real relation to creation then God's relation to creation is not real but creation's relation to him is.[11]

Simply put, in sum, the economic activity of creation *ex nihilo* does not alter God, as creation is a temporal manifestation of the eternal divine

---

8. Ibid., 1:397-99.

9. Anselm, *Monologion*, 41.

10. Of course, the metaphysical conversation pertaining to the nature of relations is vast. In terms of jurisdiction, if the purpose of this research project was to *defend* divine immutability or persuade *toward* divine immutability, a longer discussion of relations would be necessary. However, given that the primary goal of this book is to work toward soteriological implications of divine immutability, we will save that discussion. For the curious reader, see Anna Marmodoro and David Yates, *The Metaphysics of Relations* (Oxford: Oxford University Press, 2016), Leila Haaparanta and Heikki J. Hoskinen, *Categories of Being* (Oxford: Oxford University Press, 2012), Robert Pasnau, *Metaphysical Themes: 1274–1671* (Oxford: Oxford University Press, 2011).

11. Tyler Wittman, *God and Creation in the Theology of Thomas Aquinas and Karl Barth* (Cambridge: Cambridge University Press, 2019), 118.

will and all relational mutability is inherent exclusively on the part of the creature. While the creature experiences the movement temporally and in time, this nevertheless entails a change in the creature, not in the one bringing about the creature.

Matthew Levering helpfully resurfaces the language of 'divine ideas' when discussing creation in relation to the doctrine of God. He writes, 'within the broader doctrine of creation, the doctrine of divine ideas underscores most importantly that God's infinitely actual intelligence makes possible the countless array of created presences.'[12] Levering makes use of a number of proponents in articulating denials and affirmations of divine ideas, yet the one most helpful in our discussion pertaining to Genesis 1:1 is Augustine.

Augustine, in *De Trinitate* notes, 'It is true of all his [God's] creatures, both spiritual and corporeal, that he does not know them because they are, but they are because he knows them. He was not ignorant of what he was going to create. So, he created because he knew, he did not know because he had created.'[13] As we read Genesis 1:1, we need not read God's economic activity as contrary to His ontology. Rather, recalling the inalterability of God when reading the opening salvo of Holy Scripture helps prevent a number of hermeneutical and theological errors.

Progressing in the Pentateuch into the book of Numbers, Balaam's discourse in the twenty-third chapter attests to God's immutability pertaining to His volition and word. 'God is not man, that he should lie, or a son of man, that he should change his mind' (Num. 23:19). Standing in the plains of Moab, Balak was eyewitness to the development of a particular blessing of the covenant – God's people were multiplying. In fact, the Israelites were growing numerically at a rate which made foreign countries worried that they would take all the geographical resources for themselves and 'as an ox licks up the grass of the field' (Num. 22:4) these people would take what once belonged to the Moabites. In response, Balak desires to overtake the Israelites but wants to do so only after he

---

12. Matthew Levering, *Engaging the Doctrine of Creation: Cosmos, Creatures, and the Wise and Good Creator* (Grand Rapids: Baker Academic, 2017), 70.

13. Augustine, *De Trinitate*, 414, quoted in Levering, *Engaging the Doctrine of Creation*, 45. For another brief conversation pertaining to divine immutability and creation, especially as it relates to modern evangelical shortcomings, see Richard C. Barcellos, 'Change in God Given Creation?' in *Trinity and Creation: A Scriptural and Confessional Account* (Eugene, OR: Resource Publications, 2020), 49-79.

has secured a prophet to utter a curse against the people. Balak sends for the son of Beor, Balaam, to utter a curse against those who are beginning to 'cover the face of the earth' (Num. 22:5). With the 'fees for divination' in hand, the elders of Moab and Midian approach Balaam and beseech him to curse the Israelites. Balaam, after hearing from the Lord that he is to do no such thing, denies the request. Balak demonstrates persistence and raises the fees offered to Balaam and eventually gets the prophet to come with him to see the people for himself.

Three separate times Balak requests Balaam to curse God's people that the Moabites might overtake them. In each scene – Moab, Kiriath-huzoth, and Zophim – Balak erects seven altars and sacrifices seven bulls and seven rams. To Balak's dismay, the Lord instructs Balaam not to curse, but to bless the people of Israel. Growing frustrated with Balaam, Balak rebukes him for his work amongst the Israelites. In response, Balaam says:

> Rise, Balak, and hear;
> Give ear to me, O son of Zippor:
> God is not man, that he should lie,
> Or a son of man, that he should change his mind.
> Has he said, and will he not do it?
> Or has he spoken, and will he not fulfill it?
> Behold, I received a command to bless:
> He has blessed, and I cannot revoke it (Num. 23:18-20).

In this scene, the second oracle of Balaam, we witness the consistency in God's outward action. His faithfulness toward the Israelites is predicated on the Creator-creature distinction. A distinguishing mark between the Creator and the creatures is that the Creator is not man nor the son of man – and, therefore, unlike man, He will not lie. God has covenanted to these people and has told their father, Abraham, 'Behold, my covenant is with you, and you shall be the father of a multitude of nations' (Gen. 17:4). God's immutable will and promise means that He will not allow the Moabite king, Balak, to bring harm to His people.

Samuel alludes to this clause when he rebukes Saul and delivers the word to him that the kingdom of Israel will be torn from his leadership. Saul begs Samuel to return with him so that Saul might repent in hopes that the Lord would relent of His punishment He had promised would come upon Saul and His people. However, Samuel informs Saul, 'the Glory of Israel will not lie or have regret, for he is not a man, that he should have regret' (1 Sam. 15:29). Saul and Balaam both appeal to the reality that due to God's *otherness* – that is, that He is not a man – He will not do what is contrary to His nature and lie.

Volitional inconsistency entails falsehood, which moves the lying party from honest to dishonest or moves the will from one object to another. In either case, Balaam's discourse rejects such movement from God. Irenaeus makes this point. Commenting on this passage, he notes, 'He thus shows that all men are indeed guilty of falsehood, inasmuch as they change from one thing to another (μεταφερόμενοι); but such is not the case with God, for he always continues true, perfecting whatever he wishes.'[14] Or, as another patristic Father said:

> But all that God speaks, in whom there is no passion, no weakness, he speaks for well-deserving reasons; and therefore, he can never be frustrated, since whatever is brought forth by reason cannot lack reason … what he himself speaks – that is, God – will he not also do it? And what has been spoken, will not also continue in these things? It is certain that men do not do what they say, and by a blemish of human weakness they do not continue in those things that they speak; for man is mutable, but God is immutable.[15]

What we see in the story of Balak and Balaam is not a surprise to readers familiar with God's faithfulness throughout the Old Testament. Deuteronomy tells us, 'Know therefore that the LORD your God is God, the faithful God who keeps covenant and steadfast love' (Deut. 7:9). God's insistence that Balaam does not curse God's people is in keeping with His immutable faithfulness to His people. As the narrative of Israel throughout the Old Testament ebbs and flows, we see even in her rebellion God faithfully preserves a remnant of His people – though they deserve destruction – which is a first fruit of locking God's *ad extra* activity with His *ad intra* life; the God of Israel is immutably faithful to His promises in the covenant as He Himself is unchangeable.

Continuing in the book of Deuteronomy, we read, 'the eternal God is your dwelling place, and underneath are the everlasting arms'

---

14. Irenaeus, *Fragments from the Lost Writings of Irenaeus* (*ANF*, 1:572).

15. Origen, *Homilies on Numbers*. Trans. Thomas P. Scheck, ed. Christopher Hall (Downers Grove: IVP, 2009), 92-93.

(Deut. 33:27). Here, again, we encounter some of the fruit of bringing ontology and soteric function together. God's immutable eternality is a rock in which the people of God dwell forever. Bringing ontology into the conversation is a buttress of assurance, as His people know this rock will never wane or diminish, nor in Him is there any shadow of change. This rock is contrasted with the 'rock' of the wicked just a chapter before. God threatens that the assurance of the pagan is futile: 'Then he will say, "where are their gods, the rock in which they took refuge, who ate the fat of their sacrifices and drank the wine of their drink offerings? Let them rise up and help you; let them be your protection!"' (Deut. 32:37-38).

The Psalms resound with an unchanging God of love. The God of the psalmists is a 'complete God' who dwells in perfection. Using Psalm 19:7, 'The law of the LORD is perfect, reviving the soul,' Christopher Holmes shows how divine simplicity and divine goodness relate to God's unchangeability throughout the Psalms. Holmes writes:

> God is not in motion 'because the whole is possessed at once.' To talk in terms of God's simplicity is to talk about how God is perfect, having no future and past, because he possesses himself entirely. Put somewhat differently, God is not in motion, so as to become something new as before. God is simple and as such possesses himself entirely, having no need of improvement. God is utterly incapable of renovation because he is entire, complete, and, as we will see the pure act of being itself. What is said of the law in terms of, for example, its being 'perfect,' 'sure,' 'right,' 'clear,' 'pure,' 'true,' and 'righteous altogether,' is said of God, who is all these things at one and the same time.[16]

Of the infinite reasons God is found to be praiseworthy, His simple and unchangeable goodness is one of them throughout the Psalms. While the 'fools say in their hearts, "there is no God"' (Ps. 14:1), the righteous, on the contrary, 'give thanks to the LORD, for he is good; his steadfast love endures forever!' (Ps. 118:1).

In the Psalms, on numerous occasions, the divine perfection of immutability is tied closely with God's love and kindness toward His people.[17] We see a God whose will and counsel do not alter, which for the

---

16. Christopher Holmes, *The Lord is Good: Seeking the God of the Psalter* (Downers Grove, IVP, 2018), 11-12.

17. On this word pairing, see James Luther Mays, *Micah: A Commentary*, The Old Testament Library (Philadelphia, PA: The Westminster Press, n.d.), 168, when he notes:

psalmist is rest for the righteous and terror for the wicked. The psalmist says, 'the counsel of the LORD stands forever, the plans of his heart to all generations' (Ps. 33:11) On the contrary, 'The LORD brings the counsel of the nations to nothing' (Ps. 33:10). His will alone stands unshakable and His prerogative alone frustrates the counsel of the foreign nations. His people, however, enjoy blessing because He has chosen them as His heritage. Perhaps no Psalm demonstrates this better than Psalm 136 as the psalmist repeats the refrain 'for his steadfast love endures forever' twenty-six times in as many verses.

Atemporality and immutability are the foundation for the unchanging God of love in the Psalms. This becomes explicit in Psalm 102:

> Of old you laid the foundations of the earth,
> and the heavens are the work of your hands.
> They will perish, but you will remain;
> they will all wear out like a garment.
> You will change them like a robe, and they will pass away,
> but you are the same, and your years have no end
> (Ps. 102:25-27).

Of this verse, Mastricht wrote, 'Amidst all the changes and vicissitudes, so many and so great, of the whole universe, he stands unmoved, and wholly unmovable. Indeed, the author of all change in all things exists himself unmoved.'[18] Contrary to those who might insist that creation brings about alteration in God, the psalmist notes that not only does the divine action of creation not initiate renovation in God's being but even as the elements of that creation come and go, God remains the same.

Moreover, while we will treat Hebrews in the coming pages, we ought to note here that the unknown author of Hebrews relies on Psalm 102 in building his case for the supremacy of Christ. The book

---

'ḥesed is combined with faithfulness (ˀemet) in the familiar hendiadys used so often in the Psalms as a word-pair for YHWH's beneficent history with Israel. Gracious faithfulness will form the future of the remnant. Abraham and Jacob are used as characterizing names for the people as the corporate objects of YHWH's election (the former only here in the Old Testament). The invocation of the names of the patriarchs also prepares for the following reference to the fathers. The hymn concludes with an appeal to the very beginning of Israel's history and the oath by which YHWH initiated it. That oath created the relation which ḥesed fulfils and ˀemet maintains.' I'm grateful for Russ Meek pointing out the significance of this hendiadys.

18. Mastricht, *TPT*, 2:161.

of Hebrews opens up with a series of questions the author poses in asking of which angels did God say such things? This series of Old Testament allusions include passages from Psalm 2, 2 Samuel, Deuteronomy 32, Psalm 104, Psalm 45, Psalm 110, as well as Psalm 102:25-27. In the use of Psalm 102, the author of Hebrews intends to show the same immutable and atemporal essence of the Father belongs to the Son. The author of Hebrews emphasizing the unchanging eternality of the Lord is no surprise as this is the same author who argues that the second person of the Trinity is 'the same yesterday and today and forever' (Heb. 13:8).

Along with the witness of the Torah and the Writings, the Prophets proclaim an unchanging God as well. As Isaiah pleads with the people of Israel to forsake their propensity to trust in foreign nations, namely Egypt, over the God of Jacob, he continually reminds them of the Lord's unchanging covenantal faithfulness. He states, 'Why do you say, O Jacob, and speak, O Israel, my way is hidden from the LORD, and my right is disregarded by my God? Have you not known? Have you not heard? The LORD is the everlasting God, the Creator of the ends of the earth. He does not faint or grow weary' (Isa. 40:27-28). The ontological change that takes place as an individual grows faint or weary is foreign to the God of Isaiah's book. Whether Isaiah aims to remind the Israelite people of God's steadfast covenant faithfulness or threaten His unwavering wrath for wickedness, he is clear that the Lord's volitional will is steady and will take place. He writes, 'My counsel shall stand, and I will accomplish all my purpose, calling a bird of prey from the east, the man of my counsel from a far country. I have spoken, and I will bring it to pass; I have purposed, and I will do it' (Isa. 46:10-11).

Though we have already looked at, and will look at again,[19] the important passage of Malachi 3:6, it is vital to note the significance of the verse in our treatment of divine immutability in the Old Testament. It is hard to overestimate the importance of Malachi 3:6 in theological antiquity when it comes to defending immutability. In fact, many early church and medieval fathers felt comfortable to simply cite Malachi 3:6 as a conclusive defense of the doctrine of divine changelessness. For example, in the *Prima Pars*, after Aquinas lists the three objections which persist against divine immutability, he begins his answer by

---

19. See especially the treatment of Malachi 3 in Chapter Six.

simply saying: 'On the contrary, it is written, "I am the Lord, and I change not.""[20]

Unlike some of the references in the biblical data to divine immutability, what makes Malachi 3 rather unique and important to the discussion is that the referent to 'do not change' is *God Himself.* Whereas texts like Numbers 23:18-20 and 1 Samuel 15:29 reference God not changing His mind, Malachi 3:6 references God not changing in Himself. The same could be said of Psalm 102 – these two pericopes come together in affirmation that it is not the case that the Lord is unchanging in *this* or *that* way, but that the Lord is unchanging in His essence.[21] Any model of immutability which could be rendered as *mere* consistency of character might have a hard time reconciling Malachi's predication of immutability to God's *essence* in his third chapter.

God's unchanging essence, in Malachi 3, should be rendered as good news to the people of Israel. There are two hermeneutical keys in the clause of verse 6 – both demonstrating this to be a covenantal proclamation. First, the covenantal name, Yahweh, is used in 'For I the LORD do not change.' Second, a covenantal title for Israel is invoked in calling them the 'children of Jacob.' God is reminding the people of Israel that He has covenanted with their fathers and while He has been faithful to His covenant as generations have come and gone, the same cannot be said for the Israelites.

The fickleness of the Israelites is on display even in the book of Malachi. Against the backdrop of Israel's unrighteousness Malachi 3:6 becomes both informative and awe-inducing. God tells the rebellious people that their propensity toward wayward infidelity should have resulted in Him destroying them in their disobedience. Instead of rightfully destroying them, God is faithful to the covenant. His changeless faithfulness to His

---

20. Aquinas, *ST,* Ia9. Of course, Aquinas goes on to elaborate and treat the objections with sophistication. However, it is worth noting that he proceeds to argue toward divine immutability on the sure foundation of Malachi 3:6. Lewis Ayres lists Malachi 3:6 amongst the texts the fourth-century theologians made foundational in discerning divine ontology, especially as it relates to articulating departures from orthodoxy (Ayres, *Nicaea and Its legacy,* 4).

21. In modernity, it is becoming popular to argue that we should conceive of the doctrine of divine immutability as 'constancy' instead of unchangeability of essence. However, references like Malachi 3 and Psalm 102 make this argument hard to uphold. Moreover, this is why we uphold divine immutability not from a mere gathering of prooftexts, but from the wisdom of the biblical logic together.

covenant and His covenant people is rooted in the changelessness of His essence. It is *because* God does not change that the children of Jacob are not consumed.

'Heirs of the Promise': Divine Immutability in the New Testament

The proclamation of an unwavering and unchanging God is not bound to one Testament alone. On the contrary, the New Testament has an equally strong emphasis on the fixed nature and will of the Lord. Paul, in his epistles to Timothy, proclaims an 'immortal' God who is 'faithful' even when His followers are faithless (1 Tim. 1:17; 2 Tim. 2:13). God's eternal and immutable will is not thwarted even by the fickle nature and wayward acts of those He redeems.

This is a will that has been established before all things, for Paul elsewhere declared, 'in him we have obtained an inheritance, having been predestined according to the purpose of him who works all things according to the counsel of his will' (Eph. 1:11). God's will in election took place 'before the foundation of the world' (Eph. 1:4), and in His sovereignty He bends all things – people, places, plagues, and power – toward accomplishing His purposes. This immutable will was set in motion before time began and will continue after it concludes. The New Testament's witness to the immutable essence of God has an exclamation point as it concludes with the proclamation that God is 'the Alpha and the Omega,' the one 'who is and who was and who is to come, the Almighty' (Rev. 1:8).

In this brief section, we focus on a few New Testament passages that aid in bolstering a robust doctrine of divine immutability. We examine James 1:17, 1 Peter 1:3-5, and 1 John 1:1-4 before lingering in the book of Hebrews (as it bears much significance in this discussion).

James 1:17

Within the General Epistles, it takes less than twenty verses until the reader is confronted with God's immutability. In his letter, James writes: 'Every good gift and every perfect gift is from above, coming down from the Father of lights with whom there is no variation or shadow due to change' (James 1:17). In this text James employs astronomical language to depict God's unchanging nature. He calls God the 'father of lights,' which invokes His creative power. The connection to God's creativity is clear in the next verse: 'of his own will he brought us forth by the word of truth, that we should be a kind of firstfruits of his creatures.'

God is the Father – Creator – of both humans and the stars that hang above them. Keeping with his astronomical metaphor, James states that within God there is 'no variation or shadow due to change.' Of this clause, Doug Moo said: 'James is not writing a scientific treatise but is using general language about the constant motion of the heavenly bodies to make a point about God: he does not change like the heavens do.'[22] As astronomical beings wax and wane, there is no such movement in God.

James also acknowledges this resistance to change as a distinguishing mark between the Creator in verse 17 and the creature in verse 18. Commenting on this passage, Turretin noted:

> In the latter not only change is denied of him, but even the shadow of change, that he may be contrasted with the sun, the fountain of material light, liable to various changes and eclipses by which its light is intercepted. But God, the father of lights, acknowledges no tropics and can be obscured by no clouds since there is nothing to intercept his influence .... All causes of change are removed from him: dependence a priori; passive power; error of mind; inconstancy of will.[23]

This text bares soteric weight that comes into clarity as it is kept in its proper exegetical context. James' statement about God's unchangeable essence comes into play as he deals with the Lord's impeccability. In verse 13 James writes, 'Let no one say when he is tempted, "I am being tempted by God," for God cannot be tempted with evil, and he himself tempts no one.' The reason James even brings up divine immutability is that God, the Father of lights, is unchanging in His designation of good gifts among His children. He does not bring temptation toward the redeemed; rather, He brings 'good and perfect' gifts toward those who love Him. The assurance of believers that God will not exchange His good gifts for the sour prize of temptation is rooted in His unchanging nature which knows no shadow of turn.

---

22. Douglas J. Moo, *The Letter of James*, Pillar New Testament Commentary (Grand Rapids, MI: Eerdmans: 2000), 79.
23. Turretin, *IET*, III.XI.3.

1 Peter 1:3-5

The Petrine epistles depict a great inheritance awaiting those who have been united to Christ. Peter writes:

> Blessed be the God and Father of our Lord Jesus Christ! According to his great mercy, he has caused us to be born again to a living hope through the resurrection of Jesus Christ from the dead, to an inheritance that is imperishable, undefiled, and unfading, kept in heaven for you, who by God's power are being guarded through faith for a salvation ready to be revealed in the last time.

Regarding this passage, Thomas Schreiner points out the fixed permanence rooted in the three words translated as 'imperishable, undefiled, and unfading.'[24] The inheritance on the horizon for believers is nothing short of eternal life.[25] This eschatological benefit of union with Christ is preserved in such a way that believers can trust that it will be pristine and pure. Peter tells his readers that it is by God and His power that this reward is kept this way. Peter can only have the confidence in the immutable nature of the church's eternal reward based on the immutable fidelity and essence of the One holding it together.

1 John 1:1-4

John opens his series of three brief epistles with a striking introduction in which he wastes no time. He writes:

> That which was from the beginning, which we have heard, which we have seen with our eyes, which we looked upon and have touched with our hands, concerning the word of life – the life was made manifest and we have seen it, and testify to it and proclaim to you the eternal life, which was with the Father and was made manifest to us – that which we have seen and

---

24. Thomas Schreiner, *1, 2 Peter, Jude, New American Commentary* 37 (Nashville: Broadman & Holman, 2003), 63. He shows the regular use of these three adjectives elsewhere in the New Testament, saying: 'Elsewhere we are told that God is imperishable (Rom. 1:23; 1 Tim. 1:17) and that our resurrection bodies are incorruptible (1 Cor. 15:52). The inheritance cannot "spoil" (amianton) or perhaps better is "undefiled." The inheritance will not lose its luster and beauty. It will never become stained or filthy. The same word is used to denote Jesus' sinlessness (Heb. 7:26), the purity of marriage (Heb. 13:4), and genuine religion (James 1:27). Finally, the inheritance will never "fade" (amaranton). It will last forever, just as the crown of reward that elders receive will never fade away (1 Pet. 5:4).'

25. Ibid., 63.

heard we proclaim also to you, so that you too may have fellowship with us; and indeed our fellowship is with the Father and with his Son Jesus Christ. And we are writing these things so that our joy may be complete.

John begins with mention of 'that which was from the beginning.' Several commentators have read an allusion here to the author's Gospel, in which he opens with, 'In the beginning was the Word.' While consensus is out regarding the validity of seeing an allusion in verse 1, what is not in debate is the centrality of the incarnation of Jesus in this opening salvo. The Word, which was in the beginning, is now present in such a way that it can be heard with our ears, touched with our hands, seen with our eyes, and proclaimed with our mouths. The ontological humanity of Jesus Christ is pivotal for the argument of 1 John.

This soteric significance of Christ's ontological humanity is again proven true as the author turns to fellowship with the Triune God. John tells his readers that the message they have proclaimed is a message of 'eternal life' (1:2). Of this eternal life, he says that it 'was with the Father and was made manifest to us.' In the humanity of Christ, then, is the revelation of eternal life to God's people. This is significant as John moves on to describe the life of the believer as that of 'fellowship with the Father and with his Son Jesus Christ.'

The believer's access to life eternal is predicated on fellowship with the Triune God, which can only happen via the pneumatological work of union with Christ. This union is a prevalent theme in the epistle of 1 John.[26] Robert Peterson points out that the concept of abiding or living 'in Christ' permeates this short epistle. In 1 John 2:4-6, John writes: 'Whoever says "I know him" but does not keep his commandments is a liar, and the truth is not in him, but whoever keeps his word, in him truly the love of God is perfected.' He continues, 'By this we may know that we *are in him*: whoever says he abides in him ought to walk in the same way in which he walked' (emphasis added).

In the same chapter John reminds his readers that truth must abide in their inner being as they rid themselves of those who are seeking to deceive them with false teaching. He says: 'let what you heard from the beginning abide in you. If what you heard from the beginning abides

---

26. Although, as Robert Peterson points out, the theme 'does not appear in 2–3 John.' See Robert Peterson, *Salvation Applied by the Spirit: Union with Christ* (Wheaton, IL: Crossway, 2015), 249.

in you, then you too will *abide in the Son and in the Father*' (emphasis added). He again restates this imperative just a few verses later: 'just as it has taught you, abide in him' (2:27).

This emphasis on union with Christ carries over into the author's understanding of maturity in Christ and the mortification of sin: 'you know that he appeared in order to take away sins, and in him there is no sin. No one who abides in him keeps on sinning; no one who keeps on sinning has either seen him or known him' (3:5-6).[27] However, the apex of emphasis in this epistle comes in the fourth chapter as John writes: 'By this we know that we abide in him and he in us, because he has given us of his Spirit. And we have seen and testify that the Father sent his Son to be the Savior of the world.' He continues: 'Whoever confesses that Jesus is the Son of God, God abides in him, and he in God. So, we have come to know and to believe the love that God has for us. God is love, and whoever abides in love abides in God, and God abides in him' (4:13-16).

As if the soteric consequence of such a union between the sinner and saint were not obvious, John states that a consequence of this vital union is that 'we may have confidence for the day of judgment.' This is the point of John's final use of union language in the final chapter of 1 John when he writes: 'We know that the Son of God has come and has given us understanding, so that we may know him who is true; and we are in him who is true, in his Son Jesus Christ. He is the true God and eternal life.'

This final quote, combined with the others, aids readers in seeing the connection between ontological immutability and soteriology. John articulates an eternal life such that the entry point is fellowship with the Triune God. The plight, at least one of many, is the chasm that separates the Creator and the creature ontologically. Without the mystical union of Christ, there is no way for the finite, mutable, and temporal to share in the divine life of the infinite, immutable, and atemporal. Yet in this

---

27. Just a few verses later there is another piece of evidence for the soteriological importance of ontology. Though it refers to Christ's omniscience, as opposed to the ontological category of immutability we are focusing on here, John writes, 'By this we shall know that we are of the truth and reassure our heart before him; for whenever our heart condemns us, God is greater than our heart, and he knows everything' (1 John 3:19-20). John calls on the perfection of divine knowledge as comfort for the believer in assurance that everything has been forgiven.

union, as the finite is grafted into the infinite, the mutable man can participate in eternality in ways impossible without the Spirit's saving work. John's emphasis on union with Christ is the death of this worry and positions abiding in God at the apex of the soteric enterprise. Though he was referring to the Pauline corpus, this is why Kevin Vanhoozer can say, 'to be or not to be in Christ was, for Paul, the only question.'[28] Constantine Campbell affirmed Vanhoozer's assessment of Pauline emphasis and said: 'The theme of union with Christ in the writings of the apostle Paul is at once dazzling and perplexing. Its prevalence on every page of his writing demonstrates his proclivity for the concept.'[29]

Whether in the Pauline corpus or the epistles of John, union with Christ is an important soteriological theme, and it is where the mutable man finds the necessary ontological conditions for eternality. Moreover, with the sinner's union to Christ there is an unshakable foundation, as we will see, for all other soteric benefits that come from being found in the Vine.

The Book of Hebrews

Writing on the authorship and canonicity of Hebrews, Calvin wrote: 'There is, indeed, no book in Holy Scripture which speaks so clearly of the priesthood of Christ, which so highly exalts the virtue and dignity of that only true sacrifice which he offered by his death.'[30] While Calvin is correct in pointing out the major emphasis on the functional aspects of Christology found in the pages of Hebrews, there is nevertheless a significant feature played by the doctrine of divine immutability as it relates to the Christology of Hebrews. The author writes of the work of Christ and positions Him as 'the greater' version of a number of Old Testament saints, pointing out with each in turn that the work of Christ fulfilled both the mission of God and the needs of Israel with greater fulfillment.

28. Kevin J. Vanhoozer, 'From "Blessed in Christ" to "Being in Christ": The State of Union and the Place of Participation in Paul's Discourse, New Testament Exegesis, and Systematic Theology Today,' in *"In Christ" in Paul: Explorations in Paul's Theology of Union and Participation*, ed. Michael J. Thate, Kevin J. Vanhoozer, and Constantine R. Campbell (Grand Rapids: Eerdmans, 2014), 3. Emphasis original.

29. Constantine R. Campbell, *Paul and Union With Christ: An Exegetical and Theological Study* (Grand Rapids: Zondervan, 2012), 21.

30. John Calvin, *Hebrews*, 1. cited in F. F. Bruce, *The Epistle to the Hebrews*, New International Commentary on the New Testament (Grand Rapids: Eerdmans, 1964), xlvii.

However, for all the words spent on functional Christology, the author of Hebrews spends time as well detailing several articles regarding ontological Christology. One of these pieces of concern for the author of Hebrews is the immutability found in the divine life of the Trinity *ad intra* and in the person of Jesus Christ. In fact, readers cannot escape even the first chapter of Hebrews without confronting the unchangeable essence of God. Using one of seven consecutive allusions and quotes from the Old Testament and pulling directly from Psalm 102, the author writes: 'You, Lord, laid the foundation of the earth in the beginning, and the heavens are the work of your hands; they will perish, but you remain; they will all wear out like a garment, like a robe you will roll them up, like a garment they will be changed, but you are the same and your years will have no end' (Heb. 1:10-12). Other scriptural passages speak of humans as coming and going in passing, yet Hebrews has even greater permanence in mind. Not only will mankind come and go individually while the Lord remains; so, too, will even the foundations of creation.[31] James Thompson helpfully highlights this point: 'With the claim that *you remain* (1:11a) and *you are the same* (1:12c), the author contrasts the eternity of the Son with the impermanence of the creation and introduces a major theme of the book.' He continues: 'Forms off *menein* appear regularly throughout the book (cf. 7:3, 24; 10:34; 12:27; 13:14) to describe the eternity of the Son and high priest and the Christian possession in contrast to the transitoriness of everything that belongs to this creation.'

In Hebrews 7 the author turns to a sophisticated argument dealing with a significant problem. The issue is Jesus' credentials for performing the sacrifice of the atonement, which is potentially problematic because He descends from the line of David and not from Levi. Performing unauthorized sacrifices has been enough to get other men killed in the Scriptures (Lev. 10), yet Jesus performs the sacrifice of sacrifices with David's blood in His veins. The author articulates a lineage stemming from Melchizedek, which is superior to that of Levi. What is more, this demonstration of the superiority of Christ's priestly heritage has greater consequence than it first seemed, for not only is the heritage greater, but the sacrifice is also greater. This reality, however, is not built only upon the premise of a superior lineage but a superior ontology.

---

31. James W. Thompson, *Hebrews*, Paideia Commentaries on the New Testament (Grand Rapids: Baker Academic, 2008), 55.

The author writes, 'the former priests were many in number, because they were prevented by death from continuing in office, but he holds his priesthood permanently, because he continues forever. Consequently, he is able to save to the uttermost those who draw near to God through him, since he always lives to make intercession for them' (7:23-25). This text will prove important in not only establishing the thesis of this chapter, but also in bringing together multiple aspects of the project into a single argument. For, in this single verse, what separates Jesus from all former priests who have come is that He does not experience the change of death. Readers see elsewhere in the book of Hebrews that the quality of their sacrifice also comes into question (Heb. 10). However, even if they could muster perfect sacrifices on behalf of Israel, it would be insufficient, for they, each in turn, come to perish as they are mere mutable men. Yet Christ, the immutable Creator, preforms a single sacrifice that is maximally efficacious and stands as long as He does. The soteric efficiency of Christ's sacrifices is rooted squarely in the immutable ontology of His person. The ties that bind person and work in Christology are perhaps nowhere more evident.

However, the glory of the verse becomes even more apparent as the reader keeps in mind redemptive history and union with Christ. As we saw earlier, union with the ontologically immutable Christ nullifies the plight of man wherein their common finitude makes communion with the divine life impossible. Yet, a finite essence is not the only roadblock on the path of Trinitarian communion – there is also holiness. The passage of Hebrews above and another important passage (Heb. 6:18) are aided by keeping in mind redemptive history.

Michael Horton said that the Old Testament interprets history 'as the story of a covenant made and a covenant broken' and that the New Testament builds on this interpretation.[32] The drama of the covenant broken begins in the garden wherein Adam fails in his role as covenant representative and therefore brings about the soteric plight of his posterity – the need for and inability to obtain righteousness.

It is into this postlapsarian setting that Christ assumed human nature in the incarnation. In so doing, Jesus serves as the covenant redeemer overcoming sin and fulfilling the law. Brandon Crowe, emphasizing the

---

32. Michael Horton, *Lord and Servant: A Covenant Christology* (Louisville: Westminster John Knox, 2005), 121.

life of Jesus and not only His death, said, 'As the last Adam, Jesus is the obedient Son who serves a representative capacity, vicariously attaining the life through obedience that Adam did not.'[33] The scriptural statement of this reality is found in the fact that, according to Romans 5, 'many were made righteous' through Christ. Further, 2 Corinthians 5:21 states that those who are 'in him' would become 'the righteousness of God.'[34] So then, while those 'in' the first Adam have a personally insurmountable plight in their need of righteousness, their cosmic need finds solution in the imputed obedient righteousness of the Son, the Last Adam.

Returning to our present passage in Hebrews, this immutable salvation rooted in an immutable Savior has union with Christ at its core. The author of Hebrews says that Christ is 'able to save to the uttermost' those who are brought 'near to God *through* Christ' (emphasis added). This salvation to the uttermost is unfading and imperishable, 'since he always lives to make intercession for them' (Heb. 7:25). Putting all this exegetical reasoning together, the soteric significance of divine immutability becomes glaring. Sinners are removed from God's immutable position toward sin through an immutable salvation by union with an immutable Christ who has an immutable intercession on their behalf wherein He turns the eyes of God on His immutable righteousness.

Finally, one last passage for consideration:

> For when God made a promise to Abraham, since he had no one greater by whom to swear, he swore by himself, saying, 'Surely I will bless you and multiply you.' And thus Abraham, having patiently waited, obtained the promise. For people swear by something greater than themselves, and in all their disputes an oath is final for confirmation. So when God desired to show more convincingly to the heirs of the promise the unchangeable character of his purpose, he guaranteed it with an oath, so that by two unchangeable things, in which it is impossible for God to lie, we who have fled for refuge might have strong encouragement to hold fast to the hope set before us. We have this as a sure and steadfast anchor of the soul, a hope that enters into the inner place behind the curtain, where Jesus has gone as a forerunner on our behalf, having become a high priest forever after the order of Melchizedek (6:13-20).

---

33. Crowe, *The Last Adam*, 203.

34. As Crowe, *The Last Adam,* 204, points out, however, the necessity and reality of the obedient life of Jesus is not a teaching isolated to the Epistles.

This text, addressed to the 'heirs of the promise,' invokes memories of God's oath to Abraham. Again, Thompson notes: 'The author elaborates on the certainty of the oath by piling images for certainty drawn especially from the law court. That is, people swear by something greater.'[35] Yet, in this case, there was nothing greater for God to swear by than His own unchanging essence and will.

This passage also instructs the 'heirs of the promise' and those who 'have fled for refuge' that 'it is impossible for God to lie.' Far from a minor passing detail, this clause contains significant systematic importance. For this project is arguing for the continued mended relationship between the functional and ontological aspects of the divine life. A consequence of repairing the dichotomy between divine person and work is that the function resembles the ontology. We must be careful here not to collapse theological categories and reduce the divine life *ad intra* and *ad extra*. Yet, if we permit that God's attributes *are* His essence, our doctrine of divine simplicity will not allow us to separate what must be joined together.

In this situation then, along with others, it makes sense for the speech to match the speaker. God's speech pours forth in truth with the impossibility of bearing falsehood because God Himself cannot do so. While not the purpose of this project, bringing together the divine speech with the divine speaker has far-reaching implications in one's bibliology and hermeneutics. Since the divine ontology of the speaker can speak nothing but truth to the heirs of promise and since He has sworn by Himself – since there is nothing greater – the hearers are to 'hold fast to the hope set' before them. Indeed, the text articulates an emphatic image that those who have fled to this unchangeable God and His unchangeable Word have 'this as a sure and steadfast anchor of the soul.'

This chapter brought to our attention several passages and pericopes which attest to God's changelessness. As we bring this portion to a close, it is important to remind ourselves of the Richard Muller quote at the beginning of the chapter. Muller wrote: 'The argument for divine immutability does not rest merely on the several texts that deny change in God.'[36] While the biblical data thus far examined brings

---

35. Thompson, *Hebrews*, 138-39.
36. Muller, *PRRD*, 3:314.

together a strong case for divine immutability in the Scriptures, the succeeding chapter unfolds another important aspect of putting together constructive witness for divine changelessness – biblical logic.

Not only is divine immutability *explicitly* argued for throughout the pages of Scripture, but there is a coherent and convincing argument to be made for divine immutability in looking at the whole of Scripture and not just the parts. In the next chapter, we examine corollary divine perfections such as simplicity, atemporality, aseity, impassibility, infinitude, and the like. These corollary perfections, themselves a result of biblical wisdom and good and necessary consequence, come together as their own witness to divine changelessness. In sum, the *parts* of God's divine disclosure in the Scriptures declare that He is indeed changeless (Mal. 3, Ps. 102, James 1, etc.). But, also, the *whole* of God's divine disclosure in the canon declares that He is inalterable.

Therefore, a wholistic biblical articulation of divine immutability should include at least three considerations: (1) the covenant context weaved throughout the Scriptures, as we have seen, which shows that God is unwaveringly faithful to His people; (2) the particular biblical passages and pericopes which bring forward the pertinent grammar and wisdom needed to affirm divine immutability; and (3) a wholistic approach to the divine life *ad intra* which utilizes theological reasoning to demonstrate the coherence of God's being.

In Chapter Five, I aim to treat the doctrine of divine immutability in relation to its corollary perfections. Using theological reasoning, we work *toward* divine immutability and *from* divine immutability with assistance from the other divine perfections. However, before we move on from the biblical considerations of God's changelessness, it is necessary that we take an excursus of sorts to treat a few remaining concerns regarding the doctrine of divine immutability in the Scriptures.

In this excursus, we treat two topics: (1) What are we to make of the numerous passages which seem to indicate change in God? Are there any good hermeneutical or theological reasons to treat passages that indicate change in God as anthropomorphic while treating passages seeming to indicate immutability as literal? (2) Second, we briefly examine whether God is the only being properly said to be immutable, especially considering angels and glorified humans.

Excursus on Biblical Concerns Pertaining to God's Changelessness

Biblical Use of Anthropomorphism and Anthropopathism

Interlocutors in the conversation surrounding God's changelessness often cry foul over passages that seem to indicate clear change in God. What are we to make of passages, for instance, that seem to indicate, at the very least, emotional change in God as He moves from kindness to wrath, or vice versa? Kelly James Clark remarks that in the face of these texts any hermeneutic that still positions immutability or impassibility as viable is disingenuous at best: 'While the Scriptural record can be made to fit the hypothesis of divine impassibility, the fit is at best forced and unnatural. There is a certain naturalness of the passibilist interpretation given Scripture.'[37]

What makes the problem more significant is that passages seeming to indicate change are multifold. It is one thing to argue a hermeneutic that seeks to make peace with one wayward text; it is quite another to advocate an analogous reading method that impacts many passages. Bavinck demonstrates just how vast pericopes that depict change, at least on the surface level, are throughout Scripture:

> Now at first it may seem that this immutability is unsupported by Scripture. The Bible everywhere represents God as being in very close contact with the world. In the beginning he created heaven and earth; hence, from the state of noncreative activity he proceeded to that of creative activity. Ever since that beginning he lives the life of the world, as it were; in a very special sense he lives the life of Israel; he comes and goes; he reveals himself and hides himself; he withdraws his countenance, and lifts up the light of his countenance. He repents, Gen. 6:6; 1 Sam. 15:11; Amos 7:3, 6; Joel 2:13; Jonah 3:9; 4:2; he changes his purpose, Exod. 32:10-14; Jonah 3:10; he becomes angry, Num. 11:1, 10; Ps. 106:40; Zech. 10:3; and he turns from the fierceness of his anger, Deut. 13:17; 2 Chron. 12:12; 30:8; Jer. 18:8, 10; 26:3. He assumes a different relation to the believer than to the unbeliever, Prov. 11:20; 12:22; with the pure he shows himself pure, and with the

---

37. Kelly James Clark, 'Hold Not Thy Peace at My Tears: Methodological Reflection on Divine Impassibility,' in *Our Knowledge of God: Essays on Natural and Philosophical Theology*, ed. Kelly James Clark (Boston: Kluwer, 1992), 186.

perverse he shows himself froward (a wrester, an opponent), Ps. 18:25, 26; in the fulness of time he becomes flesh in Christ and through the Holy Spirit he comes to dwell in the church; he rejects Israel, and accepts the Gentiles. Similarly, the people of God experience at one time God's wrath, then again, his love; at one time his absence, then again his closeness; at one time they are burdened with the consciousness of their guilt, at other times they rejoice because of forgiveness of sins.[38]

Are not these passages clear, and should they not be given interpretive priority over the more abstract pericopes concerning ontology? This is a valuable question that should not be merely shrugged off, and it is a question that will inevitably lead to discussions of the biblical usage of anthropomorphisms and anthropopathisms.

There are, of course, theologians across the spectrum who disavow the employment of anthropomorphism and anthropopathism as a useful hermeneutical tool. For instance, evangelical theologian John Frame writes:

> The historical process does change, and as an agent in history, God himself changes. On Monday, he wants something to happen, and on Tuesday, something else. He is grieved one day, pleased the next. In my view, *anthropomorphic* is too weak a description of these narratives. In these accounts, God is not merely *like* an agent in time. He really *is* in time, changing as others change. And we should not say that his atemporal, changeless existence is more real than his changing existence in time, as the term *anthropomorphic* suggests. Both are real.[39]

There is problem enough with Frame's positing two modes of existence in the immanent divine life – one temporal and one atemporal. Yet, even if this issue is put aside, Frame's question remains worthwhile: Is it proper to posit anthropomorphism and anthropopathism as a sufficient hermeneutical tool to resolve the issues of paradoxical biblical passages? In this brief section, I aim to argue in the affirmative on the basis of two theological realities – divine incomprehensibility and divine inspiration.

First, it is important to note that while theologians may disagree about the nature and prevalence of anthropomorphisms, their existence in Scripture should not be taken as a serious debate. The Scriptures, with

---

38. Bavinck, *Doctrine of God*, 146.

39. John Frame, *Systematic Theology: An Introduction to Christian Belief* (Phillipsburg: P&R Publishing, 2013), 377.

great frequency, attribute to God bodily characteristics. God is said to have sight (Deut. 11:12; Amos 9:4; Ps. 34:15), feet (Gen. 3:8; Exod. 24:10; Isa. 66:1), hands (Exod. 31:18; Isa. 5:25; 49:2), ears (2 Kings 19:16; Dan. 9:18), a face (Lev. 20:6; Num. 6:25), arms (Ps. 89:10; Deut. 4:34; 5:15), and a shadow (Pss. 36:7; 91:1; Isa. 49:2; 51:16). The Scriptures even attribute non-human characteristics to the Lord, such as wings (Deut. 32:11; Pss. 17:8; 36:7; 57:1; 61:4; 63:7; 91:4; Jer. 49:22).

Anthropopathisms abound throughout the canon as well. We read of God's experiences of human emotions, such as His being jealous (Exod. 20:5; 34:14; Deut. 4:24; 2 Cor. 11:2), angry (Exod. 15:7; 32:10-11; Deut. 9:8; Job 4:9; Jer. 32:29), and regretful (Gen. 6:6-7; 1 Sam. 15:11; 2 Sam. 24:15-16; Jonah 4:2; Ps. 106:45; Amos 7:1-6).

The presence of passages like these – and many more could be brought to attention – disallows a mere denial of the existence of biblical anthropomorphisms and anthropopathisms. The question remains, however, if these two interpretive tools can do justice in the conversation pertaining to God's immutability in the face of problem texts that seem to favor a more mutable understanding of the divine essence.

Hermeneutics and the Creator/Creature Distinction

The first reason readers should affirm immutability as hermeneutically faithful even in the face of 'problem texts' is due to the Creator/creature distinction and the doctrine of divine accommodation. In Exodus 33 Moses presents a remarkable request to the Lord: 'Please show me your glory' (Exod. 33:18). The Lord responds that the very sight of God's glorious face would bring death to Moses and therefore passes by, allowing Moses a glimpse of His back from the shelter of a cleft. This pericope is instructive on a number of points, but one is certainly the unique supremacy of God. What we see in Exodus 33 is that God is not simply different than His creatures by mere degree; He is altogether different in kind. 'Like us, but bigger' simply fails to capture the grandeur of God's majesty.

This distinction between the Creator and the creature entails the doctrine of divine incomprehensibility. We cannot comprehend that which we may not even gaze upon without life-ending consequence. The ontological otherness of God renders theological inquiry a grace, as theologians are out of their depth in attempting articulations of an incomprehensible God. Apart from the grace of revelation, theology would be a hopeless enterprise. For this reason, when God sets out on the economic activity of revelation, He does so in accommodating Himself to our human limitations.

This is why Calvin famously described the act of divine revelation in terms of God 'lisping with us as nurses are wont to do with little children.'[40] It is for our good that God 'lisps' with us; for, according to Calvin, 'His immensity surely ought to deter us from measuring him by our sense.'[41] However, divine accommodation predates the Reformation and was used by a number of patristic exegetes.[42] Irenaeus writes:

> By their manner of speaking, they ascribe those things which apply to men to the Father of all, whom they also declare to be unknown to all; and they deny that he himself made the world, to guard against attributing want of power to him; while, at the same time, they endow him with human affections and passions. But if they had known the Scriptures, and been taught by the truth, they would have known, beyond doubt, that God is not as men are; and that his thoughts are not like the thoughts of men. For the Father of all is at a vast distance from those affections and passions which operate among men.[43]

Or, as Gregory of Nyssa puts it:

> Though, that is, there is a certain sort of force, and life, and wisdom, observed in the human subject, yet no one from the similarity of the terms would suppose that the life, or power, or wisdom, were in the case of God of such a sort as that, but the significations of all such terms are lowered to accord with the standard of our nature. For since our nature is liable to corruption and weak, therefore is our life short, our strength unsubstantial, our word unstable. But in that transcendent nature, through the greatness of the subject contemplated, everything that is said about it is elevated with it.[44]

---

40. John Calvin, *Institutes of the Christian Religion*, 1.13.1.

41. Ibid., 1.13.1.

42. For a helpful treatment of patristic use of divine accommodation, along with anthropomorphism and anthropopathism, see Mark Sheridan, 'God is not like Humans' in *Language for God in Patristic Tradition: Wrestling with Biblical Anthropomorphism* (Downers Grove, IL: InterVarsity Press, 2015), 27-44.

43. Irenaeus, *Against Heresies* (*ANF* 1:374).

44. Gregory of Nyssa, *The Great Catechism* (*NPNF*, 5:475).

Augustine argues that the purpose of divine accommodation is that 'the human mind might be purged from falsities.' Augustine notes: 'Holy Scripture, which suits itself to babes has not avoided words drawn from any class of things really existing, through which, as by nourishment, our understanding might rise gradually to things divine and transcendent.'[45]

Concluding these remarks on the Creator/creature distinction and why divine accommodation bears hermeneutical import, we can reasonably conclude that divine accommodation is one reason the interpreter might deduce that those passages that ascribe change to God should be read analogously as opposed to those articulating His ontology. Simply put, one method of divine accommodation, as revealed in the Scriptures, is anthropomorphism and anthropopathism.

Hermeneutics and Divine Inspiration

The second argument as to why biblical interpreters should make the exegetical decision to interpret passages describing change as analogous: anthropomorphism or anthropopathism is founded on the doctrine of inspiration. Divine authorship, like divine incomprehensibility, entails hermeneutical implications as the singularity of God's authorship brings about canonical unity.

The Princeton theologian B. B. Warfield is instructive here as he recognizes the uniqueness of both the human and the divine author of Scriptures. Warfield sees that the human authorship of divine revelation entails diversity and says:

> On first throwing open this wonderful volume we are struck immediately with the fact that it is not a book, but rather a congeries of books. No less than sixty-six separate compositions immediately stare us in the face. These treatises come from the hands of at least thirty distinct writers, scattered over a period of some fifteen hundred years, and embrace specimens of nearly every kind of writing known among Men. Histories, codes of law, ethical maxims, philosophical treatises, discourses, dramas, songs, hymns, epics, biographies, letters both official and personal, vaticinations, – every kind of composition known beneath heaven seems gathered here in one volume.[46]

---

45. Augustine, *On the Trinity* (*NPNF*, 3:18).

46. B. B. Warfield, 'The Divine Origin of the Bible,' in *Revelation and Inspiration* (Grand Rapids: Baker, 2003), 436.

He goes on to expound the diversity represented in the canon by showcasing that the diversity does not just lie in type of literature but with the authors as well: 'Their writers, too, were of like diverse kinds. The time of their labors stretches from the hoary past of Egypt to and beyond the bright splendor of Rome under Augustus.' Even in language and ethnicity, Warfield points out diversity: 'One half is a mass of Hebrew writings held sacred by a race which cannot look with patience on the other half, which is a mass of Greek writings.'[47]

However, the diversity represented amongst the human authors does not negate the unity that is consequential of the whole book being conducted by one author. To this point Warfield writes:

> We may look, however, on a still greater wonder. Let us once penetrate beneath all this primal diversity and observe the internal character of the volume, and a most striking unity is found to pervade the whole; so that, in spite of having been thus made up of such diverse parts, it forms but one organic whole. ... The same doctrine is taught from beginning to end, running like a golden thread through the whole and stringing book after book upon itself like so many pearls.[48]

The unity of the canon insists that of the options available in the interpretive range, assuming contradiction is not among them. When presented with the apparent contradiction of passages that seem to indicate mutability and passages that seem to indicate immutability, one must make an interpretive decision that comports with the unity brought about by the divine author. This brings us back to the first point pertaining to anthropomorphism and anthropopathism: the unity of the canon excludes contradiction, and the reality of divine accommodation entails the reasonableness of concluding that those passages that depict mutability should be seen as analogous.[49]

---

47. Ibid., 436.
48. Ibid., 437.
49. Of course, an interlocutor might suggest that a third way exists. See, for example, the argument of Bruce Ware outlined in Chapter Two. Dr Ware argues for an onto-ethical immutability together with relational and volitional mutability. As we will see in Chapter Five, we ought not opt for this interpretive option because it undermines a classical understanding of divine immutability and divine simplicity. This option could only be rendered viable if God is composed of parts such that some parts undergo change while additional parts remain unaltered.

Is God the Only Immutable Being? The Case of Angels and Glorified Humans

Another pertinent question in articulating a biblical understanding of divine immutability is whether or not God alone is immutable? Are there not three other beings that could properly be said to be immutable – angels, humans in glorification, and the reprobate in their waywardness? In the ninth question of the *Prima Pars*, Aquinas treats this very question. His first two objections for the ninth question are most pertinent for our purposes here. The first objection protests that since angels and souls have not matter, they are not moved and are therefore immutable. The second objection opines that anything in motion is moving toward some end, yet since some creatures – as those glorified in heaven – have already obtained their end, they are immutable.

Aquinas responds in the negative, denouncing the idea that these figures are indeed immutable. He argues that a creature might be immutable or mutable in two ways – by a power within themselves or a power residing outside themselves. Ultimately, Aquinas argues that these figures – angels and humans in their final state – only have immutability by the power and will of God. Of these creatures, Aquinas notes, 'Therefore as it was in the Creator's power to produce them before they existed in themselves, so likewise it is in the Creator's power when they exist in themselves to bring them to nothing.' This premise causes Aquinas to conclude: 'In this way therefore, by the power of another – namely, of God – they are mutable, inasmuch as they are producible from nothing by him, and are by him reducible from existence to non-existence.'[50]

Richard Muller also treats the issue of possible non-divine immutable beings. He considers the case of 'fallen angels and the reprobate in their wickedness' and 'holy angels in their perfection.'[51] Muller concludes that neither example has true immutability, for 'the former is not a perfection or an excellence, and the latter is a "conferred" immutability.'[52] Muller's argument against the nature of these figures being immutable is instructive, for it demonstrates that a biblical understanding of immutability

---

50. Aquinas, *ST*, Ia3.2.
51. Muller, *PRRD*, 3:313.
52. Muller, *PRRD*, 3:313.

is not *mere changelessness*. Rather, a biblical understanding of divine immutability must render God's immutability a divine perfection and therefore an 'essential changelessness' such that there can be 'no shadow of turning.'

Conclusion

To the question, 'Is divine immutability a biblical doctrine?', we should answer with an emphatic yes. We can affirm the biblical foundation of divine immutability with a three-fold articulation. First, we affirm the biblical foundation of divine immutability in a canonical context as we read of God's immutable covenant faithfulness to His people throughout the entirety of Scripture. Second, we affirm the biblical foundation of divine immutability bringing forth the pertinent passages and pericopes which deal with God's changelessness, such as Numbers 23, Psalm 102, Malachi 3, James 1, and Hebrews 6. Third, we affirm the biblical foundation of divine immutability when we look to corollary perfections – as we will do in Chapter Five – and see that by good and right reason, we can deduce the need for God's changelessness to make sense of the entirety of Scripture. This threefold model of defending the biblical basis of divine immutability gives us a stronger footing than merely pointing out a collection of loosely related prooftexts.

Moreover, when confronted with the hermeneutical issue that the Scriptures seem to predicate both immutability and mutability to the Lord, we have exegetical and theological reasons to prioritize those passages which indicate changelessness. We interpret passages depicting mutability as analogous and anthropomorphic due to the hermeneutical implications of divine incomprehensibility and divine inspiration.

CHAPTER FIVE

Theological Witness: Divine Immutability in Christian Reason

The 'Enamel' of All Perfections: Theological Reasoning and Divine Immutability

We turn now to the third portion of our trifold witness of divine immutability. In the previous two chapters we examined the historical and biblical witness of God's changelessness. We here turn toward a theological-metaphysical witness to round out a constructive treatment of the doctrine. As we look out of the halls of history and up from the pages of Scripture toward metaphysical theological affirmations, this methodological move need not be seen as contrary to Scripture. Rather, like scores of dogmatic theologians within the theological antiquity, we aim to provide constructive theological claims, bringing the process of Christian reasoning to the data points of biblical, historical, and philosophical reality.

As we examine the corollary divine perfections in relation with divine immutability, a reciprocal relationship of necessity comes into view. Divine immutability necessitates corollary divine perfections, and the corollary divine perfections necessitate divine immutability.[1] In this light,

---

1. It is worth reiterating here that the phrase 'divine perfection' is being used in a loose sense and does not intend to entail claims of proper predication. Along with immutability, in this chapter other apophatic predicates come under examination. Instead of issues concerning predication of attributes – both apophatic and cataphatic, this section is meant to examine the relationship between corollary predicates and negative names.

then, comes our third reason to affirm a classical articulation of God's changelessness. We affirm classical immutability on the basis of exegesis because the doctrine does justice to the biblical data; we affirm classical immutability on the basis of history because the church has historically given witness to her unchanging God in the face of variegated protests; and as we will see in this chapter, we affirm classical immutability on the basis of Christian reason because metaphysical inquiry demonstrates the coherence of a classical conception of the divine essence.

Given the simple essence of our Triune God, it is no surprise to see dogmatic connections between the divine perfections. In fact, theologians throughout the history of the Church have noted this very reality as it relates to divine immutability. Bavinck, for example, notes that a danger in denying divine immutability is simply that one would necessarily need to deny all of God's attributes.[2] What's more, we can see theologians treating the connection of divine immutability and the other divine perfections from two different directions. Some treat all remaining perfections from the vantage point of immutability, demonstrating that immutability protects and secures the others. For example, calling divine immutability the 'enamel' of all other perfections, Charnock notes:

> Immutability is a glory belonging to all the attributes of God. It is not a single perfection of the divine nature, nor is it limited to particular objects thus and thus disposed … immutability is the centre wherein they all unite. There is not one perfection but may be said to be, and truly is, immutable; none of them will appear so glorious without this beam, the sun of immutability, which renders them highly excellent without the least shadow of imperfection. How cloudy would his blessedness be if it were changeable; how dim his wisdom if it might be obscured; how feeble his power if it were capable to be sickly and languish; how would mercy lose much of its lustre if it could change into wrath, and justice much of its dread if it could be turned into mercy, while the object of justice remains unfit for mercy, and one that hath need of mercy continues only fit for the divine fury? But unchangeableness is a thread that runs through the whole web, it is the enamel of all the rest; none of them without it could look with a triumphant aspect.[3]

---

2. See Bavinck, *Doctrine of God*, 147: 'That the rejection of the doctrine of God's immutability implies the rejection of all God's attributes: if God is changeable, he cannot be eternal, omniscient, etc.'

3. Charnock, 1:381.

While Charnock here details a methodology which begins with divine immutability and then works toward other divine perfections, other theologians treat the connection between changelessness and the divine perfections by starting first with the corollary perfections and work toward divine immutability. The Genevan theologian Benedict Pictet – who works from omnipotence, simplicity, immensity, atemporality, and omniscience toward divine immutability – represents this second approach. He writes:

> There is no mutation in God; neither in his essence, nor in his eternity, nor in his understanding, nor in his will. Therefore, there is no mutation, &c. Thus, the minor is proved: not in his *essence*, for being *first*, he cannot be superseded by any prior being; being *all-powerful*, he cannot be injured by any; being most *simple,* he can be corrupted by none; being *immense*, he cannot be augmented or diminished; being *eternal*, he cannot fail. Nor in his eternity, for where there is no succession, there is no mutation. And so forth. Nor in his *understanding*, for the knowledge of God is all-perfect. Nor in his *will*, for the will of God is all-wise, to which nothing unforeseen can happen, so as to compel him to change his intentions for the better. Again, nothing can prevent and resist his will; he does, indeed, will the various changes of things, but his will itself remains unchangeable.[4]

Whether working from immutability toward metaphysical implications of other divine perfections or reversing the process and moving from alternate attributes toward divine immutability, the perfections are interconnected. The goal of this chapter is to briefly work through the systematic connection of the divine perfections, using both dogmatic methods, in order to develop a theological witness for a classical conception of divine immutability. We will examine eight doctrines altogether – simplicity, impassibility, aseity, atemporality, infinitude, and the three 'omnis' of omniscience, omnipresence, and omnipotence.

All That Is in God, Is God: Divine Simplicity and Divine Immutability

Divine simplicity, as an apophatic perfection, denies composition in God. Maintaining that God is maximally self-sufficient, the doctrine

---

4. Benedict Pictet, *Christian Theology*, trans. Frederick Reyroux (London: Seeley and Sons, 1834), 100.

of divine simplicity argues that there is nothing in God that is not God. In other words, God's attributes and perfections *are* His essence. In this light, God does not merely possess attributes; rather, He *is* them. For example, God does not *have* love; God *is* love (1 John 4:8). God does not *have* beauty; rather, He *is* beauty. Due to divine simplicity, even the 'communicable' attributes of God cannot be said to be univocal since the creature only shares in these attributes in an analogical and ectypal way. On the contrary, the so-called communicable attributes of God are not accidents to His essence.

Defining divine simplicity, James Dolezal writes that 'if God were not ontologically identical with all that is in him, then something other than God himself would be needed to account for his existence, essence, and attributes. But nothing that is not God can sufficiently account for God.'[5] The Reformed scholastics used two Latin phrases that help get at the center of the guardrails of divine simplicity: *Quicquid est in Deo, Deus est* ('Whatever is in God, is God') and its negative corollary, *Nihil est in Deo, nisi Deus* ('Nothing is in God but God').[6]

With this working definition, the question at hand is whether or not we can reason toward divine changelessness. Put another way, what is the relationship between the non-compositional essence of God and the doctrine of divine immutability? Charnock made the relationship clear, noting, 'Immutability depends on his simplicity.'[7] Charnock continues: 'he is unchangeable in his essence, because he is a pure and unmixed spiritual Being. Whatsoever is compounded of parts may be divided into those parts, and resolved into those distinct parts which make up and constitute the nature.'[8]

Steven Duby puts forward a trifold answer to the question of the relationship between simplicity and immutability. The first line of

---

5. James Dolezal, *God without Parts: Divine Simplicity and the Metaphysics of God's Absoluteness* (Eugene, OR: Pickwick, 2011), xvii.

6. For a treatment of divine simplicity, see Muller, *PRRD*, 3:275. Muller works through Maccovius, Gomarus, Binning, Charnock, Ridgley, Gill, Polanus, Alting, Hottinger, Leigh, Cocceius, Turretin, à Brakel, van Mastricht, Wyttenback, Burman, and Pictet in order to show the unity and diversity in teaching on divine simplicity within the Reformed orthodox. For more on these two Latin phrases, see also Samuel D. Renihan, *Deity and Decree* (Renihan, 2020), 33-47.

7. Charnock, 1:267. Elsewhere, Charnock says it succinctly, 'Mutability belongs to contingency.' 1:381.

8. Ibid., 1:267.

reasoning deals with *actus purus*. Duby argues that God's changelessness entails pure actuality. This point will become exceedingly important as we move toward evaluating the soteriological significance of divine immutability but proves important here as well. If God really is pure act, then He is not a complex composition of actuality and potentiality.[9] Duby does note that the reason could be worked the other way. He writes:

> From another vantage point – that of divine constancy – we add now that God's immutability implies that he is already established as he is and is therefore *actus purus* with no passive potency by which he should become or develop. The attributes of aseity and immutability join together in anchoring the claim that God is wholly in act: because of the plentitude and perfection of God, the attribute of immutability encapsulates not only that God cannot change but indeed that he *need not* change, for in so doing he would undergo a process of becoming or self-actualization inimical to his perfection and superfluous to the advance agility of his working *pro nobis*.[10]

Second, Duby notes that immutability renders God always the self-same, for, in God's changelessness, He shall never take on new '*qualitates* or *habitus* that might change or bolster his being or his ability to act.'[11] Consequently, God is fully absolute and lacking no essential or accidental property that would further complete His existence. Duby's third line of reasoning deals with indivisibility. If God is truly unchanging, it would make impossible any notion of complexity. As Duby puts forward, 'mutability and divisibility are consequents of complexity and composition.'[12]

In conclusion, divine simplicity has an important relationship with divine immutability. For, in God's non-composite essence we see protection from change by virtue of addition or subtraction. God will not gain or lose 'parts' such that render Him different than He was. Furthermore, divine simplicity protects divine immutability in ensuring that there are no accidents in God which may alter or potency by which He may be activated. Rather, whatever is *in* God, *is* God and therefore simplicity and immutability come together as a witness to God's inalterability.

---

9. Duby, *Divine Simplicity*, 145.

10. Ibid., 145.

11. Ibid., 145.

12. Ibid., 145.

God as Agent, Not Patient: Impassibility and Immutability

Like divine changelessness, the doctrine of impassibility has fallen on tough times in modern theology. Toward the close of the twentieth century, Moltmann can, with rejoicing, celebrate the 'disappearing' of impassibility from a respectable treatment of the doctrine of God.[13] Setting up modern theology's rising of affirmation of a passible God, Thomas Weinandy puts forward a myriad of voices, including Marcel Sarot, who wrote, 'during this present century the idea that God is immutable and impassible has slowly but surely given way to the idea that God is sensitive, emotional, and passionate.' Sarot concludes: 'By now the rejection of the ancient doctrine of divine impassibility has so much become a theological common place, that many theologians do not even feel the need to argue for it.'[14]

Contrary to denials by some modern theologians, the concept of an impassible God had wide acceptance throughout the ecclesial antiquity until the nineteenth and twentieth centuries.[15] For a working definition of impassibility, Weinandy proves helpful as he gives a clear and succinct definition of both impassibility and passibility, saying:

> God is impassible in the sense that he cannot experience emotional change of state due to his relationship to and interaction with human beings and the created order. This understanding of impassibility does not imply … that God is not utterly passionate in his love, mercy, and compassion.
>
> For God to be 'passible' then means that he is capable of being acted upon from without and that such actions bring about emotional changes of state within him. Moreover, for God to be passible means that he is capable of freely changing his inner emotional state in response to and interaction with

---

13. Jürgen Moltmann, *History and the Triune God* (London: SCM, 1991), xvi.

14. M. Sarot, 'Suffering of Christ, Suffering of God?,' *Theology* 95 (1992): 113, quoted in Thomas Weinandy, *Does God Suffer?* (Notre Dame: University of Notre Dame Press, 2000), 1.

15. For a study of divine impassibility in the early church, see Paul Gavrilyuk, *The Suffering of the Impassible God: Dialectics of Patristic Thought* (Oxford: Oxford University Press, 2004). After denouncing the assumption that classical theology was enslaved to Hellenistic thought and setting up the apophatic nature of divine impassibility, Gavrilyuk works through Christological heresies with an eye toward demonstrating how impassibility might protect the church's teaching. Gavrilyuk shows that impassibility can protect the church from Docetism, Arianism, and Nestorianism (Gavrilyuk, 173).

the changing human condition and world order. Last, possibility implies that God's changing emotional state involve 'feelings' that are analogous to human feelings. Thus, one can speak, for example, of God's inner emotional state as changing from joy to sorrow, or from delight to suffering.[16]

Weinandy's definition of impassibility and passibility gives us the first ingredient needed in relating divine impassibility to divine immutability. The second point needed is an understanding of passion. Based on the Latin word *passio*, the English term 'passion' carries a notion of being 'the patient.' Aquinas defines passion as 'the effect of the agent on the patient.'[17] The patient is the one who undergoes or suffers from the action of the agent. Reflection on the modern usage of 'passionate' reveals just as much, for to be 'passionate' about something is to have a level of affection for an item that one is moved to care intensely for it.[18] Dolezal connects the state of being the patient in passibility to mutability, stating: 'As a *received* state of actuality, every passion produces a change in the subject as the consequent of some agent's action on it.'[19]

These two ingredients – a working definition of impassibility and an understanding of 'passions' – come together and demonstrate immutability's connection to a passion-less God.[20] If what it means

---

16. Weinandy, *Does God Suffer?*, 38. Weinandy also makes use of the *Oxford Dictionary of The Christian Church*, which, speaking of impassibility, denies emotional change in God in three various forms: '(1) external passibility or the capacity to be acted upon from without, (2) internal passibility or the capacity for changing the emotions from within, and (3) sensational passibility or the liability to feelings of pleasure and pain caused by the action of another being.' R. Creel, 'Impassibility of God,' in *The Oxford Dictionary of the Christian Church*, ed. E. A. Livingstone, 3rd ed. (Oxford: Oxford University Press, 1997), 823.

17. Aquinas, *ST, Ia-IIae*26.2.

18. For example, Dolezal gives the example of the loveliness of a wife: 'My wife's loveliness, for instance, is the efficient cause that draws me to her. My love for her is passionate to just the extent that I am affected and moved by her loveliness. A similar account can be given of the other passions, both good and bad. Each is a state of affective actuality into which one enters through a process of being acted on by some cause and receiving from that cause a new (accidental) state of being' (James Dolezal, 'Strong Impassibility' in *Divine Impassibility: Four Views of God's Emotions and Suffering*, ed. Robert J. Matz and A. Chadwick Thornhill [Downers Grove, IL: IVP Academic, 2019], 17).

19. Ibid., 17. Emphasis original.

20. For a conciliar connection of divine immutability and divine impassibility in the first few centuries, see Giles Emery, 'The Immutability of the God of Love and the Problem of Language Concerning the "Suffering of God,"' in *Divine Impassibility and the Mystery of Human Suffering*, ed. James F. Keating and Thomas J. White (Grand Rapids: Eerdmans, 2009), 28-35.

to undergo passion is to be acted on by an outside agent such that one is moved from one emotional state to another, it is obvious that impassibility is intrinsically tied to immutability. These two doctrines have a dogmatic connection such that to denounce one would necessitate a denial of the other. For God to move from one state of emotion to the next would entail that He possesses some sort of passive potency that needs to be actualized by an outside agent.

On the contrary, since God is pure act, He does not suffer at the hands of anyone outside Himself nor by virtue of His own divine life. Instead, God, as pure act, is the agent who causes others to move or to undergo passion. While not moved by another, He is, as Aquinas called Him, the unmoved mover.

In conclusion, the perfection of impassibility acts as a witness to divine immutability by securing the reality that God will not undergo change due to passions as He is without passions. Unlike the pagan gods of old, the God of Isaac and Jacob is not tossed to and fro with passions such that His people need to worry themselves about which mood their covenantal God may be in on any given day. On the contrary, God is pure act, and His lack of passive potency includes potency of passion. In this way, divine impassibility and divine immutability come together as reciprocally necessary and a metaphysical witness to God's immutability.

Life in Himself: Divine Aseity and Divine Immutability

Pressing into Aquinas' conception of God as the unmoved mover, we come here to the doctrine of divine aseity. Key to finding truthfulness in the idea of an unmoved mover would be the lack of ontological origin and sufficiency outside of oneself. Rather, divine aseity speaks to God's having life in Himself. John Webster will prove helpful in articulating a working definition of divine aseity, as the late theologian argued for more than simply understanding aseity as a comparative doctrine alone, distinguishing the Creator from the creature. While aseity does indeed render the Creator as differing in kind, not just grandeur, from the creature, it is important to maintain both the *negative* and *positive* aspects of God's life in Himself.

Webster differentiates the negative and positive aspects of divine aseity when he observes: 'God's aseity is to be understood, not formally but materially. Aseity is not to be defined merely in negative terms, as the mere absence of origination from or dependence upon an external cause.' He continues: 'if this is allowed to happen, then a subordinate characteristic of aseity (God's "not being from another") comes to eclipse its primary meaning (God's "being in and from himself").'[21]

Webster's distinction is important here since it might appear that aseity is an apophatic perfection only. However, we treat aseity by way of negation, according to Webster, only as a 'corollary' of a more constructive and positive understanding of God's perfection of life in Himself. Moreover, Webster is right to root God's life-in-Himselfness in the eternal relations of origin. In this way, God is *a se* by virtue of the Father's unbegottenness, the Son's eternal generation, and the Spirit's eternal procession. Webster writes:

> These activities are personal relations, that is, modes of subsistence in which each particular person of the Trinity is identified in terms of relations to the other two persons. To spell this out fully would require an account of (for example) the act of the Father in begetting the Son, and the acts of the Father and the Son in spirating the Spirit. Expressed as relations, God's life *a se* includes the Son's relation to the Father as the one whom the Father begets (passive generation), and the relation of the Spirit to the Father and the Son (passive spiration). By these activities and relations, each of the persons of the Trinity is identified, that is, picked out as having a distinct, incommunicable personal property: paternity, filiation, spiration. Together, these acts and relations *are* God's self-existence.[22]

It is due to the positive application of God's perfection of aseity that the negative corollary comes into focus. Since God is the 'sufficient condition'[23] of the divine life, there is an 'absence of derivation.'[24] As God reminds Job in His response, 'Who has first given to me, that I should

---

21. Webster, *God without Measure*, 1:19.

22. Webster, *God without Measure*, 1:20. For more on ascribing aseity as a positive perfection, see Grant Macaskill, 'Name Christology, Divine Aseity, and the I Am Sayings in the Fourth Gospel,' *JTI* 12, no. 2 (2018): 217-41; and Duby, *Divine Simplicity*, 118-31. While this project seeks to find the soteriological significance of a classical understanding of divine immutability, Webster's essay is a great example of moving from divine perfections toward God's *ad extra* work in the economy via divine aseity. Webster, *God without Measure*, 1:19.

23. Dolezal, *God without Parts*, 71.

24. Webster, *God without Measure*, 1:20.

repay him? Whatever is under the whole heaven is mine' (Job 41:11). Yes, the 'cattle on a thousand hills' (Ps. 50:10) belong to the Lord, not only by virtue of possession but even by virtue of existence and contingency. They, and all creatures like them, exist as contingent beings relying on the Triune God, who has no contingencies Himself. Rather, as Paul preaches in Acts, this is the God who 'made the world and everything in it, being Lord of heaven and earth, does not live in temples made by man, nor is he served by human hands, as though he needed anything, since he himself gives to all mankind life and breath and everything' (Acts 17:24-25).

This absence of derivation means that there is no outside cause that can claim the privilege of giving ontological origin or meaning to God's immanent life. In other words, because of God's having fullness of life in Himself, He possesses no contingencies. So then, the positive affirmation of God's *a se* life entails corollary conclusions: (1) the negative application of God's lack of contingency and absence of derivation, and (2) the ability to bend divine aseity in the direction of comparison distinguishing the Creator from the creature.

Concerning the negative side of aseity, Mastricht denounces four types of 'causes' in God: (1) an efficient cause; (2) a material cause; (3) a formal cause; and (4) a final cause.[25] Denouncing these four causes, Mastricht can declare that God is 'absolutely first being' and reject any notion of God's *receiving* existence, form, and direction. Furthermore, while Mastricht here emphasizes the negative side of aseity – God's non-contingency – nevertheless, God's non-contingency indeed has implication for the creature who is utterly contingent. For this reason, Mastricht notes: 'God intended to say that he has such an essence from which is derived, and upon which depends, all the essence of all things, that he has such an essence that comes from no one and nothing, and accordingly that he is the first being, not in this or that species only, in the way that Adam was the first being among men, but absolutely first.'[26]

Moving the discussion from definition to dogmatic connection, divine immutability and divine aseity are important to keep together. For, in the *a se* life of God we see the sufficient conditions of God's pure life untainted by actuality or mutation. In his *Confessions*, Augustine notes: 'See, heaven

---

25. Mastricht, *TPT*, 2:82.
26. Mastricht, *TPT*, 2:83.

and earth exist, they cry aloud that they are made, for they suffer change and variation. But in anything which is not made and yet is, there is nothing which previously was not present. ... You are, for they are.'[27] As Augustine here notes, both the heavens and earth lack the sufficient conditions of life in themselves and therefore find their contingency in another. This contingency breeds mutability, as both heaven and earth must be actualized into their potential, even the potential to exist. This is not an actuality God is awaiting, as He is not moved from non-existence to existence. It should not come as a surprise to the insightful reader that one tie that binds aseity and immutability is, again, pure actuality. Steven Duby notes God's aseity, rooted in pure actuality, protects Him from 'casual susceptibility.'[28] Of this casual susceptibility, Duby notes, 'without being moved or, indeed, a capacity to be moved – and therefore without the root of such casual susceptibility, namely, passive potency. ... Aseity inflected independence or *primitas* thus implies that God is fully in act.'[29]

In conclusion, divine aseity and divine immutability come together to declare that God immutably has life in Himself. By derivation, God is unchangeably independent and as the only independent being who lacks all contingency no creature may cause Him change. God's life in Himself is a maximal life and renders Him in need of nothing. Therefore, God does not become actualized to a greater state of 'completeness' by virtue of creation *ex nihilo* or in the salvation and union with His people. He lacks nothing and is changed by nothing and therefore the doctrine of divine aseity is another witness to the essential reality of God's immutability.

No Beginning, No End, and No Succession: Divine Atemporality and Divine Immutability

There is a natural dogmatic connection between divine aseity and divine atemporality. Aseity not only gets at God's fullness of life, but

---

27. Augustine, *Confessions* (Oxford: Oxford University Press, 1991), XI.4.6, quoted in Webster, *God without Measure*, 1:14.

28. Duby, *Divine Simplicity*, 121.

29. Ibid., 121. Asbill makes this connection as well, saying: 'The God who exists in aseity is *immutable*, or rather, *constant*. Creates change because, not inherently having life in themselves, they are potential, caused and composite. However, since God is "entirely uncaused", God is "incapable of generation or corruption"' (See Brian D. Asbill, *The Freedom of God for Us: Karl Barth's Doctrine of Divine Aseity* [London: Bloomsbury, 2015], 9, emphasis original).

it is also considered a divine perfection. As such, God does not have *a se* essence such that it might decline as time wanes. Rather, aseity necessitates atemporality. This is why Pictet argues that God's eternity can be claimed by reason alone.[30] Of course, Pictet goes on to quote both Psalm 102 and 1 Timothy 6 in his defense of God's eternality. His point stands, however, that the eternal life of God can be deduced from proper theological reasoning about God's aseity and pure actuality (and immutability, as we will see). Pictet concludes, regarding divine atemporality, that God's eternal life 'denotes three things – to be without beginning, without end, [and] without succession.'[31]

Wilhelmus à Brakel helps distinguish forms of 'eternity' embedded in human language, especially as it is seen in the Scriptures. For example, à Brakel demonstrates four uses of eternity in Scripture. First, there is the notion of eternity as seen in Genesis 17:13, wherein circumcision is supposed to fulfill the 'eternal covenant.' This method of eternality denotes an object 'has fulfilled its purpose.'[32] Second, à Brakel notes that, as is the case with Deuteronomy 15:17, which states 'he shall be your servant forever,' the idea of eternity can communicate a commitment or reality that endures so long as a man lives. Third, eternity can designate that which displays substantial stability and endurance. À Brakel makes use of the biblical portrayal of 'hills,' which Deuteronomy 33:15 and Genesis 49:26 refer to as eternal. Finally, à Brakel discusses the eternal felicity of the saints in the afterlife. Pulling from John 10:28, the Dutch theologian points out that the life of those in Christ is *eternal* life.[33] À Brakel concludes that these four uses of the term eternal and the way we are to properly speak of God's eternality have 'neither commonality nor resemblance.'[34]

One more note about the biblical usage of eternity and time will prove helpful in this discussion. Like most perfections within the system known as classical theism, the biblical data – taken at face value – might seem to pose an issue. For, God seems to not only interact with His creatures but to interact with them in real time and space. The pages of Scripture depict a God, who, *at a certain time*, showed up to rescue the Israelites from the

---

30. Pictet, *CT*, 2:97.
31. Ibid., 2:98.
32. à Brakel, *CRS*, 1:91.
33. Ibid., *CRS*, 1:90-92.
34. Ibid., *CRS*, 1:92.

oppression of the Egyptians. In fact, is not every *ad extra* interaction in the economy between a non-incarnate God and His people an instance of God's involvement in time? Paul Helm is helpful here and shows that along with the hermeneutical tools of anthropomorphism and anthropopathism, we need the exegetical insight of an anthropochronic tool.[35] Like anthropomorphism and anthropopathism describe God's accommodation by virtue of His 'features' and 'emotions,' anthropochronism is the idea that God can and does accommodate His incomprehensibility in His self-revelation to creatures in relation to time.

Here, critics of classical theism might cry foul at the thought of employing three exegetical tools that render most, if not all, of God's *ad extra* activity as analogical. However, this should come as no theological surprise given the classical notion of God's incomprehensibility. Considering classical theists' insistence on the incomprehensibility of God's essence, and our insistence of the Bible's concursus nature, it need not be alarming that the unchanging God of the Scriptures be described in heavily analogical terms. Therefore, on the basis of the Creator/creature distinction, and utilizing anthropomorphism, anthropopathism, and anthropochronism, theologians denounce the notions of God's having body parts, passions, and successive moments of time.

Drawing the connection between divine changelessness and atemporality is not a difficult task given the definition above. In fact, in her 2016 Aquinas Lecture, Eleonore Stump begins her section on God's eternality by simply stating, 'eternity implies immutability.'[36] Stump further elaborates, 'on the doctrine of eternity, God is outside time; but change requires succession, which is characteristic of time, and so nothing that is outside time can change.'[37]

As Eleonore Stump demonstrates, there can be no coherent conception of divine immutability together with the notion of a God who

---

35. Paul Helm, *Eternal God: A Study of God without Time* (Oxford: Oxford University Press, 2010), 2. Helm writes: 'But may not such representations of God be anthropomorphic (or anthropochronic) in order to render his relations to his creation more intelligible to us? For it is agreed that there are anthropomorphisms in the Bible. ... References to God being in space are anthropomorphic while references to him being in time are, apparently, not anthropomorphic. Is there prejudice here?'

36. Eleonore Stump, *The God of the Bible and the God of the Philosophers* (Milwaukee: Marquette University Press, 2016), 26.

37. Ibid., 26. Elsewhere Stump treats Aquinas' understanding of divine eternality and there also connects the doctrine to divine immutability. See Eleonore Stump, *Aquinas* (London: Routledge, 2003), 131-59.

experiences successive moments of time. Such a God would change, by the second, as He experiences each passing moment. This is one of many ways that divine eternality and atemporality distinguish the creature from Creator. For, the creature lives and moves in a world in which not only do they change, but they have nothing in themselves that can help but change. In their continual process of *becoming*, creatures are in an ever-fluctuating state of growth. Seconds and milliseconds culminate in the creature's inability to cease ontological movement. On the contrary, God does not suffer these alterations at the hands of time. In this way, then, Stump is correct in asserting that immutability entails eternality; to denounce of God atemporality one would necessarily need to simultaneously denounce divine immutability.

Aquinas makes this point as well, noting succinctly that, 'Everything that begins to be or ceases to be does so through motion or change. Since, however, we have shown that God is immutable, he is eternal, lacking all beginning or end.'[38]

Of course, it should be understood, and is stated above, that along with successive moments of time, atemporality rules out both beginning and end in God. Again, Aquinas is helpful here:

> Again, those beings alone are measured by time that are moved. For time, as is made clear in *Physics* IV, is 'the number of motion.' But God, as has been proved, is absolutely without motion, and is consequently not measured by time. There is, therefore, no *before* and *after* in him; he does not have being after non-being, nor non-being after being, nor can any succession be found in his being. For none of these characteristics can be understood without time. God, therefore, is without beginning and end, having his whole being at once. In this consists the nature of eternity.[39]

However, Turretin desired to stress the issue of successive moments of change, over notions of origin and end, based on what he perceived to be a clear scriptural testimony to a God without beginning and end. Indeed, Turretin notes that even Socinus and Vorstius must, on the basis of exegesis, deny a beginning or end in God. Yet, successive moments of passing and change need a bit of a stronger defense.[40]

---

38. Aquinas, *SCG* I, c15.2.
39. Aquinas, *SCG* I, c15.3.
40. Turretin, *IET*, III.X.1.

Turretin's defense of a non-successive God has two points of interest for the current project. First, Turretin argues for eternality using the passage from which this book draws its name. James 1:17 exclaims a God who exists without variableness nor shadow of turning. Turretin notes that 'the succession and flow of the parts of duration (which exist successively) necessarily involve a certain species of motion (which cannot be applied to God.)'[41] Second, Turretin invokes both divine immutability and divine simplicity in his arguments against successive change in God. He writes: 'The eternity of God cannot have succession because his essence, with which it is really identified, admits none. This is so both because it is perfectly simple and immutable.'[42] According to Turretin, simplicity and immutability are contrary to succession because chronological succession entails that the former be able to change into the latter, the past be able to change into the present, the present be able to turn into the future – all of which involve succession and all of which is unthinkable given a simple and immutable essence.

In conclusion, divine atemporality protects divine immutability by ensuring that God remains changeless regarding time. God does not experience passing succession of moments. In God there is no beginning, no ending, and no passing of successive moments. Rather, God is atemporal and His atemporality provides another metaphysical witness to His immutability as He stays the same age-to-age as there is no age in Him.

No Quantity, Dimension, or Locality: Divine Infinitude and Divine Immutability

In the eleventh chapter of Job, Job's friend, Zophar, questions Job, saying:

> Can you find out the deep things of God?
> Can you find out the limit of the Almighty?
> It is higher than heaven – what can you do?
> Deeper than Sheol – what can you know?
> Its measure is longer than the earth
> and broader than the sea (Job 11:7-9).

---

41. Ibid., III.X.3.
42. Ibid., III.X.5.

In this passage, Zophar gets at what many theologians have referred to as divine infinitude.[43] While disagreements pertaining to infinitude abound, in its simplest form, infinitude is an apophatic attribute predicated to mean that God's perfections are without limit. To help with articulating a doctrine of divine infinitude we will turn to three theologians spanning three differing eras or traditions – Gregory of Nyssa, Wilhelmus à Brakel, and John Flavel.

Foundational to the Nicene faith is the notion that 'We believe in one God, the Father almighty, maker of heaven and earth, of all things visible and invisible.' The Cappadocian theologian, Gregory of Nyssa, was vital in the Church's internalizing of this opening salvo of believing in 'one God.' Gregory's work, *On 'Not Three Gods,'* was crucial in defending the concept of unity in Trinity in Christian theology. In this work, Gregory deals with the concept and name of 'Godhead' as it relates to what would come to be called the inseparable operations of God.[44]

Gregory turns toward the doctrine of divine infinitude in response to those who would insist on three Gods by virtue of operations. He writes: 'For we, believing the Divine nature to be unlimited and incomprehensible, conceive no comprehension of it.' He continues, 'but declare that the nature is to be conceived in all respects as infinite: and that which is absolutely infinite is not limited in one respect while it is left unlimited in another, but infinity is free from limitation altogether.'[45] God's being free from 'limitation altogether,' as Gregory put it, is a staple we see throughout the development of the doctrine throughout theological antiquity.

Another facet of Gregory that we see throughout theological antiquity, as in Wilhelmus à Brakel, is the notion that divine infinitude

---

43. For a helpful overview of the doctrine of divine infinitude, see Muller, *PRRD*, 3:325-35.

44. On inseparable operations, Gregory is helpful, writing: 'Since, then, the character of the superintending and beholding power is one, in Father, Son, and Holy Spirit, as has been said in our previous argument, issuing from the Father as from a spring, brought into operation by the Son, and perfecting its grace by the power of the Spirit; and since no operation is separated in respect of the Persons, being fulfilled by each individually apart from that which is joined with him in our contemplation, but all providence, care, and superintendence of all, alike of things in the sensible creation and of those of supramundane nature, and that power which preserves the things which are, and corrects those who are amiss, and instructs those which are ordered aright, is one, and not three.' Gregory of Nyssa, *NPNF*, 5:334-35.

45. Gregory of Nyssa, *On 'Not Three Gods,' NPNF* 5:335.

can only be comprehended by way of analogy and any effort to put qualitative parameters around the perfection will fall short. For example, à Brakel notes that, 'Occasionally, when referring to something of which the limits are not known, we refer to infinity in a hypothetical sense, as when we speak of the total number of grains of sand, blades of grass, or stars.'[46] These are to be understood only by analogy of divine infinitude. Differentiating between the two, à Brakel writes: 'When we define God to be infinite, however, we do so in the literal sense of the word, thereby conveying that his Being is truly without any parameters or limitations. His power is infinite, his knowledge is infinite, and his Being is infinite.'[47] To elaborate on removing quantity from consideration of divine infinitude, à Brakel argues that our articulation of God's freedom from parameters should 'exclude the concepts of quantity, dimension, and locality.'[48]

We witness one area of disagreement in how theologians have referenced divine infinitude here in à Brakel. For, à Brakel's insistence that infinitude requires no quantity, dimension, or locality ends up making his understanding very similar to omnipresence, for example. If infinitude is a non-parameter of locality, for instance, how is this distinguishable from God's omnipresence? In fact, à Brakel himself says outright, 'Infinity and omnipresence are identical in God.'[49] However, this issue is resolved when à Brakel states that this may be the case only in relation to God's infinitude and omnipresence in terms of space. Omnipresence, then, for à Brakel is just one aspect of divine infinitude. In this vein Muller, writing of disagreements within the Reformed orthodoxy's articulation of this perfection, says: 'Like Aquinas and the medieval doctors, the Protestant scholastics define divine infinity not as the endless extension of the categories of finite being, but as the transcendence of those categories.'[50] Infinitude cannot be understood,

---

46. Wilhelmus à Brakel, *CRS* 1:93.

47. Ibid. à Brakel argues that divine infinitude is necessitated logically from three realities: (1) God's perfect being since a being without limitation is greater than a being with limitations, (2) God's having infinite power – which we would be unable to say of any finite being, and (3) As a necessary consequence of reading the Scriptures, particularly scriptures like Psalms 145:3 and 1 Kings 8:27.

48. Ibid., 1:93.

49. Ibid., 1:94.

50. Muller, *PRRD* 3:330.

then, by contemplating the notion of infinity by way of series. If addition or subtraction be at all possible, then we risk misunderstanding the concept of divine infinitude. Any parameter which may be increased or decreased must be denied of God such that He is not simply the greatest in an infinite series but transcends the notion of series and limit altogether.

Our final theologian of consideration, John Flavel, is helpful in articulating a definition and implications of divine infinitude. By way of definition, Flavel writes that God's infinity 'signifies that which hath no bounds or limits, within which it is contained, as all created things are.'[51] Extrapolating on this definition, Flavel argues that God can be understood to be infinite in three respects: first, God is infinite in respect of 'the perfection of his nature; his wisdom, power, and holiness, exceed[ing] all measures and limits'; second, God is infinite in respect to time and place since 'no time can measure him'; third, and finally, 'God is infinite in respect to his incomprehensibleness.'[52]

In conclusion, to see the relationship between divine infinitude and divine immutability, we return once more to the Cappadocian, Gregory of Nyssa. Gregory argues that 'neither diminution nor increase attaches to any nature.'[53] A true understanding of divine infinitude is protected by and necessitates divine immutability. For God to transcend quantity or series, He is beyond sequence or scope, He must not simply be the greatest in a quantitative – even infinite – numerical collection. Rather, God must transcend the notion of parameter, limit, quantity, or series completely. To transcend these concepts, there must not be even the possibility of diminution nor increase. If the possibility of increase or decrease existed within God, the notion of infinitude would become measurable and therefore cease to be true infinitude. In this way, divine immutability and divine infinitude bolster and necessitate one another. God's infinitude renders Him changeless beyond limits and divine infinitude is but another witness to divine changelessness.

---

51. John Flavel, *An Exposition of the Assembly's Catechism* in *The Works of John Flavel*, Volume Six, (Edinburgh: Banner of Truth Trust, 1982), 6:147.

52. Flavel, *An Exposition of the Assembly's Catechism*, 147. For each of these points, Flavel cites a passage of Scripture. For the first, he notes 1 Samuel 2:2 and 1 Kings 8:27. For the second, he cites Isaiah 57:15. Finally, for third, he references Job 11:7.

53. Gregory of Nyssa, *NPNF* 5:335.

Wisdom, Power, and Presence: The 'Omnis' and Divine Immutability

It is not only the so-called incommunicable attributes that possess systematic connection to divine immutability. The communicable perfections as well can be derived using theological reasoning from or toward God's changelessness. In this brief section we will examine three 'omnis' of God in search of their relationship to the classical conception of divine immutability – omniscience, omnipotence, and omnipresence.

Writing on omniscience, the seventeenth-century English Protestant scholastic theologian Edward Leigh utilized the *via triplex,* a threefold method of predication, in attributing omniscience to God. Leigh demonstrated that, by the way of negation, ignorance is an imperfection and therefore must be denied of God. By way of causation, Leigh noted: 'God governs all things in the whole Universe, and directs to convenient ends even those things which are destitute of all Knowledge.'[54] Finally, by way of eminence, Leigh predicated omniscience to God. He writes: 'God hath made creatures intelligent and full of knowledge, *viz.* Angels and men; therefore, he knows and understands in a far more perfect and eminent manner.'[55]

Leigh also describes six key differences between the knowledge of the Creator and knowledge obtained by the creature. One of these differences relates both to immutability and our previous section of eternality. Leigh notes that as the creature grows in his/her knowledge, we must do so successively; meaning, we increase in wisdom and insight by 'pains of discourse' as we proceed from ignorance toward insight.[56] We also move from an insight by gradation – increasing or decreasing in understanding. On the contrary, Leigh notes that it is by derivation

---

54. Edward Leigh, *SBD*, 2:192.

55. Ibid., 2:192.

56. Ibid., 2:194. Leigh's other five differences between knowledge in the creature and knowledge in the Creator are: (1) We have our knowledge by 'helpers' – others, God, etc., yet God knows without aid; (2) we vary by extent as creatures only know in part, yet God knows all particulars and generalities in full; (3) our knowledge is finite, but God's is infinite; (4) creatures have knowledge by virtue of 'species or images,' whereas God knows by His essence; and (5) we know 'doubtingly,' which differs from God's knowledge of perfection. He knows all things past, present, and future and knows all contingencies and connections.

of divine simplicity and divine immutability that God does not increase nor decrease in omniscience. God knows Himself – and therefore all things – fully, not by succession of movement but as they actually are for all time.

Moving to God's omnipresence, Benedict Pictet once again proves helpful, as he gives five realities present in the doctrine of divine omnipresence. Pictet's five rules of divine omnipresence can be summarized as:

1. God's omnipresence should not be understood as the 'diffusion of the divine essence through all things.'

2. God's omnipresence is derived by His power, energy, and operation.[57]

3. God's omnipresence is not unbecoming of His own divine majesty. Since what is Spirit cannot be touched by what is corporeal, God can be said to 'be in the most impure places, without being contaminated.'

4. God's omnipresence does not necessitate that He is unable to be present in a *particular* manner in an individual location.

5. God's omnipresence entails that God is not confined to any one place or any one space.[58]

For these reasons, and more, Scripture can analogically and really depict God with verbs of movement such as ascending, descending, approaching, and departing without violating the doctrine of divine immutability. By relation and derivation, the implication of divine immutability on the presence of God is what allows the psalmist to declare in Psalm 139:7-10:

---

57. This point of omniscience might need further elaboration. Pictet here does not intend to denounce that God is omnipresent by virtue of His own essence. Rather, 'He is omnipresent in regard to his *operation*, for he works all in all. … Now since he works all this by his power, we say that he is omnipresent by virtue of that power. And as this is not different from the divine essence, we maintain that he is omnipresent in regard to his essence' (Pictet, *CT*, 2:95-96).

58. Ibid., 2:95-97.

Where can I go from your Spirit?
Or where shall I flee from your presence?
If I ascend to heaven, you are there!
If I make my bed in Sheol, you are there!
If I take the wings of the morning
And dwell in the uttermost parts of the sea,
Even there your hand shall lead me,
And your right hand shall hold me.

As God does not increase nor decrease by virtue of His wisdom and insight, nor does He increase or decrease regarding His presence. The changelessness of God necessitates a God of omnipresence.

Finally, as it pertains to God's omnipotence and power, Aquinas argued that 'the fact that he is immovable and impassible is not repugnant to his omnipotence.'[59] Not only may we affirm Aquinas' conclusion here, we may go further and argue that immutability is not repugnant to divine omnipotence but essential for it. By virtue of God's non-composite nature, the Lord has not power but rather *is* omnipotent. Given that a simple *esse* renders any divine action as essence in act, the relationship between divine simplicity, immutability, and omnipotence is vital because it is derivative of God's immutability that He has no alteration in His omnipotence and therefore no alteration in His ability to pursue divine action. God did not expend a portion of His power, for example, when He created, exercised providence, or redeemed His people. It is the same *actus purus* power that God exercises yesterday, today, and forevermore without increase or decrease.[60]

In conclusion, omniscience, omnipotence, and omnipresence all give witness to God's immutability as there is no increase nor decrease in His wisdom, power, or presence. The perfections of the 'omnis' while being 'communicable' with the creature nevertheless are a powerful demonstration of the Creator/creature distinction in the reality that God's wisdom, power, and presence are immutably glorious and supreme.

---

59. Aquinas, *ST*, Ia25.3, cf. Ia3.1.

60. For more on the connection between divine simplicity and power, see Andrew Radde-Gallwitz, *Basil of Caesarea, Gregory of Nyssa, and the Transformation of Divine Simplicity* (Oxford: Oxford University Press, 2009), 21. For more on divine action and divine simplicity, see Duby, *God in Himself*, 185.

Conclusion

In the second portion of this book – A Three-Fold Witness for Divine Immutability – the aim was to leverage three fields of study to argue for a constructive and classical articulation of divine immutability. First, we saw how the saints of the past provide a witness for divine immutability by working through each of the major eras of history in search of how theologians of yesterday nuanced and advanced the church's understanding of her unchanging Triune God. Second, we turned to the pages of Scripture itself for an affirmation of divine immutability based on the biblical data. We saw in the biblical data hermeneutical and exegetical implications of divine immutability and the reciprocal relationship between theology proper and Christian Scripture. Third, in this chapter we moved from the halls of history and the pages of Scripture to theological reasoning, exploring how each of God's divine perfections relates to, necessitates, or is necessitated by divine immutability. In this third witness of divine immutability, we see that to deny divine immutability one must work through corollary perfections because each is systematically connected with one another. In conclusion, by virtue of the biblical data, the confessions and confessors of the church, and theological reasoning, we affirm that in God there is no variableness nor shadow of turning.

PART THREE

Divine Immutability and Soteriology

CHAPTER SIX

Divine Immutability and the Economy of Redemption

From Constructive Articulation to Soteric Application

Much of the previous material aimed at building a constructive articulation of divine immutability. With the theological construction behind us, we can now move from construction to application. More specifically, we can turn our attention to examining the soteriological import of the doctrine of God's immutability; doing so helps bring the general thesis and the specific thesis together. The doctrine of God must not be marginalized or maligned in developing the economy of redemption. Divine immutability gives a helpful test case in demonstrating the advantages of situating God's economy in and under God's life in Himself. As Webster reminded us in the first chapter: 'The doctrine of God is prior to the economy of God's works, both materially and so also logically, since the being of God in and for himself is the ground of God's works.'[1]

Part One of the book sought to demonstrate the problem in conversations surrounding the doctrine of divine immutability. First, there is the problem of metaphysics falling out with dogmatic theology as modern theologians have a growing allergy to metaphysical contemplation in the Christian theological method. The second,

---

1. Webster, '*Rector et iudex super omnia*,' 46.

and related to the first, is that divine immutability has drastically decreased in favor in modernity's conception of God as theologians, spanning the spectrum of ecclesial communities, deviate from or outright deny God's inalterability.

In Part Two, 'A Three-Fold Witness to Divine Immutability,' the aim was to move beyond deconstruction and leverage historical theology, biblical data, and theological reasoning to develop a constructive articulation of classic divine immutability. These three chapters provided the material needed to work toward the specific thesis as we utilize the conclusions of this three-fold witness to divine immutability and contemplate how God's inalterability entails soteriological significance.

In our attempt to parse the soteriological significance of divine immutability, we will work under four headings. First, we once again turn to the biblical data to demonstrate that the relating of God's changelessness to soteriological assurance of God's people is a biblical paradigm. Second, we look specifically at the work of Jesus of Nazareth in hopes to understand how the changelessness of Jesus' divine nature impacts functional Christology. Third, we return to the metaphysical relations of the divine perfections in hopes of seeing how immutability relates soteriologically to corollary divine perfections. Fourth, and finally, we consider how divine immutability might relate to the doctrine of union with Christ as sinners are made one with their Savior.

These four headings will help us see that a classical articulation of divine immutability both protects and promotes God's soteriological acts in the economy of redemption. Pausing to take a moment and explain what we mean by saying that God's changelessness both 'protects' and 'promotes' the economy of redemption is worthwhile.

By arguing that divine immutability 'protects' salvation I simply mean that God's unchanging nature keeps intact certain elements in the economy of redemption without which sinners would be doomed. For example, for the economy of redemption to be good news to a wayward people, it is crucial that God's decree in their justification not alter or wane. We can be confident that God's declaration of sinners' justification is immutable because it is rooted in the immutable righteousness of the Son. This is but one way the doctrine of divine immutability 'protects' God's soteric activity in the economy of redemption.

By arguing that divine immutability 'promotes' salvation I simply mean that God's essential inalterability perpetuates His soteric activity. For example, bringing *actus purus* to bear in the economy of redemption promotes God's soteric activity as we see God's lack of potency means that He need not be actualized to save His people. Rather, God's pure actuality means He redeems out of the fullness of life in Himself. Redemption is not an afterthought or accident in God but rather the action of His essence in relation toward His people. Ironically, then, we see the counter-narrative to the modern complaint against immutability that changelessness renders God a stoic being incapable of salvation. On the contrary, it is God's unchanging pure act that promotes – not negates – the soteriological development in the economy of redemption.

Grounding God's economic activity in His immanent life will be to the benefit of the church as those who have hung their earthly joy and eternal hope on Christ's unique qualification and ability to unite them into right relationship with the Triune God. In any chapter exploring the soteric significance of divine immutability there will be a mingling of theology proper, Christology, soteriology, and related theological fields. However, what will come to fruition in an examination of these related areas of theological inquiry is that God's redemption is an unchanging redemption because it is rooted in an unchanging Redeemer.

Working on the classical doctrine of inseparable operations, Adonis Vidu notes:

> 'A thing acts in so far as it is in act,' Aquinas wrote. By no means an esoteric principle of the Common Doctor, this axiom merely expresses the simple idea that the activity of a particular thing is determined in its nature by the kind of thing that it is. A rock can't speak, but it can break; water can flow, but it can't break; and so on. The kind of actions, or action *types* that an agent may do, are directly related to the range of possibilities inscribed in its nature.[2]

Building off Aquinas, Vidu here makes an important observation regarding the relationship between the action of a thing and its being. Of this relationship, Vidu says, 'since actions are grounded in natures, the

---

2. Adonis Vidu, *The Same God Who Works All Things: Inseparable Operations in Trinitarian Theology* (Grand Rapids: Eerdmans, 2021), 92. The quote from Aquinas that begins this section comes from q.18, a.1, ad. 2.

nature of the action is determined by the nature of the agent.'[3] Following Vidu's logic would mean, for instance, that water may flow, but it may not break, as 'breaking' is not within the 'range of possibilities inscribed' in the nature of water. Theologically, then, we may not predicate to God any economic activity outside the range inscribed by His own nature. So then, as rock may break but not speak, God may redeem, but He may not go back on His word as it is against God's nature to lie (Num. 23:19).

Another reason one might be tempted to cry foul at this juncture is on the basis that we may only know the immanent life of God by virtue of His gracious economic activity. Along with recalling readers to Chapter Four in which we discussed the reciprocal relationship between the immanent and economic life of God, Vidu also proves helpful here. He notes that 'while it is natural that one starts with the divine economy and proceeds to an understanding of the immanent Trinity, the knowledge of the divine economy should be regarded as provisional.'[4] With the limited, or 'provisional,' epistemic insight about the immanent life of God students of theology gain by way of examining His economic activity, they must return to the *ad extra* once again. This circular epistemological tension causes Vidu to conclude: 'Thus, our principle does not yield a simplistic and unidirectional application but rather a creative tension, whereby the immanent pole is ascribed a principled priority, with full awareness that the two poles cannot be divorced and are unavailable apart from one another.'[5]

We here turn to attempt exactly what Vidu and Webster suggest by way of method – grounding the soteric *ad extra* activity of God in the divine life by examining how a classical articulation of divine immutability impacts the economy of redemption.

Lessons from Divine Immutability's Biblical Pattern

As we saw in Chapter Four, there is a great deal of biblical data concerning the changelessness of our Lord. However, not only is the content of these passages vital for examination in conversations

---

3. Vidu, *The Same God Who Works All Things,* 91. Vidu also provides a helpful corrective when dealing with epistemology and the *ad extra.*

4. Ibid., 92. Vidu calls this provisional knowledge 'a sort of first naïveté.'

5. Ibid., 93. Of course this is only describing epistemology in the theological journey as we could, with great ease, entertain the notion of God without His economic activity.

concerning divine immutability, so too, is the pattern in which this biblical data appears. The biblical pattern exhibits a strong correlation between divine immutability and God's inalterable and sure salvation. Even the most cursory exploration of the scriptural material reveals that when explicit mention of divine immutability appears, it is often accompanied with a soteriological concern and emphasis. This paradigm holds true even in the major passages discussed in Chapter Four. For example, consider the oft-cited passages of Malachi 3:6; Numbers 23:19-24; Hebrews 6:13-20; Hebrews 7:22-28; and James 1:16-18. Each of these five passages – two in the Old Testament and three in the New Testament – comes up frequently when discussing the doctrine of divine immutability yet it is easy to miss the soteriological concern of each; I will list them here at length that I may reference them in the remaining pages:

> For I the LORD do not change; therefore you, O children of Jacob, are not consumed (Mal. 3:6).

> God is not man, that he should lie,
> or a son of man, that he should change his mind.
> Has he said, and will he not do it?
> Or has he spoken, and will he not fulfill it?
> Behold, I received a command to bless:
> he has blessed, and I cannot revoke it.
> He has not beheld misfortune in Jacob,
> nor has he seen trouble in Israel.
> The LORD their God is with them,
> and the shout of a king is among them.
> God brings them out of Egypt
> and is for them like the horns of the wild ox.
> For there is no enchantment against Jacob,
> no divination against Israel;
> now it shall be said of Jacob and Israel,
> 'What has God wrought!'
> Behold, a people! As a lioness it rises up
> and as a lion it lifts itself;
> it does not lie down until it has devoured the prey
> and drunk the blood of the slain (Num. 23:19-24).

For when God made a promise to Abraham, since he had no one greater by whom to swear, he swore by himself, saying, 'Surely I will bless you and multiply you.' And thus Abraham, having patiently waited, obtained the promise. For people swear by something greater than themselves, and in all their disputes an oath is final for confirmation. So, when God desired to show more convincingly to the heirs of the promise the unchangeable character of his purpose, he guaranteed it with an oath, so that by two unchangeable things, in which it is impossible for God to lie, we who have fled for refuge might have strong encouragement to hold fast to the hope set before us. We have this as a sure and steadfast anchor of the soul, a hope that enters into the inner place behind the curtain, where Jesus has gone as a forerunner on our behalf, having become a high priest forever after the order of Melchizedek (Heb. 6:13-20).

This makes Jesus the guarantor of a better covenant. The former priests were many in number, because they were prevented by death from continuing in office, but he holds his priesthood permanently, because he continues forever. Consequently, he is able to save to the uttermost those who draw near to God through him, since he always lives to make intercession for them. For it was indeed fitting that we should have such a high priest, holy, innocent, unstained, separated from sinners, and exalted above the heavens. He has no need, like those high priests, to offer sacrifices daily, first for his own sins and then for those of the people, since he did this once for all when he offered up himself. For the law appoints men in their weakness as high priests, but the word of the oath, which came later than the law, appoints a Son who has been made perfect forever (Heb. 7:22-28).

Do not be deceived, my beloved brothers. Every good gift and every perfect gift is from above, coming down from the Father of lights, with whom there is no variation or shadow due to change. Of his own will he brought us forth by the word of truth, that we should be a kind of firstfruits of his creatures (James 1:16-18).

In each instance, the reality of God's immutability is directly related to His being qualified and able to save. In the first example, Malachi 3:6, the implication of the indicative, 'I the LORD do not change,' is good news for Israel as it prevents God's people from being consumed.[6] The Israelites were surrounded by foreign nations that came and went by the sovereign providence of their God. Even though the history of Israel was a story of waning and waxing faithfulness, the people need not fear being consumed by the Lord thanks to His inalterability.

In Balaam's oracles in the book of Numbers, to Balak's disappointment, God gives the Mesopotamian prophet a word concerning Israel. Though hired by his sponsor to pronounce judgment and cursing on God's people, Balaam instead thrice over blesses the Israelites. In his second oracle, recorded in Numbers 23:18-24, Balaam blesses Israel and reminds the people of God's care for them. This providential care is painted as a mighty force as Balaam compares YHWH to a shouting king (23:21), the horns of a wild ox (23:22), and a roaring lion on the hunt for its prey (23:24). The strong king of Numbers 23 will protect His people from harm and the people may rest assured in this reality. The assurance lies a few verses prior as Balaam declares that this strong God is, 'not man, that he should lie, or a son of man, that he should change his mind' (23:19). The contrasting of the divine consistency and inalterability with the frailty of man's wavering means that the prophet can ask, rhetorically, 'Has he said, and will he not do it? Or has he spoken, and will he not fulfill it?' The logic of the passage is founded upon God's unchanging nature, which results in the assurance of God's people that what He has said, He will accomplish; and it is for their good, as 'what he has said' happens to be their ultimate protection by virtue of His unchanging power and providence.

Turning toward the three examples from the New Testament, we will treat Hebrews 6 with greater detail as we examine the relationship between divine immutability and functional Christology in the next section. However, it is worth mentioning in the current section as we seek to see the biblical pattern of a soteriological emphasis of divine immutability in the pages of Scripture. As for Hebrews 6, this pattern is not hard to spot. For, in this vital passage, 'the heirs of the promise' – that is, the promise of Abraham – may know more convincingly

---

6. It is for this reason that Walter Kaiser, *Malachi: God's Unchanging Love* (Grand Rapids: Baker, 1984) 77, notes the two emphases of the pericope covering the material from Malachi 2:17 through 3:12 should be God's unchanging ways, especially as it relates to His justice and faithfulness toward Israel.

the unchanging nature of God's work by virtue of His swearing by Himself. The scene that unfolds in these few verses is vital as, to borrow from and tweak Anselm a touch, God is seen as *that-which-there-is-nothing-greater-to-swear-by*. Since people swear by something greater than themselves, and there is nothing greater than God, He swears by Himself, showing the utter inalterability of His covenant faithfulness. Now, two unchanging elements have been brought into the discourse – God's own nature and His word of promise – which results in the 'strong encouragement' and 'sure and steadfast anchor for the soul.'

The biblical pattern of emphasizing the soteriological concern of immutability carries into chapter 7 of Hebrews as well. Juxtaposing the high priests of the people of Israel with Christ's work as priest, the author of Hebrews invokes Jesus' unique quality of atemporality, and therefore immutability, when describing Christ's priestly work. Of the former priests, the author points out that there were many in number. Israel's priests came and went as they each perished in death. The priests' mortality and temporality necessitated an ever-increasing proliferation in priests as 'they were prevented by death from continuing in office' (Heb. 7:23). Contrary to the former priests, Jesus' priestly qualification descends through the line of Melchizedek, and His eternality uniquely qualifies Him to serve as a better priest than any who descend from the loins of Levi. Jesus, unlike the former priests, is unchanging and eternal, which renders Jesus 'the guarantor of a better covenant' (7:22). The author bends the indicative of Jesus' ontological eternality and immutability in the direction of soteriology explicitly with the adverb 'consequently.' The consequence of Jesus being the guarantor of a better covenant due to His eternality is that 'he is able to save to the uttermost those who draw near to God through him, since he always lives to make intercession for them.'

Finally, looking briefly at the passage from which this book takes its name, James 1:17 brings together the doctrine of divine immutability and soteriological benefits in a single sentence. James writes: 'Every good gift and every perfect gift is from above, coming down from the Father of lights, with whom there is no variation or shadow due to change.' The first clause in this cosmically beautiful sentence hints at the notion that in the bank of blessings that believers enjoy, not one deposit was made by anyone other than God Himself. What's more, God's people may have assurance of the permanence of these good gifts *because* their God is the Father of lights and as such experiences no shadow of turning. Lights come, lights fade; supernovas obliterate the luminance of even the brightest stars and eclipses cast a shadow on even the brightest moons. However, with this God – the Father of lights – there is no such turning or variableness that could cause believers to doubt the good gifts they have received from Him.

To bring these five examples together in a more succinct view, and to demonstrate the biblical pattern of emphasizing Scripture's soteriological concern more easily when dealing with divine immutability, this chart may prove helpful:

Passage	Emphasis on Divine Immutability	Soteriological Concern and Emphasis
Malachi 3:6	'For I the LORD do not change.'	'therefore you, O children of Jacob, are not consumed.'
Numbers 23:19-24	'God is not man, that he should lie, or a son of man, that he should change his mind.'	'Has he said, and will he not do it? Or has he spoken, and will he not fulfill it?'
Hebrews 6:13-20	'So, when God desired to show more convincingly to the heirs of the promise the unchangeable character of his purpose, he guaranteed it with an oath, so that by two unchangeable things, in which it is impossible for God to lie.'	'we who have fled for refuge might have strong encouragement to hold fast to the hope set before us. We have this as a sure and steadfast anchor of the soul, a hope that enters into the inner place behind the curtain, where Jesus has gone as a forerunner on our behalf, having become a high priest forever after the order of Melchizedek.'

Passage	Emphasis on Divine Immutability	Soteriological Concern and Emphasis
Hebrews 7:22-28	'The former priests were many in number, because they were prevented by death from continuing in office, but he holds his priesthood permanently, because he continues forever.'	'Consequently, he is able to save to the uttermost those who draw near to God through him, since he always lives to make intercession for them.'
James 1:16-18	'With whom there is no variation or shadow due to change.'	'Every good gift and every perfect gift is from above, coming down from the Father of lights.'

Table 6.1. Scripture's Soteriological Concern with Divine Immutability

While it would be imposing a pattern on the scriptural data that is not univocally present to say that all biblical mentions of divine immutability have a corollary soteriological emphasis, it is nevertheless a consistent theme. These five passages provide an important lesson for how the Scriptures speak about divine immutability, which is often with soteriology and God's covenant faithfulness in view. The lesson we learn from these five pericopes, and others like them, is that our conversations pertaining to God's *ad extra* work must not be divorced from contemplation of God's life *ad intra*. Simply put, *theologia* (theology) and *oikonomia* (economy) must be kept in that proper order, and the *oikonomia* – while worthy of theological exploration itself – will have richer meaning when contemplated as a derivative of *theologia*.

This is the heart of this book's general thesis – to recapture the divine life as the primary aim of Christian theological contemplation and reprioritize God's own Triune nature as the foundation of proper theological method. As Ivor Davidson notes: 'Soteriology's particular but spacious remit is to retell the grand sweep of this divine economy as announced in Scripture: to identify the source, occurrence and

182

consequences of salvation by speaking of the nature of the one who lets us know him as he really is.'[7]

Moreover, these five passages not only get at the heart of the general thesis but also the specific thesis. The pattern of these five passages reveals that when the biblical writers brought up God's inalterability, they did so to invoke assurance in their hearers. In God's economic activity He has set His providential power toward the good of His people, and the good news of God's care is inalterably good news, for He is an inalterable God. Divine immutability is the foundation of God's covenant faithfulness, and God's covenant faithfulness is the foundation of the church's assurance. This connection becomes clearer as we continue to look at the biblical drama of salvation and examine the relationship between God's immutability and functional Christology.

Divine Immutability and Functional Christology

Jesus Christ is the cornerstone of the Christian enterprise. As such, it should not be surprising that the theological field that bears His name spans both continents and millennia. Christology as a theological discipline has expanded and evolved over the centuries as the church seeks to best describe the Second Person of the Trinity. In her attempt to articulate the doctrine of her Lord, the church's Christological conversation has shifted with the contextual junctures throughout antiquity. Consistent, however, in this ever-changing conversation about Christ has been questions regarding His *person* and *work*.

Theologians often categorize these two concepts under the umbrella of ontological and functional Christology; ontological pertaining to that which belongs to Christ's being or person and functional referring to the works which Christ performed.[8] Throughout this project, there has been

---

7. Ivor Davidson, 'Introduction: God of Salvation' in *God of Salvation*, 7. In the same collection of essays, John Webster makes a similar observation. See, Webster, '"It was the Will of the Lord to Bruise Him": Soteriology and the Doctrine of God,' in *God of Salvation*, 16.

8. It is important to note both of these phrases, ontological and functional, have gone through revisions. Consequently, this definition is not universally used in modern theology. For example, Stephen Wellum agrees that ontological Christology is that branch of Christology that refers to Christ's 'nature or being.' However, Wellum states that ontological Christology 'usually stresses Christ's deity over against his humanity' (Stephen Wellum, 'Jesus as Lord and Son: Two Complementary Truths of Biblical Christology,' *Criswell Theological Review* 13.1 [2015]: 24). Wellum is not alone in using ontological

a repetition of the reality that we should not attempt to render asunder God's essence and His activity. This is true not only of Trinitarianism in a broad way but also specifically of Christology. Christological studies are at their best when Christian theologians refuse to divorce these two categories of ontological and functional Christology.

However, the relationship between these two Christological categories is a story of ebbing proximity and distance. In the modern era there is a perceived distance between the ontological and functional aspects of Christology. Of this problem, Veli-Matti Kärkkäinen stated: 'the integral link between the person and work of Christ has led theologians to a growing realization of the connection between "functional" (what Christ has done for us) and "ontological" (who Christ is in his person) Christologies. Yet at the same time, works of Christology tend to focus on one or the other.'[9]

As scholars 'focus on one or the other,' there is an 'ever-widening fissure'[10] between the person and work of Christ. Of this fissure, Marcus Peter Johnson said, 'in far too many evangelical expressions of the gospel, the saving work of Christ has been so distanced from his person that the notion of a saving *personal* union with the incarnate, crucified, resurrected, *living* Jesus strikes us as rather outlandish.'[11]

Christology synonymously with Christ's divinity, and he is right to express the *primary* conversation regarding Christ's ontology focuses on divinity. However, since we can talk of Christ's ontological humanity, this chapter will instead employ Grant Macaskill's understanding of the categories. Macaskill says: 'the use of the word "ontology" may imply an assumption about the way in which Paul considers Jesus to be "divine".... [T] he word "ontology" is simply used to describe what Paul considers God and Jesus to "be" or what he understands as the constituent elements of their "being"' (Grant Macaskill, 'Incarnational Ontology and the Theology of Participation in Paul,' in *"In Christ" in Paul: Explorations in Paul's Theology of Union and Participation,* ed. Michael J. Thate, Kevin J. Vanhoozer, Constantine R. Campbell [Grand Rapids: Eerdmans, 2014], 87).

9. Veli-Matti Kärkkäinen, *Christology: A Global Introduction,* 2nd ed. (Grand Rapids: Baker Academic, 2016), 4. Kärkkäinen has elsewhere discussed this issue. Drawing a dichotomy between the way theologians have done Christology in the past with the methodology of the present, he says, 'Ontology and functionality cannot be distinguished in such a categorical way as older theology did, nor is it useful to do so. Who Jesus Christ is determines what he does; what he does reflects and grows out of who he is.' See Veli-Matti Kärkkäinen, *Christ and Reconciliation: A Constructive Christian Theology for the Pluralistic World,* 4 vols. (Grand Rapids: Eerdmans, 2013) 1:40.

10. Marcus Peter Johnson, *One with Christ: An Evangelical Theology of Salvation* (Wheaton: Crossway, 2013), 15.

11. Ibid., 15. Elsewhere, Johnson has insightfully pointed out typical evangelical language as evidence of this dichotomy. He says, 'let us take a moment to consider our habits of

In line with Kärkkäinen's assessment regarding the need to bring ontological and functional Christology together, a number of contemporary scholars have consciously made this shift. For instance, Oliver Crisp presented readers with a '"joined-up" account of the person and work of Christ.'[12] Stephen Wellum argued ontology and functionality can never truly be torn asunder for, 'who Christ is determines what he does; what he does reveals who he is.'[13] Moreover, Wellum's Christology, *God the Son Incarnate*, is a full-length treatment exhorting readers in the mending of this relationship by seeing Christ in His being as the Son without losing the work of His incarnation.[14] In the field of biblical theology, Brandon Crowe offered readers an examination of the importance of Christ's *life* during His incarnation as opposed to focusing solely on His *death*.[15] In doing so, Crowe's work in the Gospels mends the gap between Jesus' person and work.

As we examine the unfolding drama of God's redemption of His people, the need to keep connected Christ's person and work becomes evident. Michael Horton said that the Old Testament interprets history 'as the story of a covenant made and a covenant broken' and that the New Testament builds on this interpretation.[16] The drama of the covenant broken begins in the Garden wherein Adam fails in his role as covenant representative and therefore brings about the soteric plight of his posterity – the need for and inability to obtain righteousness.

The inability to obtain this needed righteousness becomes the recurring refrain of the entirety of the Old Testament. From the firstfruits

---

speech. We often talk, for instance, about trusting the finished work of Christ rather than the living person of Christ for our salvation. We talk about our sins being nailed to the cross rather than our sins being borne away in the body and soul of Christ' (Marcus Peter Johnson and John C. Clark, *The Incarnation of God: The Mystery of the Gospel as the Foundation of Evangelical Theology* [Wheaton: Crossway, 2015], 104. Emphasis original).

12. Oliver D. Crisp, *The Word Enfleshed: Exploring the Person and Work of Christ* (Grand Rapids: Baker, 2016), xi.

13. Stephen Wellum, *Christ Alone: The Uniqueness of Jesus as Savior* (Grand Rapids: Zondervan, 2017), 107. Emphasis original.

14. Stephen J. Wellum, *God the Son Incarnate: The Doctrine of Christ* (Wheaton: Crossway, 2015).

15. Brandon D. Crowe, *The Last Adam: A Theology of the Obedient Life of Jesus in the Gospels* (Grand Rapids: Baker, 2017).

16. Michael Horton, *Lord and Servant: A Covenant Christology* (Louisville: Westminster John Knox, 2005), 121.

of the patriarchs' sinful rebellion against the God who established them as the covenant people to the postexilic period's propensity to abandon the God of their fathers, what we read throughout the entire of the Old Testament is covenantal infidelity on the part of God's chosen people.

It is into this postlapsarian setting that Christ assumed human nature in the incarnation. In so doing, Jesus served as the covenant redeemer, overcoming sin and fulfilling the law. Brandon Crowe, emphasizing the *life* of Jesus and not only His death, said: 'As the last Adam, Jesus is the obedient Son who serves a representative capacity, vicariously attaining the life through obedience that Adam did not.'[17] The scriptural statement of this reality is found in the fact that, according to Romans 5, 'many were made righteous' through Christ and that, in another Pauline passage, those who are 'in him' would become 'the righteousness of God' (2 Cor. 5:21).[18] So then, while those 'in' the first Adam have a personally insurmountable plight in their need of righteousness, their cosmic need finds solution in the imputed obedient righteousness of the Son, the Last Adam.

In the covenantal relationship between God and His people, and Christ's role in rectifying the creation back to its Creator, the seriousness of sin is on full display. In covenant violation, the people of God lay down their right standing before the Triune God and pick up a need for an alien righteousness, a need for propitiation, a need for expiation, a need for atonement, a need for a mediator, and a need for someone foreign to them to provide a work they are not qualified to perform. The uniqueness of this plight is one example of the vital need of keeping the divine person in view of our soteriology. For, in the person and work of Christ we find a redemption accomplished by the only One with satisfactory qualification, and divine immutability plays a crucial role.

We saw how vital Christ's changelessness was for the economy of redemption in the book of Hebrews as it is Christ's immutability, via His divine nature, that enables Him to act as a priest on behalf of the

---

17. Crowe, *The Last Adam*, 203. Along with Brandon Crowe, on the relationship between the old Adam and new Adam as covenantal representatives, see J. V. Fesko, *Death in Adam, Life in Christ: The Doctrine of Imputation* (Fearn, Ross-shire, UK: Christian Focus, 2016).

18. As Crowe, *The Last Adam*, 204, points out, however, the necessity and reality of the obedient life of Jesus is not a teaching isolated to the Epistles.

people of God forever. Unlike the 'former priests' who were prevented by death from providing a sacrifice once and for all for the people, Christ, in His immutable eternality, can perform an immutably sufficient sacrifice on the basis of His inalterable holiness. As it was an eternal, infinite, immutable God who was offended as humankind's first parents sunk their teeth into the forbidden fruit, justice and propitiation will necessitate nothing short of an eternal, infinite, immutable sacrifice on the offender's behalf.

To pull from the book of Hebrews once again, 'Jesus Christ is the same yesterday and today and forever' (Heb. 13:8). The immutability of Christ comes as eternally good news to those who have been united to Him. It is in Christ's inalterability – by virtue of His divine nature – that many of the functional needs of the economy of redemption are met. In the immutable Christ, God's people find an unchanging mediator who ever pleads their innocence before God and in the immutable Christ, God's people find an unchanging adoption in which they'll ever be endowed the underserved script of 'Abba, Father.' In the immutable Christ, God's people find an unchanging righteousness granted them as the merits of Christ become their own. In the immutable Christ, God's people find an unchanging atonement in which the spilt blood forever pardons their darkest sins. And it is in the immutable Christ that God's people find an unchanging resurrection in which they'll ascend to the right hand of the Father and enjoy the prize of their faith evermore. The immutability of the second person of the Trinity – Jesus Christ – protects vital elements needed for the economy of redemption. Christ immutably protects the righteousness and merits needed for reconciliation, He protects the once-and-for-all sacrifice needed to propitiate the just wrath of the Father, He protects the priestly intercession needed as He pleads on our behalf, and He protects the eternal resurrection and ascension to the right hand of the Father.

Divine Perfections and Soteriology

A consequence of God's simplicity, as Steven Duby notes, is that 'Divine action *ad extra* is just God's essence with a relation to the creature.'[19] If this be true, then an important ingredient in soteriological studies should

---

19. Duby, *God in Himself,* 185. Duby continues, building off Aquinas, 'in particular, as Thomas describes it, a divine mission is just the procession with the addition of a created, temporal *terminus ad quem.*'

be the divine persons as they are in themselves. Sadly, however, the divine perfections are not only ignored but often seen as hostile toward God's economic activity. Stephen Holmes notes this unfortunate phenomenon, saying, 'Whilst what were once called the "communicable" perfections of God – love, justice, mercy, wrath perhaps – still find some deployment in accounts of soteriology, the so-called "incommunicable" perfections – eternity, aseity, impassibility, simplicity – are not only not deployed, but are routinely criticized as inappropriate accretions that should have no place in Christian theology.'[20] Holmes is wise to note that the so-called 'communicable' perfections are still utilized in soteric discussions as it is difficult to conceive of a thoroughly Christian salvation without attributes such as love, justice, mercy, and wrath. However, for the economy of redemption it should be just as nonsensical to articulate God's salvation without the classical perfections of simplicity, aseity, and atemporality.

This vital point in Christian soteriology is significant for the thesis of this project because not only do the classical divine perfections bear soteriological significance, *but they do also so immutably*. Stephen Charnock, quoted in Chapter Five, once again proves helpful here. Charnock calls the perfection of divine immutability the 'enamel' of all other perfections and says it is 'a glory belonging to all the attributes of God.'[21] Charnock discusses immutability as the 'glorious sunbeam' whose 'rays' illuminate and brighten the corollary perfections. For, none of the perfections of God would be rendered good news to the creature if they were to fade or wither. Charnock concludes:

> How cloudy would his blessedness be if it were changeable; how dim his wisdom if it might be obscured; how feeble his power if it were capable to be sickly and languish; how would mercy lose much of its lustre if it could change into wrath, and justice much of its dread if it could be turned into mercy, while the object of justice remains unfit for mercy, and one that hath need of mercy continues only fit for the divine fury? But unchangeableness is a thread that runs through the whole web, it is the enamel of all the rest; none of them without it could look with a triumphant aspect.[22]

---

20. Stephen R. Holmes, 'A Simple Salvation? Soteriology and the Perfections of God,' in *God of Salvation: Soteriology in Theological Perspective*, ed. Ivor J. Davidson and Murray A. Rae (Burlington: Ashgate, 2011), 37.

21. Charnock, *Discourse on the Existence and Attributes of God*, 1:381.

22. Ibid., 1:381.

It is therefore important for us to take another look at divine immutability's corollary perfections in hopes of demonstrating some of each perfection's soteriological import and its relationship to divine immutability in the economy of redemption. Processing the attributes with an eye toward God's *ad extra* work will allow us to accomplish two important tasks for this project: (1) We see, by virtue of immutability's simple relationship with other divine attributes, further soteriological implications of God's changelessness (accomplishing the specific thesis); and (2) We observe a brief, but important, sampling of how other divine perfections also bear soteriological implications (accomplishing the general thesis). We here keep our study to two perfections – divine simplicity and divine aseity. After looking at each of these two perfections, we then turn to the vital metaphysical category of pure actuality, which undergirds many of the divine perfections and together with immutability bears significant soteriological significance.

Divine Simplicity, Immutability, and Soteriology

We begin our venture through a few of the classical perfections with divine simplicity because doing so will remind us to take care in treating these attributes in separate categories and due to simplicity's important role in answering some of the objections against immutability raised in Chapter Two. Turretin advocates four reasons Christian theologians should argue in favor of a classical articulation of divine simplicity – God's independence, unity, perfection, and activity.[23] God is independent and therefore must be simple, as a composition would necessitate a composer,[24] or at least parts to make up the composition. God is unified and therefore 'absolutely one' such that He is unable to be divided. God, in His perfection, may not alter as to either increase nor decrease His glory (otherwise, according to Turretin, we would render God passive, dependent, and mutable). God is pure actuality and has 'no passive admixture.'

With these four deductions, Turretin arrives at simplicity and helps us situate soteriology as derivative of God Himself. On the basis of

---

23. Turretin, *IET*, III.VII.4.

24. Matthew Barrett, *None Greater*, 77. Scott Swain makes this point as well; Swain, *The Trinity: An Introduction* (Wheaton: Crossway, 2021), 58. Swain notes, 'All composition presupposes a composer.'

divine simplicity, we affirm the supreme unity of the divine essence and will. Therefore, as the Triune God sets His face toward the redemption of His creature, we can be confident that any movement *ad extra* will be an operation that cannot be properly separated amongst the persons of the Trinity. God's simplicity necessitates inseparable operations in which the three persons of the Godhead move and act in unison of essence and will. Simplicity, then, saves us from the soteric disaster of a Father's economy conflicting with the Son's economy conflicting with the Spirit's economy. Rather, each member of the Godhead, in the *ad extra*, operates inseparably and pursues the wayward sinner in unchanging unison.[25]

The issue of economic disagreement amongst the Godhead is not the only soteriological disaster from which divine simplicity saves. Another is that of pitting divine perfections against one another as if some perfections were more supremely active in God's economic relation with His creature than other attributes. For example, it is inappropriate to say that the passion of Christ and the gloriously bitter scene of His crucifixion was a demonstration of love alone. Nor would it be appropriate to explicate eschatological judgment as an exercise of God's wrath apart from other perfections. On the contrary, as salvation is God's revelation of Himself in such a way that He reorders a sin-stained world back to Himself, we ought to see the whole of the economy as God's simple essence in action. Moments in the *pactum salutis* and steps within the *ordo salutis* are not to be taken as expressions of one attribute over another but rather as a harmonious and benevolent grace of a God who is simple and pure act. Divine simplicity, then, saves us from the soteric misstep of pitting perfection against perfection, which is so often done in soteriology with something like God's love and justice.

As stated previously, the goal of this study is not to respond point by point to the deviations and denials leveraged against the doctrine of divine immutability articulated in Chapter Two. However, God's simple essence does give us an important point in assessing and answering some of the objections to a classical articulation of divine immutability. As we saw in Chapter Two, a major impetus for theologians to deviate from divine immutability is soteriological concern. How could an unchanging God *truly* relate to creatures who are in desperate need of redemption?

---

25. For more on the doctrine of inseparable operations, see Vidu, *The Same God Who Works All Things*.

How might a God of changelessness, in any meaningful way, respond to prayer, aid the hurting, reconcile the sinful, or 'move' from wrath to kindness toward a rebellious people? This soteriological conundrum has had enough explanatory power to make some contemporary theologians conclude that a denial of divine immutability is the best course of action. On the other hand, some theologians have gone not the way of outright denial; rather they have deviated from the classical articulation in hopes of keeping both an understanding of divine immutability and a true reciprocal relation of change between the Creator and the creature.

Recall Bruce Ware's articulation of divine immutability from Chapter Two, for example. Ware hopes to do justice both to God's being 'transcendently self-existent' and 'immanently self-relating.'[26] Attempting the balance between these two poles leads Ware to affirm that God possesses onto-ethical immutability while still predicating real change and alteration to God by virtue of His relationships and volition. For Ware, while God's essence and ethics remain changeless, He nevertheless undergoes real alteration as He immanently relates to the creature and undergoes volitional and relational adaptation.

However, while we should applaud Dr Ware's attempt to be thoroughly biblical and systematically consistent in his articulation of God's changelessness, I nevertheless propose that we should see Ware's project as unconvincing on the basis of divine simplicity. For God to maintain a measure of onto-ethical immutability while experiencing real change in both relations and volition, God would need to be a compositional being such that portions of Him may remain unchangeable while others undergo alteration. This is consistent with Aquinas' rebuttal that anything that changes 'remains as it was in part, and passes away in part.'[27] Charnock insisted that 'mutability belongs to contingency' and said,

> Mutability is absolutely inconsistent with simplicity, whether the change come from an internal or external principle. If a change be wrought by something without, it supposeth either contrary or various parts in the thing so changed, whereof it doth consist; if it be wrought by anything within, it supposeth that the thing so changed doth consist of one part that doth change it, and another part that is changed, and so it would not be a simple being.[28]

---

26. Ware, *Evangelical Reexamination*, 384.

27. Aquinas, *ST*, Ia9, cf. Ia3.

28. Charnock, *Works*, 1:393.

Divine simplicity's relationship to immutability and soteriology is vital, for God's non-composition both protects us from soteriological tragedies as mentioned above and, in the positive, provides a necessary ingredient for God's unified and inseparable operation in the *ad extra* to redeem an undeserving people. We will see another soteriological implication of divine simplicity when we turn our attention to the economic implications of God's pure actuality.

Divine Aseity, Immutability, and Soteriology

Affirming John Webster's assertion that divine aseity must not be understood as an apophatic doctrine only, nor only by way of negation, the doctrine of divine aseity teaches, in the positive, that God has life in Himself.[29] Four passages are important in establishing the soteriological significance of divine aseity – Exodus 3, Psalm 102, Isaiah 43, and John 5.

In Exodus 3, readers find themselves witnesses to one of the most famous theophanies in the Old Testament – the burning bush. In this scene God is recruiting a messenger who is to deliver a message of hope to His people. God says, 'I have surely seen the affliction of my people who are in Egypt and have heard their cry because of their taskmasters. I know their sufferings, and I have come down to deliver them out of the hand of the Egyptians and to bring them up out of that land to a good and broad land.' This anthem of coming hope is to be communicated back to God's people, yet Moses recognizes a problem. Moses is in an issue of authority. He is worried that, given their current plight of bondage, none of God's people will believe the message he has been sent to proclaim. So, looking to stake his message on the sender's authority, Moses asks, 'if I come to the people of Israel and say to them, "the God of your fathers has sent me to you," and they ask me, "what is his name?" what shall I say to them?' This question leads to one of the most famous answers in the Hebrew Bible as God says back to His servant, 'I am who I am.' God continues, 'Say this to the people of Israel: "I AM has sent me to you."'

In his commentary on the book of Exodus, Douglas Stuart says of this revealing name of the Lord:

> Here the revelation of the name Yahweh is first given in its first-person form, *'ahyeh*, later vocalized by the medieval Masoretes and also understood by

---

29. See, Webster, 'Life in Himself,' 13-28.

the translators of the LXX as the simple imperfect tense of the verb 'to be' (in the earliest Hb. *hwh*, later *hyh*), thus *'ehyeh*, I am,' rather than the early Canaanite causative (what later became the hiphil in Hb.), which means 'I cause to be.' The name should thus be understood as referring to Yahweh's being the creator and sustainer of all that exists and thus the Lord of both creation and history, all that is and all that is happening – a God active and present in historical affairs.[30]

While interpretations differ at points, one consistent remark regarding Exodus 3 is that what is being communicated is presence. Cole says it this way: 'since this is the only place in the Old Testament where there is any explanation of the meaning of the name YHWH, we ought therefore to take very seriously the association with "being" which is clearly stated here.'[31]

The presence of I AM is not contained to Exodus 3. Rather, as Christopher Holmes demonstrates in *The Lord is Good*, the Psalter has much to say about this *a se* being.[32] One such passage is found in Psalm 102, primarily in verses 25-28:

> Of old you laid the foundation of the earth,
> and the heavens are the work of your hands.
> They will perish, but you will remain;
> they will all wear out like a garment.
> You will change them like a robe, and they will pass away,
> but you are the same, and your years have no end.
> The children of your servants shall dwell secure;
> their offspring shall be established before you.

Reflecting on this psalm, Tremper Longman points out the connection between the immutability of the Lord and the assurance of His people. He states: 'His awareness that his life is short and fragile leads him to reflect on God's eternal nature. God was there at the beginning when he created the heavens and the earth.' He continues: 'They will not last

---

30. Douglas K. Stuart, *Exodus*, New American Commentary 2 (Nashville: Broadman & Holman Publishers, 2006), 121.

31. R. A. Cole, *Exodus: An Introduction and Commentary* (Downers Grove: InterVarsity Press, 1973), 76.

32. See, Christopher R. J. Holmes, *The Lord Is Good: Seeking the God of the Psalter* (Downers Grove: InterVarsity Press, 2018).

forever, but God will survive them. They are perishable, but God is imperishable. Since he will be there forever, he will be there in future generations, for the present generation's children and their children's children and so on.'[33] However, it is not just the doctrine of immutability that readers see in this psalm but that of aseity as well. The psalmist declares that God will change the heavens and earth like a robe. Only the One who is the basis and foundation of heaven and earth poses this kind of authority over both matter and men.

In the forty-third chapter of Isaiah the Lord declares: 'You are my witnesses ... and my servant whom I have chosen, that you may know and believe me and understand that I am he. Before me no god was formed, nor shall there be any after me. I, I am the LORD, and besides me there is no savior.' We see from this declaration that the Lord is exclusive in both His identity and His work. In His identity, He is the only who was not formed, nor was there any god before Him. In His work, He is the only one who is Savior. The causation aspect of aseity is prevalent in the clause, which asserts that God is not like that which has been formed. On the contrary, He is the party who does the forming. The Lord's exclusive *a se* identity renders Him capable of producing the heavens and earth *ex nihilo*.

Finally, and most importantly, John 5 is the most explicit of all the biblical passages mentioned thus far for the doctrine of divine aseity. While the context of the entire chapter is important, verses 25-29 provide the most significant section:

> Truly, truly, I say to you, an hour is coming, and is now here, when the dead will hear the voice of the Son of God, and those who hear will live. For as the Father has life in himself, so he has granted the Son also to have life in himself. And he has given him authority to execute judgment, because he is the Son of Man. Do not marvel at this, for an hour is coming when all who are in the tombs will hear his voice and come out, those who have done good to the resurrection of life, and those who have done evil to the resurrection of judgment.

About these verses, D. A. Carson states: 'The logical *for* (*gar*) is important: this verse explains how it is that the Son can exercise divine judgment

---

33. Tremper Longman III, *Psalms: An Introduction and Commentary* (Downers Grove: InterVaristy Press, 2014), 355.

and generate resurrection life by his powerful word.' He continues: 'It is because, like God, he has life-in-himself. God is self-existent; he is always "the living God." Mere human beings are derived creatures; our life comes from God, and he can remove it as easily as he gave it. But to the Son, and to the Son alone, God has imparted life-in-himself.'[34]

We plainly see the aseity of the Father here as the text explicitly says that the Father has life in Himself. However, as Webster described, aseity is rooted in the eternal modes of subsistence as the Father, who has life in Himself, grants that life-in-himself-ness to the Son via the eternal generation of the Son.

In the positive, these four passages show that God uniquely has life in Himself, which – in the negative, and only by derivation – means that God is not contingent upon anyone to give Him life or meaning. For this reason Stephen Holmes, discussing the soteric import of God's being *a se*, notes: 'If God is simple and *a se*, then nothing outside of God, which is to say nothing in creation, affects God's life in any way; this includes human (or angelic) sin.' Holmes continues: 'God is not damaged, lessened or hurt at all by our failures, nor is God restored, repaired, or set right in his own gracious act of salvation.'[35]

God's aseity, in relation to soteriology, means that He acts not out of a self-need – neither in response to sin nor by way of addition. It was not the case that sin's entrance into history caused an affront to God that rendered His existence lacking, nor was the enterprise of the economy of redemption pre-empted by any need in Him. God has the fullness of life in Himself, and with the fullness of life is the perfection of being. Being *a se*, God lacks nothing. From eternity to eternity, there is nothing God needs to complete Himself, nothing He's missing that would further fulfill Him, nothing outside of Him that would bring Him life. While some may be tempted to read this as bad news, we should avoid this temptation and see the soteriological wonder at play in this reality. If God's perfections, most importantly His being *a se*, means that God is supremely complete in His Triune life, we can have confidence that His redemption of a wayward people was not out of a deficiency in the divine life. Rather, God redeems the unredeemable out of the fullness of His own life and the grace

34. D. A. Carson, *The Gospel According to John*, Pillar New Testament Commentary (Grand Rapids: Eerdmans, 1991), 256.

35. Holmes, *A Simple Salvation?*, 43.

therein. Our redemption flows not out of a need in God but comes out of the God of grace. This means that the soteriological enterprise will not cease to exist when God has some felt need met. Rather, since God does not redeem on the basis of a felt need nor deficiency in Himself, those counting on Him for salvation can rest assured, knowing that He redeems out of His immutable fullness of life in Himself.

There is another soteriological consequence of God's aseity. As Webster noted, the primary definition of divine aseity should be rooted in the positive construction of the doctrine and insists on God's fullness of life in Himself. However, divine aseity does have a negative correlation of God's supreme non-contingency. The negative corollary of the ontological property of being *a se* means both that nothing gives life to God and, on the contrary, that God is the supreme contingency of all else. There is an *ex nihilo* power in God, rooted in His aseity, that gives Him the exclusive capability and qualification to bring something out of nothing. The primary place we see God exercise His *ex nihilo* power is in creation, yet this is not the only place we witness His wonder. For, the *ex nihilo* power on display in God's calling forth the cosmos out of nothing is the same omnipotence at work when the Triune God calls forth faith in rebellious sinners where no faith was before.[36] Regeneration *ex nihilo* requires a God of aseity. As the creature, we have not life in ourselves, and we have not life again in ourselves. Both our existence and our regeneration find their source in God.

Divine simplicity and divine aseity are but two perfections that bear soteriological significance. We could turn to other perfections, such as impassibility, eternality, omnipotence, omniscience, and omnipresence, in examining soteriological significance as well. However, the two classical attributes of simplicity and aseity prove to be helpful examples in showing how the divine perfections, each in their own way, bear soteriological significance – *and they do so immutably*.

Actus Purus, Immutability, and Soteriology

To elaborate on our example from the introduction of this chapter, when relating God's essence to the *ad extra* operation in the economy

---

36. Of course, this is said analogously, as the major difference exists that in creation there was no matter present whereas in regeneration there is at least matter. However, it is still out of nothing from which faith arises in the unregenerate.

of redemption, one metaphysical point becomes increasingly vital – pure actuality. When speaking of the essence of creatures it is, at least somewhat, appropriate to seek to articulate the *what-ness* that constitutes their being. However, when describing God's *esse*, we must insist on the term maintaining its proper part of speech and emphasize God's essence as a verb. God is not a *something* in act, but according to the doctrine of *actus purus*, God simply *is* pure act. Thomas Weinandy states this well:

> For the essence of God to be *ipsum esse* means that God is pure act. For God to be pure act then does not mean that God is *something* fully in act, but rather that God is act pure and simple. There is *no-thing*, no essence (in finite sense) in God to be actualized, but just act or *esse* itself. Likewise, to say that God has no potency does not mean that God in some way fully actualized all his potential comparable to a man who has fully actualized all his potential, but rather God has no potency because there is no potency to actualize. He is *actus purus*.[37]

We see, in Weinandy's description of *actus purus*, not a God who is actualized but who is pure act. Gisbertus Voetius demonstrates that *actus purus* is a necessary ingredient of perfection. For God to possess passive potency would entail He possesses that which is perfectible. Voetius writes:

> God is pure act without mixture of any potency. For, if there were potency in God, there would exist in him something imperfect or perfectible for which an act would be perfective, through which perfective act some higher perfection would encroach upon God. We demonstrate the consequence of the major proposition, because every composition is from act and potency, just as every composite is. For genus, matter, integrated part, essence, nature, and subject all have the concept of potency; and, on the other hand, difference, form, integrating part, existence, suppositum, and accidence all have the concept of act.[38]

Of course, these articulations of pure act have not come without their critiques. Rob Lister, for example, bemoans that Weinandy's conception of pure actuality would lead to God's being 'never, properly speaking, responsive.'[39] Lister's worry here is important, for it gets at the heart of

---

37. Weinandy, *Does God Change?*, 78, emphasis original.
38. Gisbertus Voetius, 'God's Single, Absolutely Simple Essence,' trans. R. M. Hurd, *The Confessional Presbyterian* 15 (2019): 13.
39. Lister, *God is Impassible and Impassioned*, 157, n. 38.

actus purus' role in Christian soteriology. Lister is worried that a God who lacks all potency has not the relational qualities for a meaningful response toward creatures. If God is pure act, without any trace of potency, how might He – in any meaningful sense – respond to my woes and worries? Lister's worry is not novel. Indeed, we have seen this in abundance throughout Chapter Two when we covered the denial of divine immutability on the predication of a soteriological/relational movement in God. Isaak Dorner, for example, lamented that God would be a 'rigid dead substance' and 'lifeless … [and] motionless in itself.'[40]

The remonstrance against pure actuality that decries immobility brings us to the meeting place of *actus purus*, divine immutability, and the economy of redemption. Contrary to Lister, Dorner, and the like, who insist that an unchanging God of pure act would be rigidly immobile, a God who is *actus purus* occupies the polar opposite side of the movement spectrum than an immobile object. To explain, Weinandy calls to mind the difference between a rock and God. Both God and the rock are said to be unmoving; however, inalterability is the only commonality they share, and they share it for antithetical reasons. A rock, says Weinandy, is unchanging on the basis that it is hardly in act at all. The rock does not move, make, speak, or do much at all and is thus unchanging. God's inalterability is on the opposite end of the spectrum, however, as His inalterability is rooted in dynamism. As Weinandy notes: 'God is unchangeable not because he is inert or static like a rock, but for just the opposite reason. He is so dynamic, so active that no change can make him more active.'[41] Weinandy relates this to the doctrine of divine immutability, saying,

> Thus, to say that God is immutable is to deny something of God that is inherent in finite reality. However, while it is a negative adjective, it is based on something positive which makes God unlike creatures, that is, the fact that God is pure act, being itself. God is immutable, then, for Aquinas, not because he is static, inert, or inactive, but precisely because he is so supremely active and dynamic, because he is pure act. He is so much in act that it is ontologically impossible to be more in act. Paradoxically God is supremely immutable because he is supremely active.[42]

---

40. Dorner, *Divine Immutability*, 137.
41. Weinandy, *Does God Change?*, 79.
42. Ibid., 78.

Charnock succinctly makes this important point, 'He is a pure act, nothing but vigour and act.'[43] At no point, based on both His divine immutability and pure actuality, is God *not* in act. When God set His face toward the rescue of the wayward in the economy of redemption, the *ad extra* operation was not a potency within God but a demonstration of His pure actuality. This means, as a soteriological significance of divine immutability, that God is not *moved* into action to redeem His people. It was not the sinner's helpless estate that so moved God that He then decided to act as the benefactor for His people. Nor was it the prevalence of sinfulness that moved God to finally send His only begotten Son. It was not the degradation of God's holy law that made the idea of redemption spring up in God as an idea or act that was not previously there. Rather, God redeems on the basis of Himself.

The significance of God's economy of redemption being a redemption of divine freedom and pure actuality can be illustrated by recalling Hartshorne's poem puzzle. Let the reader recall Hartshorne's poem predicament from Chapter Two, in which Charles Hartshorne poses a poem being read to six different audience members: (1) a glass of water, (2) an ant, (3) a dog, (4) a human being who does not speak the language of the poem, (5) a human being who knows the language but is not sensitive to poetry, (6) and finally, a person who is both sensitive to poetry and who speaks the language.[44] In hopes of demonstrating the snobbery toward relativity on display in classical theism, Hartshorne shows that we would never attribute honor to the glass of water – which is least likely to react at the reading of the poem. While the glass of water, in this case, is the most immutable and impassible, this is hardly a reason to ascribe worth, as it is the ability to respond to the reading of the poem that is worthy of honor.

Hartshorne here makes the very misstep Weinandy warned against in his rock illustration. While Hartshorne's immobile object of choice happened to be a glass of water over against a rock, the same mistake is at play. While Hartshorne is correct in his argument that creaturely honor often demands relativity instead of either immutability or impassibility,

---

43. Charnock, *Works*, 1:356. Unlike Weinandy, Charnock's statement regarding *actus purus* does not take place in his treatment of divine immutability but rather during his section on eternality and its relation to divine aseity – showing the doctrine of pure actuality's vitality across multiple perfections.

44. Hartshorne, *Divine Relativity*, 48.

there is a major difference between the divine perfections and Hartshorne's hypothetical audience. All six members of Hartshorne's cast possess potency and the need to be awakened, to varying degrees. On the contrary, God possesses no such potency and no need to be awakened. To continue with Hartshorne's poem predicament, if God were the seventh member of the audience, He would have been the only audience member to show up to the poem's reading already in pure act. So then, if it is the ability to be moved to action that makes the member of Hartshorne's audience who speaks the language of the poem and is sympathetic to the poem worthy of honor and praise, then God is to be pre-eminently praised as the only audience member who need not be moved at all but who is already in pure action.

We see the glory of God's being God in *actus purus*, for He need not be awakened to set about the business of redeeming His people. God does not need the soteriological version of Hartshorne's poem to finally *move* toward activating a soteric potency within Himself. Rather, the economy of redemption is God's essence with relation to a wicked and rebellious people. This ought to root God's people on the sturdiest grounds of assurance as they can rest in the reality that as God was not moved into actualization to redeem them, He will not one day alter into inactivity either. On the contrary, God's changelessness in His pure act promotes Christian salvation forward in an unchanging fashion. God will ever have life in Himself and will ever lack potency. Salvation will be promoted forevermore until the 'already' and the 'not yet' of the eschaton collide and our faith is turned to sight. The God of Christian salvation is the God of pure actuality who brings about an immutable redemption in an immutable redeemer.

Divine Immutability and Union with Christ

Robert Letham penned a telling line in the introduction to his treatment on the doctrine of union with Christ. After demonstrating the importance of the doctrine throughout church history, using emphatic statements from theologians ranging from the Reformation to the present, Letham said, 'When one asks what in fact this union consists in, however, what it actually *is*, there is a general silence.'[45] Letham is observant here, for

---

45. Robert Letham, *Union with Christ* (Phillipsburg: P&R Publishing, 2011), 1. Emphasis original.

when it comes to defining the doctrine of union with Christ, superlatives abound greater than articulations of definition.

Disagreement is the leading culprit aiding the difficulty of arriving at a definition. Students of the conversation's antiquity see, in short time, that the discussion tends to create more questions than answers and has the ability to divide those who are usually united. Consensus is out on a number of queries, including: What is the relationship between union with Christ and justification? Does an ontological union with an impeccable and perfect Christ render forensic soteriology redundant at best or irrelevant at worst? Is the proper language for the conversation that of 'participation' or 'mystical union'? Is union with Christ a step in the *ordo salutis*, or should it be known as an umbrella category for all soteriology? Is the 'in' of 'in Christ' locative, ontological, or a designation of sphere? Does uniting the church to Christ lead to an Eastern understanding of *theosis*?[46]

Though disagreements proliferate, what seems rather unanimous is the significance of the doctrine itself. One after another, theologians both past and present marvel at the mystical union. One of the most oft quoted instances is found in Calvin's *Institutes*:

> We must understand that as long as Christ remains outside of us, and we are separated from him, all that he has suffered and done for the salvation of the human race remains useless and of no value to us. Therefore, to share in what he has received from the Father, he had to become ours and to dwell within us ... all that he possesses is nothing to us until we grow into one body with him.[47]

---

46. A number of scholars have done the helpful work of compiling or at least bringing some of the varying positions into conversation. Cf. William B. Evans, 'Three Current Reformed Models of Union With Christ,' *Presbyterian* 41 (2015): 12-30; Stephen Clark and Matthew Evans, *In Christ Alone: Perspectives on Union with Christ* (Fearn, Ross-shire: Christian Focus, 2016); William B. Evans, *Imputation and Impartation: Union with Christ in American Reformed Theology* (Eugene: Paternoster, 2008); David Vandrunen, 'A Contested Union: Union with Christ and the Justification Debate,' in *The Doctrine on Which the Church Stands or Falls*, ed. Matthew Barrett, (Wheaton: Crossway, 2019), 469-503, and the source to which my thinking is most indebted, J. V. Fesko, *Beyond Calvin: Union with Christ and Justification in Early Modern Reformed Theology (1517–1700)* (Göttingen: Vandenhoeck & Ruprecht, 2012).

47. John Calvin, *Institutes of the Christian Religion* (Peabody: Hendrickson, 2008), 349. This quote is only rivaled by the Edwards' quote wherein he said, 'By virtue of the believer's union with Christ, he doth really possess all things. That we know plainly from Scripture. (1 Cor. 3:21-23; 2 Cor. 6:10) But it may be asked, how doth he possess all

Vanhoozer determined that the theme was so prevalent in the Pauline corpus that he stated, 'to be or not to be in Christ was, for Paul, the only question.'[48] Constantine Campbell affirmed Vanhoozer's assessment of Pauline emphasis and said, 'The theme of union with Christ in the writings of the apostle Paul is at once dazzling and perplexing. Its prevalence on every page of his writing demonstrates his proclivity for the concept.'[49] The literary exchange regarding a definition of union with Christ leaves readers uncertain and astonished. However, for the purpose of this chapter we will move forward knowing that union with Christ refers to the pneumatological work wherein the Spirit unites believers to the humanity of Christ such that what He has and is in His humanity becomes theirs as His active and passive obedience, and all their soteric benefits, is applied to them. This is not to be understood as a negation of the individual aspects of the *ordo salutis*, of course. Instead, as J. V. Fesko notes, 'union with Christ is to speak of the forest, and to talk of the *ordo salutis* is to speak of the trees.'[50]

Union with Christ is the intersection of Sinai and Zion. The author of Hebrews compares the two mountains in chapter 12. He said of Sinai that 'they could not endure the order that was given, if even a beast touches the mountain, it shall be stoned. Indeed, so terrifying was the sight that Moses said, "I tremble with fear"' (Heb. 12:20-21). This is contrasted with the joy of Mount Zion, of which the author said, 'but you have come to Mount Zion and to the city of the living God, the heavenly Jerusalem' (Heb. 12:22a).

---

things? What is he the better for it? How is a true Christian so much richer than other men? To answer this, I'll tell you what I mean by "possessing all things." I mean that God three in one, all that he is, and all that he has, and all that he does, all that he has made or done—the whole universe, bodies and spirits, earth and heaven, angels, men and devils, sun, moon, and stars, land and sea, fish and fowls, all the silver and gold, kings and potentates as well as mean men—are as much the Christian's as the money in his pocket, the clothes he wears, or the house he dwells in, or the victuals he eats.' Jonathan Edwards, 'Entry ff,' in The 'Miscellanies,' in *The Works of Jonathan Edwards*, 13:183-84, emphasis original.

48. Thate, Vanhoozer, and Campbell, "In Christ" in Paul, 3, emphasis original.

49. Constantine R. Campbell, *Paul and Union with Christ: An Exegetical and Theological Study* (Grand Rapids: Zondervan, 2012), 21. To further demonstrate the ambiguity that lingers regarding union with Christ, Campbell continued, 'yet nowhere does he directly explain what he means by it. This creates a problem for any student of Paul's theology, since union with Christ is both important yet obtuse.'

50. Fesko, *Beyond Calvin*, 29.

These two meet in the person and work of Christ, as the One who meditates the new covenant fulfills the prolegomenous requirement of accomplishing the old covenant. Rooted in Christological holiness, impeccability, and volitional consistency is the fulfillment of the law. This is indeed significant for any conversation of union with Christ, for any sinner grafted into Christ has been made one with the mediator of the new covenant who has satisfied the demands of Sinai on their behalf, thus granting them a place on the better mountain of Zion.

This brief exploration of the doctrine of union with Christ relates to our current discussion of divine immutability's significance in the economy of redemption in two ways: (1) It aids in protecting us from unnecessarily and erroneously ascribing change in God due to His salvation of sinners; and (2) we see that those blessings distributed to believers by virtue of their union with Christ are theirs irrevocably.

As we saw in Chapter Two, and again in this chapter, one remonstrance against the classical articulation of divine immutability is that it would inevitably render God incapable of meaningful soteric movement. For God would need to 'move' from wrath toward kindness in disposition toward the sinner for there to be any hope of justification of the guilty. Even if there are causal realities, such as the atonement of Jesus Christ and the imputation of His righteousness to the sinner in exchange for their disobedience paid for on Calvary, would not there still need to be change? As these salvific blessings are applied to the sinner, is it not the case that such an application to the wayward renders a change, at least in posture, in respect to the Triune God toward the sinner now turned saint?

While it is not the only protective measure, the doctrine of union with Christ proves helpful in demonstrating God's changelessness in the redemption of His people. In relating union with Christ to the economy of redemption, we can squarely place the change necessary for meaningful transformation in the creature, not the Creator. As God is divinely simple, when the creature experiences God, they cannot help but experience God *as He is*. This means, among other things, that it is not the case that the unregenerate experiences the wrath of God which is transformed to the kindness of God at a particular point in their relationship. Rather, both the sinner and the saint will one day experience God as He is since He cannot be otherwise. What will separate the sinner and the saint in their experience of God – one as justice in condemnation and one as mercy in salvation – is the means by which *they* come to Him.

At this juncture the doctrine of union with Christ becomes vitally important in Christian salvation. For, those not 'in Christ' will experience the simple and pure essence of God in a state of rebellion and unrighteousness and will therefore experience the simple essence of God as judgment that breeds righteous wrath. On the contrary, those creatures who have gone about the change of being united to Christ will experience the simple essence of God by virtue of the immutable perfect merits of their high priest. It is the robes of righteousness obtained in the believer's union with Christ that enable them to experience God's holy and simple essence as salvation instead of judgment.

We can see, then, that neither the simplicity of God nor the immutability of God is violated in the economy of redemption. In fact, the simplicity and immutability of God are vital in maintaining an orthodox understanding of Christian salvation. Instead of imposing composition or change on the Triune God, the creature undergoes the necessary change to experience the presence of God as good news in their vital union with the Second Person of the Trinity.

We now turn to examine the second benefit of relating union with Christ, divine immutability, and the economy of redemption – that the benefits of this vital union now belong to the believer irrevocably. Opening his epistle to the saints at Ephesus, Paul – in one unbroken sentence – discusses the riches which belong to those 'in Christ':

> Blessed be the God and Father of our Lord Jesus Christ, who has blessed us in Christ with every spiritual blessing in the heavenly places, even as he chose us in him before the foundation of the world, that we should be holy and blameless before him. In love he predestined us for adoption to himself as sons through Jesus Christ, according to the purpose of his will, to the praise of his glorious grace, with which he has blessed us in the Beloved. In him we have redemption through his blood, the forgiveness of our trespasses, according to the riches of his grace, which he lavished upon us, in all wisdom and insight making known to us the mystery of his will, according to his purpose, which he set forth in Christ as a plan for the fullness of time, to unite all things in him, things in heaven and things on earth.

These eight verses (Eph. 1:3-10) come together to describe the avalanche of grace in the inheritance of the saints. In this singular passage, we read of eight blessings given to God's people: (1) Being chosen and predestined before the foundation of the world; (2) being made holy and blameless before God; (3) being adopted as sons through Jesus Christ; (4) redemption through His blood; (5) forgiveness of our sins; (6) the riches of His grace lavished upon us; (7) the wisdom of the mystery of His will and purposes uniting all things in heaven and on earth; and, as if these seven were not enough, (8) the eighth blessing in the list, which actually appears first, is 'every spiritual blessing.' It is important to note that the condition to receive these blessings appears in verse 3; only those 'in Christ' will obtain these riches of Christ.

The conclusion of verse 10 does not, however, conclude Paul's lengthy sentence. It continues on till verse 14:

> In him we have obtained an inheritance, having been predestined according to the purpose of him who works all things according to the counsel of his will, so that we who were the first to hope in Christ might be to the praise of his glory. In him you also, when you heard the word of truth, the gospel of your salvation, and believed in him, were sealed with the promised Holy Spirit, who is the guarantee of our inheritance until we acquire possession of it, to the praise of his glory.

Starting, once again, on the foundation of union with Christ by the designation 'in him,' Paul brings this pericope to a conclusion. It is important here to notice the finality and assurance with which Paul writes on behalf of the believer. Those who are 'in Christ' have – in the past tense – *obtained* an inheritance. Those who are 'in Christ,' when they heard the truth of the gospel and believed, were 'sealed' by the Spirit and therefore have a 'guarantee' of inheritance. This inheritance is sure until they 'acquire possession' of it.

Paul is enabled to use such sturdy and sure language because the salvation that is found 'in Christ' is sturdy and sure. The significance of God's immutable divine life is on full display as those who are immutably grafted into Christ receive an immutable righteousness, are granted immutable access to a holy God, benefit from immutable mediation, and are immutably accredited the immutable merits of their immutable high priest.

The embarrassment of riches described in Ephesians 1:3-14 can only be described as grace that is 'lavished' upon the saints in Christ. By virtue of their union with God incarnate, the branches, now one with the vine, have Christ as their sure and sturdy head. Those who now make up the body of Christ, with Christ as their head, can rest assured of their salvific inheritance, for they are as sure as their head. Christ's immutable divine nature renders Ephesians 1:3-14 not only the riches of Christ, but the kind of riches that will not fade nor depreciate even as the cosmos wanes.

An Unchanging Redemption in an Unchanging Redeemer

On January 7, 1855, Charles Haddon Spurgeon ascended the pulpit of the New Park Street Chapel and delivered an opening of a homily that would one day receive international fame. The twenty-one-year-old preacher began his sermon with these words:

> It has been said by someone that 'the proper study of mankind is man.' I will not oppose the idea, but I believe it is equally true that the proper study of God's elect is God; the proper study of a Christian is the Godhead. The highest science, the loftiest speculation, the mightiest philosophy, which can ever engage the attention of a child of God, is the name, the nature, the person, the work, the doings, and the existence of the great God whom he calls his Father. There is something exceedingly improving to the mind in a contemplation of the Divinity. It is a subject so vast, that all our thoughts are lost in its immensity; so deep, that our pride is drowned in its infinity. Other subjects we can compass and grapple with; in them we feel a kind of self-content, and go our way with the thought, 'Behold I am wise.' But when we come to this master-science, finding that our plumb-line cannot sound its depth, and that our eagle eye cannot see its height, we turn away with the thought, that vain man would be wise, but he is like a wild ass's colt; and with the solemn exclamation, 'I am but of yesterday, and know nothing.' No subject of contemplation will tend more to humble the mind, than thoughts of God.
>
> But while the subject *humbles* the mind it also *expands* it. He who often thinks of God, will have a larger mind than the man who simply plods

around this narrow globe. … [T]he most excellent study for expanding the soul, is the science of Christ, and him crucified, and the knowledge of the Godhead in the glorious Trinity. Nothing will so enlarge the intellect, nothing so magnify the whole soul of man, as a devout, earnest, continued investigation of the great subject of the Deity. And, whilst humbling and expanding, this subject is eminently consolatory. Oh, there is, in contemplating Christ, a balm for every wound; in musing on the Father, there is a quietus for every grief; and in the influence of the Holy Ghost, there is a balsam for every sore. Would you lose your sorrows? Would you drown your cares? Then go, plunge yourself in the Godhead's deepest sea; be lost in his immensity; and you shall come forth as from a couch of rest, refreshed and invigorated. I know nothing which can so comfort the soul; so calm the swelling billows of grief and sorrow; so speak peace to the winds of trial, as a devout musing upon the subject of the Godhead. It is to that subject that I invite you this morning.[1]

This awe-inducing introduction rose to international recognition not only because it came from the mouth of 'the Prince of Preachers' but also because, one hundred and eighteen years later, it would serve as another introduction – this time to J. I. Packer's magnificent volume, *Knowing God*.[2] While over a million readers have encountered this quote from Spurgeon by the instrument of Packer's pages, what many do not know is that this homiletical introduction served as the opening words to Spurgeon's sermon entitled 'The Immutability of God.' Expositing Malachi 3, Spurgeon led his congregation to contemplate the changelessness of their Lord. While scores of readers have been stirred to doxology and worship at Packer's use of Spurgeon's quote considering the sheer, infinite depth of beauty that is Christian theology, we here conclude with Spurgeon's original intent – to be moved to doxology at not just the beauty of Christian theology in general but the glory of this changeless God in particular.

Though many are familiar with how Spurgeon's sermon begins, few know how it ends:

Remember God is the same, whatever is removed. Your friends may be disaffected, your ministers may be taken away, everything may change,

---

1. C. H. Spurgeon, 'The Immutability of God' in *New Park Street Pulpit*, XX vols. (London: Passmore & Alabaster, 1855), 1:1.

2. J. I. Packer, *Knowing God* (Downers Grove: InterVarsity Press, 1993), 18-19.

but God does not. Your brethren may change and cast out your name as vile: but God will love you still. Let your station in life change, and your property be gone; let your whole life be shaken, and you become weak and sickly; let everything flee away – there is one place where change cannot put his finger; there is one name on which mutability can never be written; there is one heart which never can alter; that heart is God's – that name Love.[3]

In his concluding remarks, Spurgeon makes one thing clear – God's immutability is impetus for worship. This simple conviction lay at the foundation of this book. There is, in our Triune God, a sure and steady anchor of salvation.

We have, in these six chapters, explored a double thesis – a general thesis and a specific thesis. The general thesis relates to theological method and claims that the proper home for soteriological study is situated within theology proper. Christian soteriology is a derivative field, finding its source in God Himself. The burden of the general thesis is that the study of God's redemption, if divorced from contemplation of God as He is in Himself, often loses both in the process. Theology proper becomes mangled when theological method launches from the starting blocks of soteriology. To force theology proper to exclusively answer to soteriology is to force soteriology to bear a weight it is not fit to uphold. Rather, we ought to affirm with the late John Webster that soteriology is most properly situated within the 'theology of the *mysterium trinitatis*'[4] and therefore that 'the bedrock of soteriology is the doctrine of the Trinity. The perfect life of the Holy Trinity is the all-encompassing and first reality from whose completeness all else derives.'[5] When rooted in theology proper, the streams of soteriology become all-the-more beautiful and life-giving, as the source becomes the fullness of God *in se*.

To demonstrate the vital methodological step defined in the general thesis, this study sought to keep theology and economy together in a way that treat the economy as a doctrine of derivation flowing from the fullness of God's life in himself. Continuing to the specific thesis, this project aimed to demonstrate this methodological commitment by demonstrating the benefit of contemplating God's unchanging essence

---

3. Spurgeon, 'The Immutability of God,' 8.

4. Webster, 'It Was the Will of the Lord to Bruise Him,' 148.

5. Ibid.,145.

as it relates to the economy of redemption. Starting with theology proper and a classical articulation of divine immutability, then, shows that the economy of redemption takes place within an inalterable God and renders the plan and prize of soteriology unchanging. Cristian salvation is the story of an unchanging redemption in an unchanging redeemer.

To arrive at this conclusion, we first stated the problem. Chapter One dealt with the fall of metaphysics in theological contemplation, especially as it relates to theological method in modernity. Chapter Two then zoomed in on one consequence of this shift in method by examining deviations and denials of divine immutability as modern theology exchanged the God of being for a God of *becoming*. Working contrary to contemporary theology, Chapters Three through Five sought to provide a constructive articulation and understanding of classical divine immutability. This constructive articulation of divine immutability utilized a three-fold witness and examined the doctrine of God's changelessness by way of a historical witness, a biblical witness, and the metaphysical-theological witness of Christian reason. These three ingredients come together to show that God is unchanging as He is *actus purus* and has the fullness of life in Himself. There is no change in God by way of potentiality, parts, passions, process, or plan – though the grass will wither, and flowers will fade, the Triune God will remain the same yesterday, today, and forevermore (Isa. 40:8; Heb. 13:8).

Far from rendering God an immovable and immobile deity whose transcendence means He has not care nor ability to redeem His creatures, a proper understanding of divine immutability makes salvation both possible and sure. The climax of this study – Chapter Six – sought to extrapolate these soteriological realities and see how the doctrine of divine immutability both protects and promotes God's soteriological work in the economy of redemption. We saw in Chapter Six that, through and through, divine immutability undergirds Christian soteriology. Consequently, the biblical pattern of discussing divine changelessness often entails a soteric export as biblical authors invoke God's inalterability to impress assurance within their hearers. Moreover, divine immutability bears soteriological significance in the economy of redemption as we see the changelessness of God's purposes of election, changelessness in God's covenant faithfulness, and ultimately, changelessness in the Triune redemption of the creature's soteric plight – the need for and inability to obtain righteousness.

This changeless redemption is realized in the creature as they are made one with Christ by virtue of their union to Him. In this union they are given Christ's unchanging righteousness as they receive – by virtue of imputation – the soteric reward of His faithfulness. In this union, justification becomes unchangingly theirs as God declares them justified forever on the basis of the merits of their high priest who now intercedes for them forever at the right hand of God. Since Jesus' mediation is immutably eternal, He ever lives to make intercession for them such that those who have been grafted into the Son can live ever secure that the Father will never turn away His only begotten Son and those found in Him. As immutably sure as the Son is, so too immutably sure the salvation found in Him is.

Moreover, as God is pure act and in His being *a se*, He gives this immutable salvation freely out of the fullness of Himself and not under compulsion or need. Therefore, those who have inherited this sure salvation might live evermore assured that God will not change His plan or purposes, as the entirety of the economy of redemption is a consequence of the never-changing fullness of life of the Triune God.

As the inseparable operations of the Trinity's missions are rooted in the eternal processions, the one immutable essence of all three persons renders salvation sure and final. The unfolding of a Trinitarian-shaped salvation is the drama of an unchanging election from the Father, secured by the unchanging righteous and atonement of the Son, forever applied in the unchanging seal of the Spirit.

The church's assurance is not grounded in frailty or fickleness. Rather, she lives with assurance since the Father has declared her righteous, and He never changes. The church can live with assurance because she bears the righteous robes of Christ, and He never changes. The church can live with assurance as the Spirit immutably seals her to her Lord, and He never changes.

To return to the general thesis, these eternal purposes and the assurance that they bear demonstrate the vital methodological step of situating soteriology within the sturdy foundation of theology proper. Christian salvation is already an unfathomably good gift. A thousand gears of grace are turning to make salvation possible. However, as wonderful as the gift of redemption is, it becomes all the more wonderful when we contemplate who it is that is redeeming us – the unchanging God Himself.

So, we close by way of a reminder from James, who instructs us as his 'beloved brother' in Christ: 'Do not be deceived, my beloved brothers. Every good gift and every perfect gift is from above, coming down from the Father of lights, with whom there is no variation or shadow due to change' (James 1:16-17).

Tables and Figures

Throughout the project, there have arisen a few lists. More specifically, five lists have proven important for advancing the thesis of this book. In hopes to serve the reader, these lists have been also made into tables and placed here. The five lists in mind are: (1) Five Reasons for the Decline of Classical Theology Proper in Modern Theology, (2) An Alliterated Definition of Divine Immutability, (3) A Taxonomy of Deviations and Denials of Divine Immutability, (4) A Three-Step Approach for a Dogmatically Informed Exegesis, and (5) The Soteriological Emphasis on Biblical Passages on Immutability.

Table One:

Five Reasons for the Decline of Classical Theology Proper in Modern Theology (From Chapter One):

Reason	Meaning
Reciprocal and relational soteriology	Can the God of classical theism, with the perfections of immutability, simplicity, aseity, impassibility, and the like, have a meaningful and reciprocal soteriological relationship with creatures? (This project answers in the affirmative.)
Decline of contemplative theology	As the desire for a pragmatic theology arises, there can be a depreciation for the kind of sustained contemplative theology needed for classical theism.
Reprioritization of theological *loci*	As theological projects arise that seek to find a 'center' to systematic theology, there can be a reprioritization which prizes the economy of theology.
The demise of pre-critical hermeneutics	As the scholarly community begins to prioritize critical or historic-grammatical interpretations only, the theological, ecclesial, and conciliar reading of the biblical data which guided pre-modern hermeneutics begins to wane.
The rise of theistic personalism and theistic mutualism	The rise of models of God which prefer a more genuine give-and-take between Creator and creature as well as a greater chance at univocal predication and articulation undermine theological tools utilized in classical theism.

Table Two:
An Alliterated Definition of Divine Immutability (From Chapter Two):

God does not change, and it is impossible for Him to change, in respect to His:	
Process	God is not in the process of becoming; instead, God is perfect in His being.
Processions	God is simply trinity, and that which distinguishes persons – eternal relations of origin – will not alter. The processions and persons will not change in God.
Potentiality	As God is pure act and possesses no passive potency, He will not undergo alteration of potentiality.
Parts	Since God's perfections are His essence and He is not composed of parts, God will not experience change regarding the addition, subtraction, or movement of parts.
Passions	Like God is without parts, He is also without passions. As God is pure act and has no passive potency, there are no passions in God such that He could undergo any actualization of passion.
Perfections	As God does not merely *have* perfections but *is* them in His essence, He will not undergo any change since all that is in God, is God, immutably so.
Plans	God's perfections and eternality demonstrate that His will and volition are perfect and need not undergo any change.

Table Three:
A Taxonomy of Deviations and Denials of Divine Immutability (From
Chapter Two):

The Problem of Relations and Soteriology	Those who deviate from or deny immutability using this problem argue that God must be mutable, at least in some respects, for there to be meaningful relationships between Him and His creatures.
The Problem of the Incarnation	Those who deviate from or deny immutability using this problem argue that the incarnation of Jesus Christ shows a demonstrative change.
The Problem of Creation and Divine Action	Those who deviate from or deny immutability using this problem argue that moments of divine action – such as creation, incarnation, Pentecost, providence, etc. – demonstrate change in God.
The Problem of Volition and Knowledge	Those who deviate from or deny immutability using this problem argue that the biblical data seems to depict God 'relenting' or 'repenting' as well as showing change in knowledge.
The Problem of Divine Freedom and Contingency	Those who deviate from or deny immutability using this problem argue that immutability threatens genuine divine freedom and makes some actions, like creation, a contingency to the divine life.

Table Four:

A Three-Step Approach for a Dogmatically Informed Exegesis (From Chapter Four)

Since there are passages and pericopes which seem to indicate both immutability and mutability in God, a method more mature than *mere* biblicism is needed. Rather, biblical reasoning will aid readers and should include consideration of the following:	
Covenantal Faithfulness	Immutability is *demonstrated* by God's unchanging faithfulness to His covenantal people. From the beginning of the Scriptures to the end, God is unchangingly faithful to His covenant.
Individual Passages	Immutability is *taught* by individual passages explicitly in Scripture. See Malachi 3:6, Numbers 23:19-24, Hebrews 6:13-20, Hebrews 7:22-28, and James 1:16-18.
Theological Reasoning	Immutability is *demanded* by theological reasoning. When one contemplates all the Scripture says about the divine essence, it becomes apparent that God *must* be unchanging for all the biblical data says of Him to be true.

Table Five:
The Soteriological Emphasis of Biblical Passages on Immutability (From Chapter Six)

Passage	Emphasis on Divine Immutability	Soteriological Concern and Emphasis
Malachi 3:6	'For I the LORD do not change.'	'therefore you, O children of Jacob, are not consumed.'
Numbers 23:19-24	'God is not man, that he should lie, or a son of man, that he should change his mind.'	'Has he said, and will he not do it? Or has he spoken, and will he not fulfill it?'
Hebrews 6:13-20	'So, when God desired to show more convincingly to the heirs of the promise the unchangeable character of his purpose, he guaranteed it with an oath, so that by two unchangeable things, in which it is impossible for God to lie.'	'we who have fled for refuge might have strong encouragement to hold fast to the hope set before us. We have this as a sure and steadfast anchor of the soul, a hope that enters into the inner place behind the curtain, where Jesus has gone as a forerunner on our behalf, having become a high priest forever after the order of Melchizedek.'
Hebrews 7:22-28	'The former priests were many in number, because they were prevented by death from continuing in office, but he holds his priesthood permanently, because he continues forever.'	'Consequently, he is able to save to the uttermost those who draw near to God through him, since he always lives to make intercession for them.'
James 1:16-18	'With whom there is no variation or shadow due to change.'	'Every good gift and every perfect gift is from above, coming down from the Father of lights.'

Bibliography

à Brakel, Wilhelmus. *The Christians Reasonable Service*, 4 vols. Trans. Bartel Elshout. Grand Rapids: Reformation Heritage Books, 1995.

Adams, Marilyn McCord. 'Praying the Proslogion' in *The Rationality of Belief and the Plurality of Faith*. Ed. Thomas Senor. Ithaca: Cornell University Press, 1995.

Alexander, T. Desmond, and Brian S. Rosner, eds. *New Dictionary of Biblical Theology*. Downers Grove, IL: InterVarsity Press, 2000.

Alfsvåg, Knut. '"With God all things are possible" – Luther and Kierkegaard on the relation between immutability, necessity and possibility.' *Neue Zeitschrift für Systematische Theologie und Religionsphilosophie,* Volume 60.1, 2018.

Allen, Michael. *Grounded in Heaven: Recentering Christian Hope and Life on God*. Grand Rapids, MI: Eerdmans, 2018.

Allen, Michael. *Sanctification*. Grand Rapids, MI: Zondervan, 2017.

Allen, Michael, and Scott R. Swain, eds. *Christian Dogmatics: Reformed Theology for the Church Catholic*. Grand Rapids, MI: Baker Academic, 2016.

Allen, Michael, and Scott R. Swain, eds. *Reformed Catholicity: The Promise of Retrieval for Theology and Biblical Interpretation*. Grand Rapids: Baker, 2015.

Allen, R. Michael, ed. *Theological Commentary: Evangelical Perspectives*. New York: T&T Clark, 2011.

Anatolios, Khaled. *Retrieving Nicaea: The Development and Meaning of Trinitarian Doctrine*. Grand Rapids, MI: Baker Academic, 2018.

Anselm. *The Major Works: Monologion, Proslogion, and Why God Became Man*. Oxford: Oxford University Press, 1998.

Aquinas, Thomas. *Commentary on the Gospel of John: Chapters 1–5*. Translated by Fabian Larcher and James A. Weisheipl. Washington, D. C.: Catholic University of America Press, 2010.

Aquinas, Thomas. *Commentary on the Gospel of John: Chapters 13–21*. Translated by Fabian Larcher and James A. Weisheipl. Washington, D.C.: Catholic University of America Press, 2010.

Aquinas, Thomas. *The Summa Theologica of St. Thomas Aquinas*. Translated by Fathers of the English Dominican Province. English Dominican Province Translation edition. New York: Christian Classics, 1981.

Aquinas, Thomas. *Thomas Aquinas' Earliest Treatment of the Divine Essence: Scriptum Super libros Sententiarum*. Book 1, Distinction 8. Trans. E.M. Macierowski. New York: University of New York Press, 1997.

Asbill, Brian D. *The Freedom of God for Us: Karl Barth's Doctrine of Divine Aseity*. London: T&T Clark, 2015.

Athanasius. *Against the Arians*, in *Nicene and Post-Nicene Fathers*, second series, edited by Philip Schaff and Henry Wace. Peabody, MA: Hendrickson, 2012.

Athanasius. *On the Incarnation*, in *Nicene and Post-Nicene Fathers*, second series, edited by Philip Schaff and Henry Wace. Peabody, MA: Hendrickson, 2012.

Augustine. *Confessions*. Oxford: Oxford University Press, 1991.

Augustine. *Letter to Dioscorus*, in *Nicene and Post-Nicene Fathers*, Volume 1. Peabody: Hendrickson, 2012.

Augustine. *On the Trinity*, in *Nicene and Post-Nicene Fathers*, Volume 3. Peabody: Hendrickson, 2012.

Ayres, Lewis. *Nicaea and Its Legacy: An Approach to Fourth-Century Trinitarian Theology*. Reprinted. Oxford: Oxford Univ. Press, 2009.

Babka, Susie Paulik. *'God is Faithful, He Cannot Deny Himself': Karl Rahner and Jürgen Moltmann on Whether God is Immutable In Jesus Christ*. PhD Dissertation, University of Notre Dame, 2004.

Baines, Ronald S., et al. *Confessing the Impassible God: The Biblical, Classical, & Confessional Doctrine of Divine Impassibility*. Palmdale: RBAP, 2015.

Barcellos, Richard C. *Trinity and Creation: A Scriptural and Confessional Account*. Eugene, OR: Wipf and Stock, 2020.

Barrett, Jordan P. *Divine Simplicity: A Biblical and Trinitarian Account*. Minneapolis, MN: Fortress, 2017.

Barrett, Matthew. *Canon, Covenant and Christology: Rethinking Jesus and the Scriptures of Israel*. Downers Grove, IL: IVP Academic, 2020.

Barrett, Matthew. *God's Word Alone: The Authority of Scripture*. Grand Rapids: Zondervan, 2016.

Barrett, Matthew. *None Greater: The Undomesticated Attributes of God*. Grand Rapids: Baker, 2019.

Barrett, Matthew. ed. *Reformation Theology*. Wheaton: Crossway, 2017.

Barrett, Matthew. *Salvation by Grace: The Case for Effectual Calling and Regeneration*. Phillipsburg, NJ: P&R Publishing, 2013.

Barrett, Matthew. *Simply Trinity: The Unmanipulated Father, Son, and Spirit*. Grand Rapids, MI: Baker Books, 2021.

Barrett, Matthew, ed. *The Doctrine on Which the Church Stands or Falls: Justification in Biblical, Theological, Historical, and Pastoral Perspective*. Wheaton, IL: Crossway, 2019.

Barrett, Matthew, and Tom J. Nettles, eds. *Whomever He Wills: A Surprising Display of Sovereign Mercy*. Cape Coral, FL: Founders Press, 2012.

Barth, Karl. *Church Dogmatics*, Edited by G. W. Bromiley and T. F. Torrance. Trans. by T. H. L. Parker, W. B. Johnston, Harold Knight, and J. L. M. Haire. Edinburgh, UK: T&T Clark, 1957.

Bavinck, Herman. *The Doctrine of God*. Edinburgh: Banner of Truth, 1977.

Bavinck, Herman. *Reformed Dogmatics*. 4 vols. Grand Rapids: Baker Academic, 2008.

Beeke, Joel R., and Paul M. Smalley. *Reformed Systematic Theology*. Vols. 1–2: Wheaton, IL: Crossway, 2019.

Beeley, Christopher A. *Gregory of Nazianzus on the Trinity and the Knowledge of God: In Your Light We Shall See Light*. Oxford: Oxford University Press, 2008.

Behr, John. *The Case Against Diodore and Theodore: Texts and Their Contexts*. Oxford: Oxford University Press, 2011.

Berkhof, Louis. *Systematic Theology*. Edinburgh: Banner of Truth Trust, 1998.

Betz, John R. 'After Heidegger and Marion: The Task of Christian Metaphysics Today.' *Modern Theology* 34, no. 4 (July 2015): 565-597.

Betz, John R. 'Theology without Metaphysics? A Reply to Kevin Hector.' *Modern Theology* 31, no. 3 (July 2015): 488-500.

Billings, J. Todd. *Calvin, Participation, and the Gift: The Activity of Believers in Union with Christ*. New York, NY: Oxford University Press, 2007.

Billings, J. Todd. *Union with Christ: Reframing Theology and Ministry for the Church*. Grand Rapids, MI: Baker Academic, 2011.

Bird, Michael, *Romans in The Story of God Bible Commentary*. Grand Rapids: Zondervan, 2016.

Bird, Michael F., and Scott Harrower, eds. *Trinity without Hierarchy: Reclaiming Nicene Orthodoxy in Evangelical Theology*. Grand Rapids, MI: Kregel Publications, 2019.

Boersma, Hans. *Heavenly Participation: The Weaving of a Sacramental Tapestry*. Grand Rapids, MI: Eerdmans, 2011.

Boersma, Hans. *Scripture as Real Presence: Sacramental Exegesis in the Early Church*. Grand Rapids, MI: Baker Academic, 2017.

Boersma, Hans. *Seeing God: The Beatific Vision in Christian Tradition*. Grand Rapids, MI: Eerdmans, 2018.

Boyd, Gregory. *God of the Possible: A Biblical Introduction to the Open View of God*. Grand Rapids: Baker Books, 2000.

Bray, Gerald L. The Doctrine of God. Downers Grove: IVP Academic, 1993.

Bray, Gerald L. *Documents of the English Reformation*, 3rd Edition. Cambridge: James Clarke Company, 2020.

Brink, G. Van den, and C. Van der Kooi. *Christian Dogmatics: An Introduction*. Grand Rapids: Eerdmans, 2017.

Brown, Robert. 'Divine Omniscience, Immutability, Aseity and Human Free Will.' *Religious Studies*, Volume 27.3, 1991.

Brown, Robert. 'Schelling and Dorner of Divine Immutability.' *Journal of the American Academy of Religion*, LIII.2.

Bruce, F. F. *1 and 2 Corinthians*. Grand Rapids, MI: Eerdmans, 1992.

Bruce, F. F. *The Epistle to the Hebrews*. Grand Rapids: Eerdmans Publishing, 1964.

Brueggemann, Walter. *Theology of the Old Testament: Testimony, Dispute, Advocacy*. Fortress Press, 2012.

Calvin, John. *Institutes of the Christian Religion*. Peabody, MA: Hendrickson Publishers, 2008.

Campbell, Constantine R. *Paul and Union with Christ: An Exegetical and Theological Study*. Grand Rapids: Zondervan, 2012.

Carson, D. A. *The Gospel According to John,* in The Pillar New Testament Commentary, Grand Rapids: Eerdmans, 1991.

Carter, Craig A. *Interpreting Scripture with the Great Tradition: Recovering the Genius of Premodern Exegesis*. Grand Rapids, MI: Baker Academic, 2018.

Carter, Craig A. *Contemplating God with the Great Tradition: Recovering Classical Trinitarian Theism*. Grand Rapids, MI: Baker Academic, 2021.

Cassidy, James J. 'No "Absolute Impeccability": Charles Hodge and Christology at Old and New Princeton' *The Confessional Presbyterian* 9, 2013.

Chalamet, Christophe. 'Immutability or Faithfulness?' *Modern Theology*, Volume 34.3, 2018.

Charnock, Steven. *Works of Stephen Charnock*. Edinburgh: Banner of Truth, 2010.

Childs, Brevard S. *Biblical Theology of the Old and New Testaments: Theological Reflection on the Christian Bible*. Minneapolis, MN: Fortress Press, 1993.

Childs, Brevard S. *The Struggle to Understand Isaiah as Christian Scripture*. Grand Rapids: Eerdmans Publishing Co., 2004.

Clark, John C., and Marcus Peter Johnson. *The Incarnation of God: The Mystery of the Gospel as the Foundation of Evangelical Theology*. Wheaton, IL: Crossway, 2015.

Clark, Kelly James. 'Hold Not Thy Peace at My Tears: Methodological Reflections on Divine Impassibility' in *Our Knowledge of God: Essays on Natural and Philosophical Theology*. Boston: Kluwer, 1992.

Clark, Stephen. *In Christ Alone: Perspectives on Union with Christ*. Fearn: Christian Mentor, 2016.

Cole, Graham A. *God the Peacemaker: How Atonement Brings Shalom*. Downers Grove, IL: InterVarsity Press, 2009.

Cole, Graham A. *He Who Gives Life: The Doctrine of the Holy Spirit*. Foundations of Evangelical Theology. Wheaton, IL: Crossway Books, 2007.

Cole, Graham A. *The God Who Became Human: A Biblical Theology of Incarnation*. Downers Grove, IL: InterVarsity Press, 2013.

Cole, R. A. *Exodus: An Introduction and Commentary*. Downers Grove: InterVarsity Press, 1973.

Craig, William Lane. *God Over All: Divine Aseity and the Challenge of Platonism*. Oxford: Oxford University Press, 2016.

Craig, William Lane. *Time and Eternity: Exploring God's Relationship to Time*. Wheaton: Crossway, 2001.

Crisp, Oliver D. *Approaching the Atonement: The Reconciling Work of Christ*. Downers Grove, IL: IVP Academic, 2020.

Crisp, Oliver D. *Divinity and Humanity: The Incarnation Reconsidered*. Cambridge: Cambridge University Press, 2007.

Crisp, Oliver D. *The Word Enfleshed: Exploring the Person and Work of Christ*. Grand Rapids: Baker Academic, 2016.

Crisp, Oliver, and Fred Sanders, eds. *Advancing Trinitarian Theology: Explorations in Constructive Dogmatics*. Grand Rapids, MI: Zondervan, 2014.

Crisp, Oliver, and Fred Sanders, eds. *The Task of Dogmatics: Explorations in Theological Method*. Grand Rapids: Zondervan, 2017.

Crowe, Brandon D. *The Last Adam: A Theology of the Obedient Life of Jesus in the Gospels*. Grand Rapids: Baker Academic, 2017.

Cumming, Nicholas A. *Francis Turretin (1623–87) and the Reformed Tradition*. Leiden: Brill, 2020.

Cunning, David. 'Descartes on the Immutability of the Divine Will.' *Religious Studies*, Volume 39, 2003.

Cyril of Alexandria. *On the Unity of Christ.* Popular Patristics Series, Vol 13. Crestwood, NY: St. Vladimir's Seminary Press, 1995.

Davidson, Ivor, and Murray A Rae. ed. *God of Salvation: Soteriology in Theological Perspective.* London: Routledge, 2011.

Davies, Brian. *An Introduction to Philosophy of Religion*, 3rd Edition. Oxford: Oxford University Press, 2004.

Davies, Brian. *Thomas Aquinas' Summa Theologiae: A Guide and Commentary.* Oxford: Oxford University Press, 2014.

Davies, Brian and Brian Leftow. *The Cambridge Companion to Anselm.* Cambridge: Cambridge University Press, 2005.

Dennison, James T. *Reformed Confessions of the 16th and 17th Centuries in English Translation*, Volumes 1–4, Grand Rapids, MI: Reformation Heritage, 2008.

Dingel, Irene. *Die Bekenntnisschriften der Evangelish-Lutherischen Kirche.* Göttingen: Vandenhoeck & Ruprecht, 2014.

Dodds, Michael J. *The Unchanging God of Love: Thomas Aquinas and Contemporary Theology on Divine Immutability, Second Edition.* Washington, D.C: The Catholic University of America Press, 2008.

Dolezal, James E. *All That Is in God: Evangelical Theology and the Challenge of Classical Christian Theism.* Grand Rapids: Reformation Heritage Books, 2017.

Dolezal, James E. *God without Parts: Divine Simplicity and the Metaphysics of God's Absoluteness.* Eugene: Pickwick Publications, 2011.

Dolezal, James E. 'Strong Impassibility' in *Divine Impassibility: Four Views of God's Emotions and Suffering*, ed. Robert Matz and A. Chadwick Thornhill. Downers Grove: InterVarsity Press, 2019.

Dorner, Isaak August, *Divine Immutability: A Critical Reconsideration.* Minneapolis: Fortress Press, 1994.

Duby, Steven J. *Divine Simplicity: A Dogmatic Account.* London: T&T Clark, 2016.

Duby, Steven J. *Divine Immutability, Divine Action and the God-World Relation.* International Journal of Systematic Theology, Volume 19.2, 2017.

Duby, Steven J. 'For I am God, Not a Man: Divine Repentance and the Creator-Creature Distinction.' *Journal of Theological Interpretation*, Volume 12, 2018.

Duby, Steven J. *God in Himself: Scripture, Metaphysics, and the Task of Christian Theology*. Downers Grove: IVP Academic, 2019.

Edwards, Jonathan. 'Entry ff' in *The 'Miscellanies,' The Works of Jonathan Edwards*, Volume 13. Ed. Harry S. Stout. New Haven: Yale University Press, 1994.

Emery, Gilles. *The Trinity: An Introduction to Catholic Doctrine on the Triune God*, trans. Matthew Levering. Washington: Catholic University of America Press, 2011.

Emery, Gilles, and Matthew Levering, eds. *The Oxford Handbook of the Trinity*. Oxford handbooks. New York, NY: Oxford University Press, 2011.

Evans, Stephen C. *Exploring Kenotic Christology: The Self-Emptying of God*. Oxford: Oxford University Press, 2006.

Evans, William B. *Imputation and Impartation: Union with Christ in American Reformed Theology*. Eugene: Paternoster, 2008.

Fairbairn, Donald and Ryan M. Reeves. *The Story of Creeds and Confessions: Tracing the Development of the Christian Faith*. Grand Rapids, MI: Baker, 2019.

Feinberg, John S., and Harold O. J. Brown. *No One Like Him*. Wheaton: Crossway, 2006.

Ferguson, Sinclair B. *The Holy Spirit*. Contours of Christian theology. Downers Grove, IL: InterVarsity Press, 1996.

Feser, Edward. *Scholastic Metaphysics: A Contemporary Introduction*. Lancaster: *editiones scholasticae*, 2014.

Fesko, J. V. *Beyond Calvin: Union with Christ and Justification in Early Modern Reformed Theology*. Göttingen: Vandenhoeck & Ruprecht, 2012.

Fesko, J. V. *Death in Adam, Life in Christ: The Doctrine of Imputation*. Ross-shire, UK: Christian Focus, 2016.

Fesko, J. V. *Justification: Understanding the Classic Reformed Doctrine*. Phillipsburg: P&R Publishing, 2008.

Fesko, J. V. *The Covenant of Works: The Origins, Development, and Reception of the Doctrine*. New York, NY: Oxford University Press, 2020.

Fesko, J. V. *The Trinity and the Covenant of Redemption*. Ross-shire, UK: Christian Focus, 2016.

Frame, John M. *The Doctrine of God*. Phillipsburg: P & R Publishing, 2002.

Frame, John M. *Systematic Theology: An Introduction to Christian Belief.* Phillipsburg: P&R Publishing, 2013.

Frei, Hans W. *The Eclipse of Biblical Narrative: A Study in Eighteenth and Nineteenth Century Hermeneutics.* New Haven: Yale University Press, 1980.

Fretheim, Terrence E. 'The Repentance of God: A Key to Evaluating Old Testament God-Talk.' *Horizons in Biblical Theology*, Volume 10, 1988.

Garner, David B. *Sons in the Son: The Riches and Reach of Adoption in Christ*. Phillipsburg, NJ: P&R Publishing, 2016.

Gathercole, Simon J. *Defending Substitution: An Essay on Atonement in Paul*. Grand Rapids, MI: Baker Academic, 2015.

Gathercole, Simon J. *Where is Boasting? Early Jewish Soteriology and Paul's Response in Romans 1–5*. Grand Rapids, MI: Eerdmans, 2002.

Gavrilyuk, Paul. *The Suffering of an Impassible God: Dialectics of Patristic Thought*. Oxford: Oxford University Press, 2004.

Gentry, Peter, and Stephen J. Wellum. *Kingdom Through Covenant: A Biblical-Theological Understanding of the Covenant*. Wheaton: Crossway Books, 2018.

Gill, John. *A Complete Body of Doctrinal and Practical Divinity*. Paris: The Baptist Standard Bearer, 2007.

Gockel, Matthias. 'On the Way from Schleiermacher to Barth: A Critical Reappraisal of Isaak August Dorner's Essay on Divine Immutability.' *Scottish Journal of Theology* 53, 2000.

Gregory of Nazianzus. *On God and Christ: The Five Theological Orations and Two Letters to Cledonius*. Crestwood, NY: St Vladimir's Seminary Press, 2002.

Gregory of Nyssa. *Against Eunomius*. In Nicene and Post-Nicene Fathers, second series, edited by Philip Schaff and Henry Wace. Peabody, MA: Hendrickson, 2012.

Grenz, Stanley J, and Roger E Olson. *20th Century Theology: God and the World in a Transitional Age*. Downers Grove, IL: InterVarsity Press, 1997.

Gunton, Colin E. *Act and Being: Towards a Theology of the Divine Attributes*. Grand Rapids, MI: Eerdmans, 2002.

Gutjahr, Paul. *Charles Hodge: Guardian of American Orthodoxy*. Oxford: Oxford University Press, 2011.

Hallman, Joseph M. 'The Mutability of God: Tertullian to Lactantius.' *Theological Studies*, Volume 42.3, 1981.

Hanson, R. P. C. *The Search for the Christian Doctrine of God: The Arian Controversy, 318-381*. Grand Rapids: Baker Academic, 2006.

Hanson, R. P. C. *The Promise of Trinitarian Theology*. 2nd ed. New York, NY: T&T Clark, 2003.

Hardy, Edward R., ed. *Christology of the Later Fathers, Icthus Edition*. Louisville: Westminster John Knox Press, 1954.

Hart, David Bentley. *The Beauty of the Infinite: The Aesthetics of Christian Truth*. Grand Rapids, MI: Eerdmans, 2005.

Hart, David Bentley. *The Experience of God: Being, Consciousness, Bliss*. New Haven, CT: Yale University Press, 2013.

Hart, David Bentley. *The Hidden and the Manifest: Essays in Theology and Metaphysics*. Grand Rapids: Eerdmans, 2017.

Hartshorne, Charles. *Creative Synthesis and Philosophic Method*. London: Open Court, 1970.

Hartshorne, Charles. 'The Dipolar Conception of Deity.' *The Review of Metaphysics*, Volume 21, 1967.

Hartshorne, Charles. *The Divine Relativity: A Social Conception of God*. New Haven: Yale University Press, 1948.

Hartshorne, Charles. *The Logic of Perfection: Neoclassical Metaphysics* Lasalle: Open Court, 1962.

Hector, Kevin. 'Immutability, Necessity and Triunity: Towards a Resolution of the Trinity and Election Controversy.' *Scottish Journal of Theology*, Volume 65.1, 2012.

Hector, Kevin. *Theology without Metaphysics: God, Language, and the Spirit of Recognition*. New York, NY: Cambridge University Press, 2011.

Hefner, Craig. '"In God's Changelessness There is Rest": The Existential Doctrine of God's Immutability in Augustine and Kierkegaard.' *International Journal of Systematic Theology*, Volume 20.1, 2018.

Helm, Paul. *Eternal God: A Study of God without Time*. Oxford: Oxford University Press, 2011.

Henry, Carl F. H. *God, Revelation, and Authority*. Vols. 1–6: Waco, TX: Word Books, 1979.

Hilary of Poitiers. *De Trinitate*, trans. Stephen McKenna. Washington: Catholic University of America Press, 1954.

Hill, Wesley. *Paul and the Trinity: Persons, Relations, and the Pauline Letters*. Grand Rapids: Eerdmans, 2015.

Hinlicky, Paul R. *Divine Simplicity: Christ the Crisis of Metaphysics*. Grand Rapids: Baker Academic, 2016.

Hodge, Charles. 'Short Notices.' *Biblical Repertory and Princeton Review*. Volume 17.1, 1845.

Hodge, Charles. *Systematic Theology*, 3 vols. Peabody, MA: Hendrickson, 2013.

Hoglund, Jonathan. *Called by Triune Grace: Divine Rhetoric and Effectual Call*. Downers Grove, IL: IVP Academic, 2016.

Holmes, Christopher R. J. *The Lord is Good: Seeking the God of the Psalter*. Downers Grove: IVP Academic, 2018.

Holmes, Stephen. *The Quest for the Trinity: The Doctrine of God in Scripture, History and Modernity*. Downers Grove: InterVarsity Press, 2012.

Horton, Michael Scott. *Justification. Vols. 1–2*. Grand Rapids, MI: Zondervan, 2018.

Horton, Michael Scott. *Covenant and Salvation: Union with Christ*. Louisville: Westminster John Knox Press, 2007.

Horton, Michael Scott. *Lord and Servant: A Covenant Christology*. 1st ed. Louisville, KY: Westminster John Knox Press, 2005.

Horton, Michael Scott. *People and Place: Covenant Ecclesiology*. Louisville: Westminster John Knox Press, 2008.

Irenaeus. *Against Heresies* in *The Faith of the Early Fathers*, Volume 1. Trans. William Jurgens. Collegeville: The Liturgical Press, 1970.

Irenaeus. *Fragments from the Lost Writings of Irenaeus. Ante-Nicene Fathers*. Volume 1, 2012.

Jansen, Henry. 'Moltmann's View of God's (Im)mutability: The God of the Philosophers and the God of the Bible.' *Neue Zeitschrift für Systematische Theologie und Religionsphilosophie*. Volume 36, 1994.

Jenson, Matt. *Theology in the Democracy of the Dead: A Dialogue with the Living Tradition.* Grand Rapids, MI: Baker Academic, 2019.

John of Damascus. *Exposition of the Orthodox Faith,* in *Nicene and Post-Nicene Fathers,* Volume 9. Peabody: Hendrickson, 2012.

Junius, Franciscus. *A Treatise on True Theology: With the Life of Franciscus Junius,* translated by David C. Noe, Grand Rapids: Reformation Heritage Books, 2014.

Junius, Franciscus. *Synopsis Purioris Theologiae / Synopsis of a Purer Theology: Latin Text and English Translation, Volume 1, Disputations 1–23,* ed. H. van der Belt, et al. Studies in Medieval and Reformation Tradition 187. Leiden: Brill, 2014.

Kaiser, Walter. *Malachi: God's Unchanging Love.* Grand Rapids: Baker, 1984.

Kapic, Kelly M., and Bruce L. McCormack, eds. *Mapping Modern Theology: A Thematic and Historical Introduction.* Grand Rapids, MI: Baker Academic, 2012.

Kärkkäinen, Veli-Matti. *Christology: A Global Introduction,* 2nd ed. Grand Rapids: Baker Academic, 2016.

Kärkkäinen, Veli-Matti. *The Doctrine of God: A Global Introduction.* Grand Rapids: Baker Academic, 2017.

Kärkkäinen, Veli-Matti. *One with God: Salvation as Deification and Justification.* Minnesota: Liturgical Press, 2004.

Le Poidevin, Robin, Peter Simons, Andrew McGonigal, Ross P. Cameron. *The Routledge Companion to Metaphysics.* New York: Routledge. 2012.

Legaspi, Michael C. *The Death of Scripture and the Rise of Biblical Studies.* New York, NY: Oxford University Press, 2010.

Legge, Dominic. *The Trinitarian Christology of St. Thomas Aquinas.* Oxford: Oxford University Press, 2017.

Leigh, Edward. *A Systeme or Body of Divinity.* London: A.M., 1662.

Leithart, Peter J. *Athanasius.* Edited by Hans Boersma and Matthew Levering. Grand Rapids, MI: Baker Academic, 2011.

Leithart, Peter J. *Traces of the Trinity: Signs of God in Creation and Human Experience.* Grand Rapids, MI: Brazos Press, 2015.

Letham, Robert. *The Holy Trinity: In Scripture, History, Theology, and Worship.* Phillipsburg: P&R Publishing, 2004.

Letham, Robert. *Union with Christ: In Scripture, History, and Theology.* Phillipsburg: P & R Publishing, 2011.

Levering, Matthew. *Engaging the Doctrine of Creation: Cosmos, Creatures, and the Wise and Good Creator.* Grand Rapids: Baker Academic, 2017.

Levering, Matthew. 'The Holy Spirit in the Trinitarian Communion: "Love" and "Gift"?' *International Journal of Systematic Theology* 16:2, 2014.

Levering, Matthew. *Scripture and Metaphysics: Aquinas and the Renewal of Trinitarian Theology.* Oxford: Blackwell, 2004.

Lister, Rob. *God is Impassible and Impassioned: Toward a Theology of Divine Emotion.* Wheaton: Crossway, 2013.

Littlejohn, Bradford. *God of Our Fathers: Classical Theism for the Contemporary Church.* Davenant Institute, 2018.

Livingstone, E. A. *The Oxford Dictionary of the Christian Church*, 3rd Edition. Oxford: Oxford University Press, 1997.

Longenecker, Richard N. *Biblical Exegesis in the Apostolic Period.* 2nd ed. Grand Rapids, MI: Eerdmans, 1999.

Longman, T. *Psalms: An Introduction and Commentary.* Grand Rapids: InterVarsity Press, 2014.

Loux, Michael J. and Thomas M. Crisp. *Metaphysics: A Contemporary Introduction.* New York: Routledge, 2017.

Macaskill, Grant. *Union With Christ in the New Testament.* Oxford: Oxford University Press, 2013.

Macaskill, Grant. *Living in Union with Christ: Paul's Gospel and Christian Moral Identity* (Grand Rapids, MI: Baker, 2019).

Malysz, Piotr. *Hegel's Conception of God and Its Application by Isaak Dorner to the Problem of Divine Immutability.* Pro Ecclesia, Volume XV.4.

Manoussakis, John Panteleimon. *God After Metaphysics.* Bloomington: Indiana University Press, 2007.

Marion, Jean-Luc. *God without Being*, trans. Thomas A Carlson. Chicago: University of Chicago Press, 2012.

Marion, Jean-Luc. 'Metaphysics and Phenomenology: A Summary for Theologians' in *The Postmodern God: A Theological Reader*, ed. Graham Ward. Oxford: Blackwell, 1997.

Mastricht, Petrus Van. *Theoretical-Practical Theology, Volumes 1–2: Prolegomena.* Edited by Joel R. Beeke. Grand Rapids: Reformation Heritage Books, 2018.

Matz, Robert J. and A. Chadwich Thornhill. *Divine Impassibility: Four Views of God's Emotions and Suffering.* Downers Grove, IL: IVP Academic, 2019.

Maximus the Confessor, *Two Hundred Chapters on Theology.* New York: St. Vladimir's Seminary Press, 2015.

McCall, Thomas H. *Which Trinity? Whose Monotheism? Philosophical and Systematic Theologians on the Metaphysics of Trinitarian Theology.* Grand Rapids, MI: Eerdmans, 2010.

McCormack, Bruce L., ed. *Engaging the Doctrine of God: Contemporary Protestant Perspectives.* Grand Rapids: Baker Academic, 2008.

McNall, Joshua M. *The Mosaic of Atonement: An Integrated Approach to Christ's Work,* Grand Rapids, MI: Zondervan, 2019.

Mercer, Jarred A. *Divine Perfection and Human Potentiality: The Trinitarian Anthropology of Hilary of Poitiers.* New York, NY: Oxford University Press, 2019.

Molnar, Paul D. *Divine Freedom and the Doctrine of the Immanent Trinity.* New York, NY: T&T Clark, 2017.

Moltmann, Jürgen. *History and the Triune God: Contributions to Trinitarian Theology.* Translated by John Bowden. New York, NY: Crossroad, 1992.

Moltmann, Jürgen. *The Crucified God.* Minneapolis, MN: Fortress Press, 2015.

Moltmann, Jürgen. *The Trinity and the Kingdom: The Doctrine of God.* Minneapolis, MN: Fortress Press, 1993.

Moo, Douglas. *The Letter of James.* Grand Rapids: Eerdmans, 2000.

Muller, Richard. *Divine Will and Human Choice: Freedom, Contingency, and Necessity in Early Modern Reformed Thought.* Grand Rapids: Baker Academic, 2017.

Muller, Richard. *Incarnation, Immutability, and the Case for Classical Theism.* Westminster Journal of Theology, Volume 45, 1983. 22-40.

Muller, Richard. *Post-Reformation Reformed Dogmatics.* Vols. 1–4, Grand Rapids, MI: Baker Academic, 2003.

Mullins, R. T. *The End of the Timeless God*. Oxford: Oxford University Press, 2016.

Mullins, R. T. 'Simply Impossible: A Case Against Divine Simplicity.' *JRT.* Volume 7, 2013.

Murray, John. *Redemption Accomplished and Applied*. Grand Rapids: Eerdmans, 2015.

Nelson, R. David, Darren Sarisky, Justin Stratis. *Theological Theology: Essays in Honour of John Webster*. London: T&T Clark, 2018.

Niemeyer, H. A. *Collectio Confessionum in Ecclesiis Reformatis Publicatarum*. Leipzig: Sumptibus Lulii Klinkhardti, 1840.

O'Brien, Peter T. *The Letter to the Hebrews*. Grand Rapids: Eerdmans Publishers, 2010.

Ortlund, Gavin. *Anslem's Pursuit of Joy: A Commentary on the Proslogion*. Washington, D.C.: The Catholic University of America Press, 2020.

Ortlund, Gavin. *Theological Retrieval for Evangelicals: Why We Need Our Past to Have a Future*. Wheaton, IL: Crossway, 2019.

Owen, John. *Biblical Theology*. Fifth Printing edition. Morgan, PA: Soli Deo Gloria Publications, 2012.

Owen, John. *The Works of John Owen*. Edited by William H. Goold. Vol. 1. Edinburgh: Banner of Truth Trust, 2000.

Packer, J. I. *Knowing God*. Downers Grove: InterVarsity Press, 1993.

Pannenberg, Wolfhart. *Systematic Theology*. Translated by G. W. Bromiley. Vols. 1–4. Grand Rapids, MI: Eerdmans, 1991.

Pârvan, Alexandra and Bruce L. McCormack, 'Immutability, (Im)passibility and Suffering: Steps towards a "Psychological" Ontology of God.' *Neue Zeitschrift für systematische Theologie und Religionsphilosophie*, Volume 59.1, 2017.

Pasnau, Robert. *Metaphysical Themes: 1274–1671*. Oxford: Oxford University Press, 2013.

Pattison, George. *God and Being: An Enquiry*. Oxford: Oxford University Press, 2011.

Pelikan, Jaroslav. *Credo: Historical and Theological Guide to Creeds and Confessions of Faith in the Christian Tradition*. New Haven: Yale University Press, 2003.

Peterson, Robert A. *Salvation Accomplished by the Son: The Work of Christ.* Wheaton: Crossway, 2012.

Peterson, Robert A. *Salvation Applied by the Spirit: Union with Christ.* Wheaton, IL: Crossway Books, 2014.

Pictet, Benedict. *Christian Theology.* Trans. Frederick Reyroux. London: Seeley and Sons, 1834.

Pinnock, Clark. *The Most Moved Mover: A Theology of God's Openness.* Grand Rapids: Baker, 2001.

Radde-Gallwitz, Andrew. *Basil of Caesarea, Gregory of Nyssa, and the Transformation of Divine Simplicity.* New York, NY: Oxford University Press, 2009.

Rahner, Karl. *The Trinity.* 3rd ed. Tunbridge Wells, Kent: Burns & Oates, 1986.

Renihan, Samuel D. *Deity and Decree.* Renihan, 2020.

Richards, Jay Wesley. *The Untamed God: A Philosophical Exploration of Divine Perfections, Simplicity, and Immutability.* Downers Grove: InterVarsity Press, 2003.

Riches, Aaron. *Ecce Homo: On the Divine Unity of Christ.* Grand Rapids: Eerdmans Publishing, 2016.

Ritschl, Albrecht. *The Christian Doctrine of Justification and Reconciliation.* Edited and translated by H. R. Mackintosh and A. B. Macaulay. Edinburgh: T&T Clark, 1902.

Rosner, Brian S. *Paul and the Law: Keeping the Commandments of God.* Downers Grove, IL: InterVarsity Press, 2013.

Sailhamer, John H. *Introduction to Old Testament Theology: A Canonical Approach.* Grand Rapids, MI: Zondervan, 1995.

Sanders, Fred. *The Triune God.* Grand Rapids: Zondervan, 2016.

Sanders, Fred and Oliver D. Crisp, eds. *Advancing Trinitarian Theology: Explorations in Constructive Dogmatics.* Grand Rapids, MI: Zondervan, 2014.

Sanders, Fred and Oliver D. Crisp, eds. *The Task of Dogmatics: Explorations in Theological Method.* Grand Rapids, MI: Zondervan, 2017.

Sanders, Fred and Scott Swain, eds. *Retrieving Eternal Generation.* Grand Rapids, MI: Zondervan, 2017.

Sangiacomo, Andrea. 'Divine Action and God's Immutability: A Historical Case Study on How to Resist Occasionalism.' *European Journal for Philosophy of Religion*, Volume 7.4, 2015.

Sarot, M. 'Suffering of Christ, Suffering of God?' *Theology*, Volume 95, 1992.

Schaff, Philip. *The Creeds of Christendom*, Volumes 1–3. Grand Rapids, MI: Baker Book House, 1983.

Schleiermacher, Friedrich. *The Christian Faith*. London and New York, NY: Bloomsbury: T&T Clark, 2016.

Schmid, Heinrich. *The Doctoral Theology of the Evangelical Lutheran Church*. Philadelphia: Lutheran Publication Society, 1876.

Schreiner, Thomas. *1, 2 Peter and Jude*. Nashville: Broadman & Holman Publishers, 2003.

Schreiner, Thomas. *Hebrews*. Nashville: Broadman & Holman Publishers, 2015.

Schreiner, Thomas. *Romans* in *Baker Exegetical Commentary on the New Testament*. Grand Rapids: Baker Academic, 2018.

Shead, Andrew G. *A Mouth Full of Fire: The Word of God in the Words of Jeremiah*. Downers Grove, IL: IVP, 2012.

Sherman, Robert. 'Isaak August Dorner on Divine Immutability: A Missing Link Between Schleiermacher and Barth.' *Journal of Religion*, Volume 7, 1997.

Sonderegger, Katherine. *Systematic Theology, Volume One, The Doctrine of God*. Minneapolis: Fortress Press, 2015.

Sonderegger, Katherine. *Systematic Theology, Volume Two, The Doctrine of the Holy Trinity: Processions and Persons*. Fortress Press, 2020.

Spurgeon, Charles Haddon. 'The Immutability of God' in *New Park Street Pulpit*, Volume 1. London: Passmore & Alabaster, 1855.

Stuart, D. K. *Exodus*. Nashville: Bradman and Holman Publishers, 2006.

Stump, Eleonore. *The God of the Bible and The God of the Philosophers*. Milwaukee, WI: Marquette University Press, 2016.

Swain, Scott R. *Trinity, Revelation, and Reading: A Theological Introduction To The Bible And Its Interpretation.* London: T & T Clark, 2011.

Swinburne, Richard. *The Christian God.* Oxford: Oxford University Press, 1994.

Swinburne, Richard. *The Coherence of Theism.* Oxford: Oxford University Press, 1993.

Tertullian. *A Treatise on the Soul,* in Ante-Nicene Fathers, Volume 3. Peabody: Hendrickson, 2012.

Thate, Michael J., Kevin Vanhoozer, Constantine R. Campbell. *'In Christ' in Paul: Explorations in Paul's Theology of Union and Participation.* Grand Rapids: Eerdmans, 2014.

Thomasius, Gottfried. 'Christ Person and Work' in *God and Incarnation in Mid-Nineteenth Century German Theology,* ed. Claude Welch. Oxford: Oxford University Press, 1965.

Thompson, James W. *Hebrews.* Grand Rapids: Baker Academic, 2008.

Torrance, T. F. *The Christian Doctrine of God: One Being Three Persons.* New York, NY: T&T Clark, 2016.

Torrance, T. F. *Incarnation: The Person and Life of Christ.* Edited by Robert T. Walker. Downers Grove, IL: IVP Academic, 2015.

Tune, Anders. *Immutable, Saving God: The Import of the Doctrine of Divine Immutability for Soteriology in Augustine's Theology.* Ph.D. Dissertation: The Catholic University of America, 1994.

Turretin, Francis. *Institutes of Elenctic Theology.* Edited by James T. Dennison. Translated by George Musgrave Giger. Phillipsburg: P & R Publishing, 1997.

Van den Brink, Gijsbert and Marcel Sarot, ed. *Understanding the Attributes of God.* Frankfurt: Europäischer Verlag der Wissenschaften, 1999.

Van Mastricht, Petrus. *Theoretical-Practical Theology.* 3 Vols. Ed. Joel R. Beeke. Trans. By Todd M. Rester. Grand Rapids: Reformation Heritage Books 2019.

Van Niewenhove, Rik. *An Introduction to Medieval Theology.* Cambridge: Cambridge University Press, 2012.

Vanhoozer, Kevin. *First Theology: God, Scripture, and Hermeneutics.* Grand Rapids: IVP Academic, 2002.

Vanhoozer, Kevin. *Is There a Meaning in This Text? The Bible, the Reader, and the Morality of Literary Knowledge.* Landmarks in Christian Scholarship. Grand Rapids, MI: Zondervan, 2009.

Vanhoozer, Kevin. *Remythologizing Theology: Divine Action, Passion, and Authorship.* Cambridge: Cambridge University Press, 2012.

Vanhoozer, Kevin J., Craig G. Bartholomew, Daniel J. Treier, and N. T. Wright, eds. *Dictionary for Theological Interpretation of the Bible.* Grand Rapids, MI: SPCK; Baker Academic, 2005.

Vidu, Adonis. *The Same God Who Works All Things: Inseparable Operations in Trinitarian Theology.* Grand Rapids: Eerdmans, 2021.

Visser, Sandra, and Thomas Williams. *Anselm.* Oxford: Oxford University Press, 2005.

Voetius, Gisbertus. *God's Single, Absolutely Simple Essence.* Trans. R. M. Hurd. *The Confessional Presbyterian*, Volume 15, 2019.

Von Balthasar, Hans Urs. 'Mysterium Paschale' in *Mystermium Salutis.* Ed. J. Feincr and Magnus Löhrer. Einsiedelm: Benziger, 1969.

Vos, Geerhardus. *Reformed Dogmatics: Theology Proper.* Translated by Richard B. Gaffin, Jr. Bellingham, WA: Lexham Press, 2014.

Ware, Bruce. *An Evangelical Reexamination of the Doctrine of the Immutability of God.* Dissertation, The Southern Baptist Theological Seminary, 1984.

Ware, Bruce. *An Evangelical Reformulation of the Doctrine of the Immutability of God.* Journal of the Evangelical Theological Society, Volume 29.4, 1986. 431-446.

Ware, Bruce. *An Exposition and Critique of the Process Doctrines of Divine Mutability and Immutability.* Westminster Journal of Theology, Volume 47, 1985. 175-196.

Ware, Bruce. *Father, Son, and Holy Spirit: Relationships, Roles, and Relevance.* Wheaton, IL: Crossway Books, 2005.

Ware, Bruce. *The Man Christ Jesus: Theological Reflections on the Humanity of Christ.* Wheaton, IL: Crossway, 2013.

Ware, Bruce A., and John Starke. *One God in Three Persons: Unity of Essence, Distinction of Persons, Implications for Life.* Wheaton, IL: Crossway, 2015.

Warfield, Benjamin B. *Biblical Doctrines.* Revised edition. Carlisle, PA: Banner of Truth, 1988.

Warfield, Benjamin B. *Inspiration and Authority of the Bible.* 2nd ed. Phillipsburg, N.J.: P & R Publishing, 1980.

Warfield, Benjamin B. *Selected Shorter Writings.* 2 Vols. Edited by John E. Meeter. Phillipsburg, N.J.: P & R Publishing, 2001.

Warfield, Benjamin B. *Revelation and Inspiration.* Grand Rapids, MI: Baker Book House, 2003.

Webster, John. *Confessing God: Essays in Christian Dogmatics II.* New York, NY: Bloomsbury, T&T Clark, 2005.

Webster, John. *The Culture of Theology.* Grand Rapids, MI: Baker Academic, 2019.

Webster, John. *The Domain of the Word: Scripture and Theological Reason,* New York: T&T Clark, 2014.

Webster, John. *God without Measure: Working Papers in Christian Theology.* London: T&T Clark, 2018.

Webster, John. *Holy Scripture: A Dogmatic Sketch.* Cambridge: Cambridge University Press, 2003.

Webster, John. 'ὑπὸ πνεύματος ἁγίου φερόμενοι ἐλάλησαν ἀπὸ θεοῦ ἄνθρωποι: On the Inspiration of Holy Scripture' in *Conception, Reception, and the Spirit: Essays in Honor of Andrew T. Lincoln,* ed. J. G. McConville and L. K. Pietersen, Eugene, OR: Cascade, 2015.

Webster, John. *Word and Church: Essays in Christian Dogmatics.* New York: T&T Clark, 2016.

Weinandy, Thomas G. *Athanasius: A Theological Introduction.* Burlington: Ashgate, 2007.

Weinandy, Thomas G. *Does God Change? The Word's Becoming in the Incarnation.* Still River, MA: St. Bede's Publications, 1985.

Weinandy, Thomas G. *Does God Suffer?* Notre Dame: University of Notre Dame Press, 2000.

Wellum, Stephen J. *Christ Alone: The Uniqueness of Jesus as Savior.* Grand Rapids: Zondervan, 2017.

Wellum, Stephen J. *God the Son Incarnate: The Doctrine of Christ.* Wheaton, IL: Crossway, 2016.

Wellum, Stephen J. 'Jesus as Lord and Son: Two Complementary Truths of Biblical Christology.' *Criswell Theological Review,* Volume 13.1, 2015.

White, Thomas Joseph. 'Divine Simplicity and the Holy Trinity.' *International Journal of Systematic Theology* 18:1, 2016.

White, Thomas Joseph. 'Intra-Trinitarian Obedience and Nicene-Chalcedonian Christology.' *Nova et Vetera* 6, 402.2, 2008.

Whitehead, Alfred North. *Process and Reality*. New York, NY: Harper and Row, 1929.

Whitney, Barry L. 'Divine Immutability in Process Philosophy and Contemporary Thomism.' *Horizons*, Volume 7, 1980.

Williams, Robert. 'I. A. Dorner: The Ethical Immutability of God.' *Journal of the American Academy of Religion*, LIV.4.

Wisse, Maarten. *Trinitarian Theology Beyond Participation: Augustine's De Trinitate and Contemporary Theology*. New York, NY: T&T Clark, 2011.

Wittmann, Tyler R. *God and Creation in the Theology of Thomas Aquinas and Karl Barth*. Cambridge: Cambridge University Press, 2019.

Wrathall, Mark. *Religion After Metaphysics*. Cambridge: Cambridge University Press, 2003.

Wright, N. T. *Justification: God's Plan & Paul's Vision*. Downers Grove, IL: IVP Academic, 2016.

Wright, N. T. *The New Testament and the People of God*. Minneapolis: Fortress Press, 1992.

Zizioulas, John D. *Being as Communion: Studies in Personhood and the Church*. Crestwood, NY: St. Vladimir's Seminary Press, 1985.

Subject Index

Scripture Index

247

Books available in the REDS series...

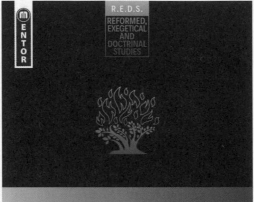

FOR THE MOUTH OF THE
LORD HAS SPOKEN

THE DOCTRINE OF SCRIPTURE

GUY PRENTISS WATERS

SERIES EDITORS J.V. FESKO & MATTHEW BARRETT

ISBN: 978-1-5271-0607-9

CHOSEN

IN CHRIST

REVISITING THE CONTOURS OF PREDESTINATION

CORNELIS VENEMA

SERIES EDITORS J.V. FESKO & MATTHEW BARRETT

ISBN: 978-1-5271-0235-4

ISBN: 978-1-5271-0391-7

R.E.D.S.
REFORMED,
EXEGETICAL
AND
DOCTRINAL
STUDIES

CRACKING THE FOUNDATION
OF THE
NEW PERSPECTIVE ON PAUL

COVENANTAL NOMISM VERSUS REFORMED COVENANTAL THEOLOGY

ROBERT J. CARA

SERIES EDITORS J.V. FESKO & MATTHEW BARRETT

ISBN: 978-1-78191-979-8

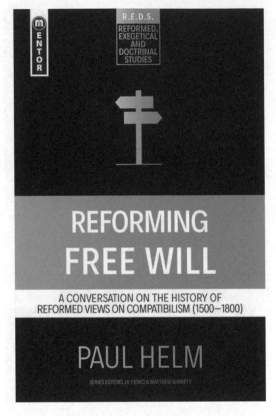

REFORMING
FREE WILL

A CONVERSATION ON THE HISTORY OF
REFORMED VIEWS ON COMPATIBILISM (1500–1800)

PAUL HELM

SERIES EDITORS J.V. FESKO & MATTHEW BARRETT

ISBN: 978-1-5271-0606-2